A New Case for the Liberal Arts

Assessing Institutional
Goals and
Student Development

David G. Winter
David C. McClelland
Abigail J. Stewart

A New Case
for the
Liberal Arts

119444

Jossey-Bass Publishers

San Francisco • Washington • London • 1981

A NEW CASE FOR THE LIBERAL ARTS
Assessing Institutional Goals and Student Development
by David G. Winter, David C. McClelland, and Abigail J. Stewart

Copyright © 1981 by: Jossey-Bass Inc., Publishers
433 California Street
San Francisco, California 94104
&
Jossey-Bass Limited
28 Banner Street
London EC1Y 8QE

Library of Congress Cataloging in Publication Data

Winter, David G., 1939-
    A new case for the liberal arts.

    Bibliography: p. 219
    Includes index.
    1. Education, Humanistic. I. McClelland, David
Clarence. II. Stewart, Abigail J. III. Title.
LC1011.W53   370.11'2   81-81963
ISBN 0-87589-502-6   AACR2

Manufactured in the United States of America

JACKET DESIGN BY WILLI BAUM

FIRST EDITION

Code 8116

The Jossey-Bass
Series in Higher Education

Preface

This book grew out of the intersection of our personal experience of liberal education with our professional orientation as behavioral scientists. All three of us enjoyed our liberal arts education as undergraduates, and we all now teach in liberal arts colleges. As persons and as teachers, then, we are firmly committed to the ideal of liberal education. Yet, having been trained in the application of empirical research to answering questions of human behavior and change, we naturally wonder why the evidence of systematic social science research is rarely brought to bear on actual decisions about educational planning or goal attainment. In faculty meetings and committee deliberations, we find ourselves questioning the varied and extravagant claims and counterclaims about the effects on students of particular educational policies and programs.

Perhaps in the land of the liberal arts, empirical evaluation will always remain a second-class activity compared to rhetoric and dialectic. Or maybe there has simply been something wrong with the research tools available for evaluating educational programs. But without good evaluation, can educators really be so certain of what they are doing? In an era when the tide of public doubt about the worth of liberal education has been rising, when the claims of higher education for resources can no longer assume an easy and confident justification, when more and more colleges are concerned with accounting and accountability, and when economic and demographic crises threaten a number of institutions, the time seems ripe for educational policy and planning to be informed and guided by research. Some educators, of course, still do not believe that liberal education faces an economic crisis. To us, however, considerations of economics and institutional survival make the tasks of defining, measuring, and systematically demonstrating educational effects not only important but urgent.

In this book, we seek to clarify the effects that liberal arts institutions are supposed to have on their students and then apply the most appropriate techniques, instruments, and analytic procedures of psychological research to determine whether they in fact have these effects, and, if so, why and how. Throughout our research, we have been determined to stay close to the liberal arts tradition. For example, rather than employing traditional psychological tests because they give reliable and cheap results in the laboratory—no matter how irrelevant— we tried to use measures adequate to the breadth and complexity of the kinds of claims that educators make for liberal education. To that task, we have each brought experience in designing nontraditional "operant" measures of personal qualities and life outcomes, rather than psychometric orthodoxy. Thus, after discussing the claims made for liberal education and organizing these claims into a series of analyzable goals in Chapter One, we describe in Chapter Two the new instruments we developed and the older instruments we adapted to measure the attainment of these goals. In Chapter Three we present the results of the three-college study that we carried out to test the effects of liberal education—a study supported by a grant to Harvard University from the Fund for the Improvement of Post-Secondary Education (FIPSE). And in the next three chapters we seek to clarify and generalize the results of this study in several ways: First, in Chapter Four, we estimate the importance in later life of the characteristics or competencies that liberal education seeks to develop, based on a further fourteen-year longitudinal study of liberal arts graduates. Then in Chapter Five we ask what aspects of the total environment of a college are responsible for which of these changes. In Chapter Six we report comparative data from several different colleges, some of which are liberal arts oriented and others of which are not. Finally, in Chapter Seven, we suggest some policy implications of our research, present our conclusions about the distinctive features of the liberal arts educational ideal as established by our research, and argue that this ideal no longer has to depend on a quasi-religious justification but can be tested and evaluated by research that is of a quality and sophistication equal to that of the educational ideal it tries to assess.

For whom have we written this book? We believe that our research helps to bridge a gap between educational policy makers and social scientists. We have written, therefore, for educational leaders, whether as members of the faculty or the administration, and other decision makers with a stake in higher education, such as political and corporate leaders, foundation officials, and even students and parents. To these readers, we hope to demonstrate that liberal arts education does have significant effects on students, as well as to illustrate the value of psychological research on educational outcomes as an aid to educational policy formation, planning, implementation, administration, and evaluation. Such a demonstration is critically needed at this time because of the dramatic increase in educational costs, combined with the decreasing pool of student applicants. Intelligent strategies to establish priorities and allocate scarce resources are now essential to institutional survival. At the same time, much of the existing research on the effects of

higher education is of little help in designing such strategies, because results are often vague, inconclusive, and even trivial. As a
result, educational policy is enmeshed in the rhetorical contro-
versies that surround the conflicting claims of educators and
their critics.

We hope that other researchers will strengthen our
"bridge" between social science and educational policy by adding to our work, and so we have also written this book for psychologists and other social scientists in the fields of personality,
social psychology, and education. For them particularly, we introduce several new "operant" measures of personality traits
and intellectual abilities. Personality psychologists will be especially interested in this approach, since the philosophy and rationale for operant measures, their psychometric credentials,
and their longitudinal importance in predicting adult life outcomes—topics covered extensively in this book—are lively current issues and problems in personality theory and research.

For such a varied audience, we decided to present the
main results in nontechnical language, with a minimum of statistical elaboration to indicate the magnitude and significance of
effects. Technical information about our instruments and methodological details are therefore presented as resources at the end
of the test. Detailed statistical tables are available, as a Supplement and at cost from us, care of McBer and Company, 137
Newbury Street, Boston, Massachusetts 02116.

Perhaps more than most research projects, this work de-
pended on the help and cooperation of many people. Most important, of course, were the hundreds of students at many different colleges who participated as research subjects, as well as
the many faculty and administrators who arranged the testing.
Since we use pseudonyms throughout the book, we can only
give a general acknowledgement here. Many other people helped
with one or another phase of the project—conceptualization, design, administration, analyis, or interpretation and writing. In
alphabetical order, they are: Derek C. Bok, Richard Boyatzis,
Sister Austin Doherty, Jacqueline Fleming, Betsy Harrington,
Joseph M. Healy, Jr., Phyllis Hirsch, Matina S. Horner, Milton
Kornfeld, Richard Lesko, Ann Litwin, Robert J. Lurtsema,

Sharyn Maclean, William G. Perry, Barbara Pontier, Paul Pottinger, Lindy Pye, David Riesman, William Rogers, Howard Russell, Michael Sokol, Paul Segel, and Dean K. Whitla. The financial support of FIPSE and McBer and Company was essential and is gratefully acknowledged. Naturally, the final responsibility for what is in this book is ours alone.

July 1981   David G. Winter
Brookline, Massachusetts

David C. McClelland
Cambridge, Massachusetts

Abigail J. Stewart
Brookline, Massachusetts

Contents

Figures and Tables

The Authors

David G. Winter is professor of psychology at Wesleyan University. He received an A.B. in social relations from Harvard University (1960), a B.A. in philosophy-politics-economics from Oxford (1962), and the Ph.D. degree in social psychology from Harvard (1967). He is the author of *The Power Motive* (1973), translator and editor of Otto Rank's *The Don Juan Legend* (1975), and co-author of *Motivating Economic Achievement* (with D. C. McClelland, 1969). He has served as director of research for McBer and Company. His current research interests include political psychology, leadership, and motive imagery in the mass media.

David C. McClelland is professor of psychology at Harvard University. He received an A.B. in psychology and sociology from Wesleyan (1938), an M.A. in psychology from the University of Missouri (1939), and the Ph.D. degree in psychology from Yale University (1941). He has written several books, including *Power: The Inner Experience* (1975), *The Achieving Society* (1961), and *The Achievement Motive* (with J. W. Atkinson, R. A. Clark, and E. L. Lowell, 1953). His research interests include human motivation in all its aspects (origins, physiological concomitants, effects on performance, and social outcomes), the identification of competencies necessary for effective performance, and the use of psychological knowledge to develop competencies.

Abigail J. Stewart is assistant professor of psychology at Boston University. She received an A.B. in psychology from Wesleyan University (1971), an M.Sc. in social psychology from the London School of Economics (1972), and the Ph.D. degree in personality from Harvard University (1975). She is the author of professional papers on individual adaptation to life changes and other topics. She has served as the director of the Henry A. Murray Research Center of Radcliffe College. Her research interests include stress and coping, strategies of personality research, and methods for studying individual and social change.

To Our Teachers

A New Case
for the
Liberal Arts

*Assessing Institutional
Goals and
Student Development*

ONE

Approaches to Evaluating Liberal Education

Liberal arts undergraduates spend several years studying broad abstractions rather than learning specific facts. While their counterparts at professional, performance, technical, or vocational colleges are learning particular action skills, liberal arts students are supposed to develop their powers of reflection upon the broad vistas of human knowledge in order to become "liberally" (rather than "vocationally") educated. By learning to distinguish abstract concepts from particularistic facts, they become, in Plato's words (Jowett, 1888, pp. 475-476, 484), philosophers: "Lover[s] not of a part of wisdom only, but of the whole . . . able to distinguish the idea from the objects which participate in the idea, neither putting the objects in the place of the idea nor the idea in the place of the objects (V, 475-476). [They have] a naturally well proportioned and gra-

1

cious mind, which will move spontaneously toward the true
being of everything" (V, 484).

Plato further argued that the welfare of the state and the
happiness of the private citizen could be secured only under the
rule of such philosophers: "Until philosophers are kings, or
the kings and princes of this world have the spirit and power of
philosophy, and political greatness and wisdom meet in one . . .
cities will never have rest from their evils . . . and then only will
this our State have a possibility of life and behold the light of
day. . . . In no other State can there be happiness private or
public" (V, 473). To select and encourage such philosophical
natures, Plato prescribed a five-year regimen that emphasized
"harmony" (the study of interrelationships) and "dialectic"
(pure intelligence or abstraction): "The sciences which they
learned without any order in their early education will now be
brought together, and they will be able to see the natural relationship of them to one another and to true being" (VII, 536).

The Flowering of Liberal Education

For over two thousand years, liberal education has been
an educational ideal of the West, for the brightest elite if not for
all students. As the universities of Europe expanded on their
original task of training the clergy and certain specialists (for
example, physicians), this ideal flowered in the English notion
of the educated gentleman. Young men first studied Greek and
Latin at preparatory school and "went up" to Oxford to "read
Greats"—classical languages and literature, classical history, and
classical philosophy. Then they "went down" to rule, whether
in the far-flung posts of the British Empire, in the civil service
or Parliament in Whitehall, or as a justice of the peace in a remote English village (Woodruff, 1953; Wilkinson, 1964). While
the strong emphasis on classical forms might not be called "liberal" by today's standards (and indeed often degenerated into
laborious toil over exercises), the very *lack* of usefulness or
practical purpose was believed to make classics an effective bul-
wark against narrow specialization or vocationalism. Classical
English education was "liberal," then, in the sense that it sought

to develop broad analytical skill rather than narrow technical brilliance—the "amateur ideal"—with supporting traits of self-assurance and self-reliance, loyalty, the sense of moral obligation, and self-control, all of this seasoned with a dash of respect for manners and ceremony (Wilkinson, 1964, pp. 67-68 and pt. 2).

This same ideal of liberal education has flowered in other times and places, again with the characteristic connection to political leadership. With a few short interludes, China was dominated by the Confucian pattern of education through several dynasties, from A.D. 618 to 1912. The roles of scholar and governor were fused, as in Plato's philosopher-king. Preparation in a classical curriculum and selection by rigorous examination produced generalists with the intellectual, personal, and ethical traits required for imperial service. Knowledge, it was believed, made the empire tranquil and happy. Among the Jesuits, secondary education traditionally emphasized the classics, reason, and debating skill; the result seemed to be priests of intellectual stature and political resourcefulness, "mission leaders who could think for themselves in novel situations far from home authority" (Wilkinson, 1964, p. 7).

In the United States, the fullest flowering of the liberal education ideal came in the two decades between the world wars—roughly coincidental with the nation's emergence as a world power. There had been precursors. Twenty years before, Cecil Rhodes had founded scholarships to bring to Oxford those young American men "who have shown . . . that they have instincts to lead" so that they would "esteem the performance of public duties as their highest aim" (Aydelotte, 1946, p. 18). A few exclusive American boarding schools had all along followed the British model in which a classical curriculum fostered a "classic personal style" (Winter, Alpert, and McClelland, 1963). In the 1920s and 1930s, several elite American universities deliberately established the liberal education ideal as the foundation of undergraduate studies. Columbia established courses in contemporary civilization and humanities. St. John's prescribed a list of "great books." At Amherst and then at Wisconsin, Alexander Meiklejohn created experimental programs that "immersed" students, first in the study of the Greek classics, then in a comparative scrutiny of American society. At Chicago, the new general education was identified with the name of the university's vigorous young president, Robert Maynard Hutchins. Wesleyan developed an interdisciplinary humanities program during the Second World War. And at Harvard, after the war, James Bryant Conant championed its program of general education.

While names and details varied, the new liberal education programs had two common features: (1) They emphasized broad abstractions and basic principles (usually across several disciplines) rather than specialized advanced work in particular disciplines. (2) They were consciously intended *not* to prepare students for vocations, or even for graduate school. Published statements of purpose mentioned preparation "to become an expert . . . in the general art of the free man and the citizen," a "broad critical sense," or "insight into general relationships" (Harvard University Committee, 1945, pp. 54, 56). Divested of platitudes, the purpose of these new programs was simply to train the nation's future leaders, at all levels, according to the ancient Platonic-Confucian-Jesuit-English ideal. The universities that took the lead in rediscovering liberal education—the Ivy League, the Little Three, Chicago, Stanford—were the very institutions that had always educated the nation's political and intellectual leaders, as well as its social aristocracy (Domhoff, 1967). After World War I, moreover, they expanded their efforts to recruit or "co-opt" promising members of the middle and lower social strata, preparing them for leadership roles in a society that was becoming more democratic and universalistic. (See Conant, 1970, chap. 12, and Riesman, 1975, for an account of this trend at Harvard.) While the new liberal education was hailed as a rediscovery of ancient virtue, it also had an unconscious element of remediation for the "classic" social background that could no longer be assumed among the new students who would become the nation's leaders.

Attacks on Liberal Education

In recent years, however, the bloom has left the flower of liberal education. Several forces and events of the 1960s and 1970s combined to create a crisis of confidence about the nature of the university in general and the value of liberal learning in particular. Dominating this era, of course, was the disastrous American participation in the Vietnam War—a continuing catastrophe that many saw as the clear culmination of policies formulated and defended by these very "brightest and best" leaders who had been liberally educated at the best colleges (Halberstam, 1973). Some of the anguish, bitterness, and cynicism aroused by the war rubbed off on the universities that had, in the minds of many, made it possible. In earlier years, Kerr (1963) and Rand (1964) had lauded the connection between universities and the power of the "establishment," whereby the university had become, in Kerr's words, "a prime instrument of national purpose" (p. 87). But Chomsky (1969) and others traced the connection between the universities and the war from a radical perspective; and if Vietnam (and the Bay of Pigs before it) was the logical outcome of liberal education, then the newest generation of the brightest and best was not having any (see Keniston, 1968). Nor can the connection between liberal education and imperialism be dismissed as a fortuitous coincidence of the 1960s. Young men in both Confucian China and Victorian England were, after all, being trained to administer an empire. Abstract conceptual rationality and an authoritative (if not authoritarian) imperial political style may have both conscious intellectual connections and deeper psychological links.[1]*

The very elite connotations of liberal education have always made it suspect in the egalitarian social and political climate of America. The heightened distrust and rejection of elites, status, and power during the 1960s (Gardner, 1965; McClelland, 1970) sometimes led students to condemn on principle any educational practice that was perceived as elitist, no matter how improbable or inconsistent that perception was, as Riesman (1975) notes from personal experience. These perceptions were not without some accuracy and justification. As consciousness of Third World issues and problems increased and the struggle of minorities and women for justice and opportunity intensified, traditional curricular offerings with titles such as "Western Thought and Institutions" did seem to reflect only a partial (even ethnocentric) white upper-middle-class male point

---

*Footnotes are collected at the end of each chapter.

of view. Some radical critics argued that the universities served
the interests of the dominant ruling groups, that this was wrong,
and that the university should become liberated or even revolu-
tionary (for example, Ohmann, 1976). Others buttressed this
same conclusion with more rigorous social and economic analysis. Bowles and Gintis (1976, p. 207) argued that the twin
trends of expansion of elite-oriented liberal education and growing "proletarianization" of the white-collar worker were bound
to conflict sooner or later, for "the educational processes best
suited to training an elite are less successful in fostering quies-
cence among followers." They did concede that institutions of
higher education will always have to provide leadership for (or
to "reproduce") society. The fault therefore lies in the capitalist, repressive nature of that society. Under alternative social
and economic relationships, Bowles and Gintis concluded, expanded liberal education could more vigorously promote personal development and social equality (pp. 265-274).

     Another coincident line of criticism started from the
premise that institutions as such are inevitably and intrinsically
opposed to essential human nature. The growth of institutions
therefore increases human degradation and misery. Rooted in
the tradition of anarchy or radical individualism, this view burst
upon the society of the 1960s as the "counterculture" (Roszak,
1969), dedicated to "restructuring" or constructing "alternative" institutions. Though hardly of the counterculture, Ivan
Illich (1971) bluntly proposed "deschooling society" because
institutionalized learning treated knowledge as a prepackaged
commodity rather than an intensely personal activity, with the
result that students learned only to be docile and dependent
"consumers." Drawing on these themes, less radical student critics proposed to replace traditional liberal education forms and
content with something else. The established must give way to
the experimental; cognition, words, and reflection must yield to
emotions, nonverbal expression, and spontaneous action (see
Brown, 1966). In more philosophical terms, knowledge as
Erkenntnis (knowing mediated by concepts) was to be replaced
by knowledge as *Erlebnis* (unmediated, direct experiencing; see
Hospers, 1946). In place of the carefully crafted essay, many

students wanted to put the accretive journal or—in extreme cases—the simple experience itself, unstructured, ecstatic, and unrecorded. Perhaps they were, in Plato's words, "the lovers of sounds and sights . . . fond of fine tones and colours and forms . . . but [not of] absolute beauty" (V, 476). Grant and Riesman (1978, especially chap. 10) chronicle the reforms, experiments, and finally the later problems and disillusionments of these years.

Perhaps the unkindest blow of all was dealt by the economic climate of the 1970s. Demographic trends and economic depression combined to shrink dramatically the job market for liberal arts undergraduates while opportunities (and earnings) at least held their own in specifically vocational fields. Students responded with demands to be taught marketable skills in preparation for specific careers rather than to study the generalized, and therefore "irrelevant," liberal arts.

A corresponding movement also emerged within the philosophy of higher education. The impact of growing numbers of "new" or "nontraditional" students, of pressures for accountability, and of concern for teaching skills demonstrably related to specific jobs combined to promote the growth of *competency-based education*. The competency perspective in education has diverse roots: American pragmatism, the "scientific management" or efficiency movement of the 1920s, the theories of John Dewey, and the wartime demands for quick training of many people in complex skills. (See Grant and others, 1979, for a general discussion and survey of the competency-based education movement.) Actually, this term is a catchall for a wide variety of particular programs; but as an ideal, it does have three central features: (1) a curriculum divided into units or competencies that are defined in terms that are narrower, sharper, and more operational than the syllabus of the traditional course, (2) measurement of competence attainment by performance tests or demonstration in use rather than by traditional exams and papers, and (3) flexibility in the preparation that is required before competence attainment is certified.

While competency-based education does not intrinsically conflict with liberal arts education, it does raise some issues and challenges to more traditional views. In principle, the ideals and goals of liberal education could be expressed as a series of competencies or performance tests. Although the criteria of successful liberal arts performance might seem subjective (for example, "Write an essay on topic X that will be judged as 'well written' by Professor Y."), they cannot logically be dismissed on that count. What makes this kind of translation seem so strange is that the whole spirit of the enterprise—breaking down broad and complex skills into smaller separate units, defining those skills in operational terms, and marking performance and growth in quantitative language—seems wholly foreign to the two-thousand-year tradition of liberal education. Surely violence is done to a great classic when one speaks of designing a performance test for the competence of "distinguish[ing] the idea from the objects which participate in the idea, neither putting the objects in the place of the idea nor the idea in the place of the objects." (No matter that for two thousand years liberal arts educators have believed that they can make intuitive judgments of this ability.) This difference in spirit, then, seems to be the true basis of whatever challenge and conflict is raised by the competency-based movement. Because it claims to define, measure, and demonstrate its accomplishments, it draws the scorn, and perhaps also the envy, of the liberal arts partisans.

We have used the word *envy* here intentionally, for one major theme in the present-day criticism of the liberal arts educational ideal is skepticism about whether liberal arts education has anything like the effects on students that it claims to have. Where is the evidence that four expensive years at a liberal arts college actually makes anyone able "to see the natural relationship [of separate studies] to one another and to true being"? The question has a special urgency nowadays. Liberal arts education is expensive, and the combination of rapidly increasing costs and limited scope for increased "productivity" means that it will become more and more expensive. Thus parents, legislators, trustees, and foundations understandably want some assurance that their sacrifices and investments are worthwhile.[2] Society as a whole demands that so vast an employment of social resources justify itself, as even Illich (1971) argued. At what point will the cost of a liberal arts college education become prohibitive to most American families? When will even the most supportive legislators and foundation executives turn to other claims on public and philanthropic funds? At times it seems as though this great intellectual ideal of the West is about to go the way of the ocean liner and the country estate—comfortable, full of happy memories, extravagant, expensive to staff, and hopelessly out of date. Perhaps this economic assault, then, is the most dramatic and dangerous one. Universities can continue to ignore the call for accountability, now grown loud and unmistakable, only at their peril.

Evaluating Liberal Education

A remarkable irony emerges when the whole range of criticism of liberal arts education is considered together. On the one hand, those with a fiscal involvement question whether it has any effects, or at least whether the effects are worth the cost. (We refer, of course, to effects on students' personalities, values, and so forth, and not to effects on income, which are reviewed by Soloman and Taubman, 1973, and Freeman, 1976.) Yet the social and political critics, as we have seen, are certain that liberal arts institutions have effects, and they are equally convinced that these effects are bad. Given the importance of knowing which view is right, and given the sophisticated techniques of education researchers, one would expect that by now there would be enough evidence to decide matters.

It is therefore sobering to realize that we have little firm evidence one way or the other about the actual effects of liberal arts education, this most enduring and expensive Western educational ideal. To be sure, there is no lack of elaborate, well-crafted, pious statements about what the goals and effects of liberal arts education *ought* to be, from Plato to the most recent report by Boyer and Levine (1981). Colleges are, Chait (1979, p. 36) suggests, "on the verge of mission madness." It is useful to review these statements in order to contrast them with what researchers have actually studied.

In 1917, Whitehead argued that the aim of education was

to arouse an "appreciation for the exact formulation of general ideas, for their relations when formulated, for their service in the comprehension of life" (1953, p. 97). In 1936, Hutchins phrased the goal of general education as "the cultivation of the intellectual virtues," which included intuitive knowledge, scientific knowledge, philosophical wisdom, art, and prudence (1936, pp. 62-63). His faculty at the University of Chicago later elaborated on these goals in more performance-oriented terms (Faust, 1950): "To develop the capacity for wise decisions in those matters with which everyone must be concerned" (p. 14). "To think for themselves rather than providing a mass of information on a host of subjects. . . . To establish an adequate relation of the mind to the things which it undertakes to grasp" (p. 17). "To formulate clearly the difference between conflicting lines of argument and to locate the critical point at which determination of relative merit and soundness of different approaches may be profitably undertaken" (p. 18). The Harvard Committee on the Objectives of a General Education in a Free Society (1945, pp. 64-73) theorized that general education fostered four traits of mind: thinking effectively, communicating thought, making relevant judgments, and discriminating among values. In introducing a discussion of evaluating general education, Dressel and Mayhew (1954, pp. 1-3) formulated two objectives: "those phases of nonspecialized and nonvocational learning which should be the *common experience* of all educated men and women" and "cultivation of the intellect and . . . the provision of an evaluation of the more significant aspects of the cultural heritage." Barton (1959) listed four rather broader intended outcomes of general education: independent and critical thinking; cosmopolitanism (versus provincialism) of knowledge, beliefs, and information; empathic ability (versus insensitivity); and egalitarian-libertarian values.

In the early 1970s, the Harvard University faculty again sought to clarify the purposes of a general liberal arts education. While reiterating many goals set forth in earlier reports, Harvard's President Bok particularly stressed critical thinking and the capacity to deal as a generalist with the ever-increasing complexity of specialized knowledge. "Above all, students should be encouraged to think clearly—to identify the issues in a complex problem, collect the relevant data, assemble arguments on every side of the question, and arrive at conclusions soundly related to the arguments and information available" (Bok, 1978, p. 5). To be sure, thinking clearly about problems requires the acquisition of "a large body of information and ideas . . . Without an ample background of facts, data, information, the mind would be too barren to sustain serious thought. Yet facts are soon forgotten and often overtaken by new discoveries. If education is to have lasting value, the curriculum must also be built around the mastery of intellectual skills" (Bok, 1978, p. 5). In other words, students are to become skillful at incorporating new information as it relates to what they already know. They must formulate general schemas of knowledge in various areas, in terms of which new information can be readily assimilated. In short, they must "learn how to learn."

Analysts of the informal or "unofficial" effects of going to college approach the task almost from the standpoint of the anthropologist. Becker (1964, p. 14), for example, argues that "Many, perhaps most, college-goers learn in college precisely what they need to know to get along as adults in a middle-class world," including qualities such as the following: independence from home; picking an appropriate mate; social poise, especially with superiors; generalized work skills (persistence, focus, deferring of gratification, organizing one's self, juggling different tasks at the same time, and simple "getting things done"); organizational skills (getting along with the rules and constraints of a bureaucracy, realizing the effect of one's actions on others, manipulation with persuasion rather than force or coercion, compromise, and using rules to one's own advantage); rehearsal for management roles; institutional motivation (to attach one's personal desires to the goals of the institution, to surmount obstacles—such as boring classes—because "they are there," and to take this as a sign of maturity and ability).

David Riesman (personal communication) suggests that one aim of liberal education is to teach students to converse and to understand conversation—that is, discourse that is not instrumental and not trivial. To do this, students must be confident and relaxed enough so that they do not worry about making a misstep, but at the same time they must also control their desires to "preen" and to impress others. Riesman also lists other goals such as "enduring frustration" and the "willingness to experience difficulties and pace one's self." Lester Thurow (personal communication) adds that while high school trains students to cooperate with friends and others of similar background, college teaches students to know and work with strangers and people from different backgrounds.

All these statements of goals and presumed effects of liberal education overlap considerably, and so we have organized them into the following list. It is much briefer than the exhaustive taxonomies worked out by Bloom (1956) and Krathwohl, Bloom, and Masia (1964), but its categories are sufficient to show the main points of agreement and divergence among the writers we have quoted.

1. Thinking critically or possessing broad analytical skill: Hutchins, Harvard Committee, Dressel and Mayhew, and Barton.
   a. Differentiation and discrimination within a broad range of particular phenomena (especially within the history of Western culture): Plato, Harvard Committee, Dressel and Mayhew, Barton, and Bok.
   b. Formation of abstract concepts: Whitehead.
   c. Integration of abstract concepts with particular phenomena or concrete instances; making relevant judgments: Plato, Whitehead, Harvard Committee, and Dressel and Mayhew.
   d. Evaluation of evidence and revision of abstract concepts and hypotheses as appropriate: Dressel and Mayhew and Bok.
   e. Articulation and communication of abstract concepts: Harvard Committee, Dressel and Mayhew, and Bok.
   f. Differentiation and discrimination of abstractions, identification of abstract concepts: Plato, Harvard Committee, Faust, Dressel and Mayhew, and Bok.
   g. Comprehension of the logics governing the relationships among abstract concepts: Plato, Whitehead, and Bok.

2. Learning how to learn: Bok.
3. Thinking independently: Faust, Barton, and Becker.
4. Empathizing, recognizing one's own assumptions, and seeing all sides of an issue: Dressel and Mayhew, Barton, and Bok.
5. Exercising self-control for the sake of broader loyalties: Plato, Rhodes, Wilkinson, and Becker.
6. Showing self-assurance in leadership ability: Plato, Rhodes, Wilkinson, and Becker.
7. Demonstrating mature social and emotional judgment; personal integration: Plato, Harvard Committee, Dressel and Mayhew, Perry, and Bok.
8. Holding equalitarian, liberal, pro-science, and antiauthoritarian values and beliefs: Dressel and Mayhew and Barton.
9. Participating in and enjoying cultural experience: Dressel and Mayhew and Bok.

While the case for liberal education in terms of these goals has never lacked rhetorical eloquence, it has not received substantial empirical support from the growing body of research on the effects of higher education. There are several reasons why. For one thing, the "guardians" of the liberal education tradition are not accustomed to thinking this kind of support is necessary. From the classical tradition, they have apparently inherited both an emphasis on the power of rhetoric and form and a distrust of the empirical method (see Wilkinson, 1964, chap. 6). If the justification of liberal education were not self-evident, therefore, it could surely be established by personal testimony and eloquent rhetorical appeals stressing the emulation of classical models, rather than by systematic collection and evaluation of empirical evidence. (Good examples of such personal testimony are Munschauer, 1979, and Ebersole, 1979, quoting a naval aviator who, as a prisoner of war, drew comfort and strength from his classical education.) Thus in the words and phrases already cited, the tone and style of the celebrant override the proof of the scientist. No wonder Bird (1975, p. 109) concludes, "The liberal arts are a religion, the established religion of the ruling class. The exalted language, the universalistic setting, the ultimate value, the inability to define, the appeal to personal witness . . . these are all the familiar modes of religious discourse."

A second reason why research has not shown that liberal education has an unambiguous pattern of effects is that the language in which the goals and presumed effects of liberal education are stated has been a major obstacle. Many liberal arts professors view important outcomes of liberal education as ineffable and incapable of being broken down and assessed systematically (Botstein, 1979). Translating their language into operational, measurable terms has not been easy and has not always been successful to date. For example, consider the following item from the Allport-Vernon-Lindzey *Study of Values*: When you visit a cathedral are you more impressed by a pervading sense of reverence and worship than by the architectural features and stained glass? (a) Yes; (b) No. A yes answer increases one's score on the *religious* value; a no answer increases the *aesthetic* value score. If liberal education is supposed to increase aesthetic sensitivity and perhaps lower adherence to religion (as might be derived from the preceding list and as will be discussed in the review of research), then going to college should increase the tendency to answer no. Yet many people would wonder whether items such as this are a fair translation of what they mean by aesthetic sensitivity or religious commitment.

Finally, the very nature of four years of college makes study of it vulnerable to several problems and pitfalls of method. One common strategy has been to test students at entrance and then at graduation (perhaps also at one or more points in between), attributing change to the intervening college experience. While longitudinal designs of this type seem to be the obvious way to test for change, they do have several technical problems (see Campbell and Stanley, 1963, and Cook and Campbell, 1979). Without certain additional control procedures, they cannot control for history (other events occurring between testings) or simple maturation. They are likely to be vulnerable to retest effects (effect of taking the same test twice). Moreover, longitudinal designs take time. Any educator who wanted to know something about the effects of a particular college would have to wait at least four years until an answer was available even in principle. A more ambitious program of innovative programs guided and modified by the feedback from research on effects could be carried out only in slow motion.

To get around these problems, many studies employ cross sectional designs in which entering and graduating students are tested at the same time, with the differences attributed to the college experience. If both groups are tested at once, then effects of history are controlled, but additional procedures are still necessary to control for the effects of simple maturation. Further, if there is substantial attrition of students (called "mortality" by Campbell and Stanley, 1963), then the characteristics of students who do *not* drop out will be erroneously taken to be change effects. Any differences in the criteria or standards used to recruit and select the two groups of students will produce similar errors.

Both the two simplest and most common designs, then, raise problems of inference and require further control procedures to rule out alternative interpretations and support the inference of college change effects. Yet these additional controls raise further problems. For example, what is the right control group for "going to college"? Students who do not go to college already differ from those who do on so many variables that they are almost useless as a control group. (Trent and Medsker, 1968, used nonattenders as controls, adjusting statistically for initial differences.) Nor do they stay in limbo for four years; rather, they get jobs, join the army, and so forth. Students attending one kind of college can be used as a control group for those at another kind of college, but this cannot fully rule out selection effects and other interaction effects involving selection.

Studies of College Effects

What conclusions can be drawn from previous research? One of the first major empirical investigations of a liberal arts college was Newcomb's now classic study of Bennington (Newcomb, 1943, 1958; Newcomb and others, 1967). According to Newcomb, Bennington was certainly liberal in many senses, and self-consciously defined its responsibility to introduce students to the world in intellectual, social, and political terms. The original study and later follow-ups showed that students changed more or less in the expected directions. However, Newcomb concluded that the principal mechanism for change was the *reference group,* or social pressure for conformity emanating from prestigious other students and faculty with whom friendship was valued, rather than any explicit mechanisms or goals, as in the previous list. Thus as a change agent, Bennington did not appear to be inherently different from any other "total institution" (see Bettelheim, 1958; Goffman, 1961). By and large, liberal political attitudes persisted into the 1960s, or over twenty years after college graduation.

The next research milestone is the report of Jacob (1957), who tried to draw together 354 studies on the effects of college. His particular focus was on values rather than the cognitive effects so extensively described in the previous list. Compared to the general population, college graduates were more concerned with status and prestige, more conservative economically and politically, more tolerant, and less religious. While Jacob (1957, pp. 4-5) did conclude that "it seems reasonable to credit these differences in value to the college experience," he argued that the mechanisms involved were conformity or a socializing pressure toward values homogeneity and selective weeding out or dropping out of students who did not fit this values pattern. Such a conclusion suggests that whatever effects colleges have are simply due to the Bennington effect on a larger, less intense, and more diluted scale—conformity to core values of the (salient) culture, in this case, middle-class college graduate American culture as a whole. "The impact of the college experience is . . . to socialize the individual, to refine, polish, or 'shape up' his values so that he can fit comfortably into the ranks of American college alumni" (Jacob, 1957, p. 4). Jacob found little evidence that general education or liberal arts curricula had effects different from professional or vocational programs, nor did particular teaching methods, particular teachers, or high-quality teaching in general have distinctive effects.

Most colleges, Jacob concluded, simply reinforce such American core values as self-confidence and self-interest, privatism or the separation of the self from civic and political affairs, tolerance, a vague and superficial religiosity, and a suspicion of "big government." Nevertheless, Jacob (1957, chap. 6) did identify certain colleges with a "particular potency," colleges that showed freshman to senior changes not typical of the general national trend:

Bennington: Radical-liberal political beliefs.
Harvard: Exceptional tolerance; individualism; creativity versus job security; political liberalism and sophistication.
Haverford: Exceptionally strong drive for success and renown; concerns for human betterment and world service.
Macalester: Public service and humanitarianism; social and political responsibility.
Reed: Antiauthoritarianism; rational theoretical interests.
Springfield: Social sensitivity; less interest in material gains and power.
Wesleyan: Moral purposiveness; concern for civic affairs, community, and world problems; group consciousness; religious concern.

While Jacob only speculated on the reasons or mechanisms responsible for this particular potency, his conclusion leaves open (however slightly) the possibility that liberal education, of a certain kind and in a certain setting, does have a special impact. "It may be that the *private liberal arts college,* with a sense of special educational mission, is more likely to have a potent influence on student values than public institutions" (Jacob, 1957, p. 115, emphasis added).

The rather gloomy conclusions of the Jacob report were soon challenged on several grounds. Smith (1958) critically analyzed the meaning and limits of the concept of value as it had guided Jacob's interpretation. Barton (1959) critically surveyed the methodology of the major studies Jacob reviewed. Riesman (1958) suggested several lines of criticism and avenues for more refined conceptual and statistical analysis, including the design of more sophisticated measures.

Over a decade later, Feldman and Newcomb (1969) again

took stock of the research literature. Their book is still generally regarded as the definitive review of the literature on college
effects (see also Sanford, 1962, and Ellison and Simon, 1973).
They approached the enormous number of research studies that
had appeared since the Jacob report with a much more sophisticated sense of method, design, and measurement issues. While
mindful of the complex and sometimes mutually contradictory
nature of changes within groups of students, they found evidence for at least seven broad effects that were characteristic of
nearly all colleges (Feldman and Newcomb, 1969, chap. 2):
increased open-mindedness, sensitivity to aesthetic and "inner"
experience, intellectual interests and capacities, independence
and dominance, and impulse-expression and *decreased* conserva-
tism and religious interest. These are, of course, only general
trends, with numerous exceptions and qualifications. For example, "Not all increases in intellectual orientation . . . are large
enough to be statistically significant. This, together with the
fact that some samples do not show any increases on some of the
'intellectuality' scales, will not be altogether encouraging to
those who feel that the primary goal of a college education is to
make young men and women more intellectually disposed"
(Feldman and Newcomb, 1969, p. 29).

After establishing these general conclusions, Feldman and
Newcomb also reviewed the evidence for the change effects of
particular types of college, particular majors, and particular residential groupings. On the whole, they are cautious and tentative, repeatedly drawing attention to the problems of distinguishing *change* effects from the effects of initial selection
(1969, pp. 48, 52, 138, 175, 209) or attrition (pp. 52-53), general maturation (p. 64), or retesting (pp. 58-59). "There are
many reasons for withholding judgment about the nature and
extent of colleges' impacts" (p. 48).

Another milestone in the study of college effects is the
massive Cooperative Institutional Research Program of the
American Council on Education (Astin, 1972, 1973, 1977).
Since 1965, random samples of students from several hundred
institutions filled out questionnaires when they entered college
and in a follow-up four years later. (Solomon and Ochsner,

1978, have followed up a similar sample three years after college.) The institutions were a representative sample of the entire population of two-year colleges, four-year colleges, and universities in the United States. By regressing the "output"—student follow-up responses—on student "input" variables (freshman year responses and background variables), it was theoretically possible to distinguish selection effects from change effects. (See Feldman and Newcomb, 1969, pp. 359-364, for a critical discussion of this technique.) Finally, the program research staff articulated a typology of effects, as shown in Table 1. For example, behavioral (or action) effects are separated from psychological (or trait-dispositional) effects, and the do-

Table 1. Typology of Possible Effects of College with
Representative Measures within Each Type

	Affective	*Cognitive*
Psychological	Self-concept, measured by 20 self-report items on 5-point scales Values, interests, and attitudes, measured by 32 Likert-scale items Religious affiliation Satisfaction with college	Grade-point average Graduation with honors
Behavioral	Self-description of engaging in 36 behaviors, grouped into 14 clusters Participation in student demonstrations Marriage Joining a fraternity or sorority	Educational attainment: persistence in college, graduate/professional school Election to student offices and committees Performance on a 30-item list of "competencies" Achievements during college in journalism, creative writing, science, theater, athletics Vocational choice Vocational attainment in 10 fields Income

Source: Adapted from Astin, 1977, p. 8.

main of the cognitive is distinguished from that of the affective (or emotional-motivation). Such a typology is much more coherent and systematic than are the loosely structured "catalogues" of variables and effects presented by previous reviewers. In many respects, therefore, the ACE study is a model of research design and a substantial improvement over previous studies.

For each of the major types of outcome outlined in Table 1, we present some illustrative results from Astin (1977, chap. 7). Attending any kind of college, for example, has the following effects: Within the *cognitive-behavioral* domain, students switch their career plans from science and engineering to law, business, and college teaching. In the *affective-behavioral* domain, they drink, smoke, and take naps more and pray less. In the *affective-psychological* domain, they become less religious. In this same domain, students at private colleges are more satisfied with faculty contact and quality than are other students. Finally, in the *cognitive-psychological* domain, private college students become more verbally aggressive in class.

Hyman, Wright, and Reed (1975) use a wholly different and novel method to study the effects of higher education. Through secondary analysis of public opinion survey results from the period 1949-1971, they were able to correlate education level with answers to questions of knowledge while controlling for some (though probably not all) potentially contaminating variables, such as social class. The effects of higher education, when estimated in this way, appear to be broad, substantial, and enduring into adult life and old age. College does increase knowledge—of popular culture, public affairs, and academic matters—while increasing the exposure to new knowledge via the print media and continuing education. Even if these conclusions are limited to "factual knowledge" rather than qualities of thinking or character, they are still more forthright and optimistic than most previous research on the effects of college, and they certainly justify further use of the method. However, Hyman, Wright, and Reed (1975) were not able to make distinctions among different kinds of higher education; so their conclusions apply to almost any kind of postsecondary education. We do not know from this study whether liberal arts education has any special effects, distinctive either in content or in magnitude.

Several recent studies of students at particular institutions could be expanded or generalized to other colleges but have not yet been. Perry (1970), for example, has classified students' intellectual and ethical growth at Harvard from stages of dualistic black-and-white thinking through relativism and toward a final position of ongoing commitment and "affirmation of identity among multiple responsibilities" (p. 10). He has provided a detailed distillation of criteria for identifying each of nine stages along this journey but has not studied how much change occurs, on the average, at different institutions. King (1973) has integrated extensive statistical data with case studies of several students to demonstrate the same kind of growth in ego strength and adaptation at Harvard. Heath (1968) has developed a theory of the maturation process from his studies of Haverford students.

Such research on the psychological effects of college gives evidence that colleges do have effects on people. Yet to the gently skeptical reviewer, the hundreds of studies, taken together, do not make a very impressive case for *liberal arts* education. Nor do they justify its great cost. After much labor, it seems that the research effort has (in the words of Isaiah) "brought forth wind." The specific justification for liberal arts education, for all the reverence paid to the ideal, still rests largely on a quasi-religious faith rather than upon systematic scientific evidence.

Toward a New Approach

The difficulty in establishing the case for the liberal arts on the basis of research can be illustrated by Astin's 1977 study, which in many respects is a model of sophisticated research design. Yet because this study was so massive—hundreds of institutions and thousands of students—it had to use measures of effects (or "student outputs") that are easy to get and simple to score. The reader who compares these measures, as shown in Table 1, with any of the liberal education statements of purpose we listed may well wonder whether there is any overlap at all. How could any conceivable changes on the Astin variables prove or disprove the case for liberal education? Take, for example, the notion of "critical thinking," which is so prominent in educational goal statements. In Astin's terms, critical thinking is either a *cognitive-behavioral* or a *cognitive-psychological* variable; yet it is difficult to see how any of the variables actually used to measure these two domains could be accepted as a measure of critical thinking *in the sense that theorists of liberal education have used the term.* And are any of the *affective-psychological* self-rating or life goal variables likely to capture what Cecil Rhodes meant by "instincts to lead" or "esteem for the performance of public duties"?

Taking the college effects research as a whole, we find that a concern for quick and easy measurement often has usurped a concern for the meaningful content of what is measured. It is not immediately clear how you can determine whether students think critically, but you can readily ask whether they applied to graduate school or graduated with honors. In the personality or affective domain of college effects, many researchers have used standard inventories or scales, seemingly because they exist rather than because the constituent variables or scales are particularly relevant to the manifest or latent goals of liberal education. For this reason, subsequent research cannot wholly invalidate the strongly worded comment of liberal educator Victor Butterfield (1946, p. 59): "I [spent] a good deal of time attempting to discuss . . . the ends or purposes of the liberal college. . . . Whereas I met many men in all fields who seemed to me to have little interest or insight into what I considered the problem . . . the proportion of such men in the field of psychology . . . is relatively great."

Finally, most of the research relies almost exclusively on variables of the "objective" type—choice of multiple responses, true-false, and so forth. While variables of this type are easy to score and seem to possess high test-retest reliability and other desirable psychometric properties, they often have a tenuous relationship to what is involved in liberal education. (Actually, the high reliability may be partly spurious; see Mischel, 1968, chap. 3.) Consider critical thinking. If it means the differentiation of particular phenomena and the integration and articulation of abstractions (and this is how educators have used the term), then why not test students by giving them some materials, asking them to perform some critical thinking, and recording what they do? Instead, even the most carefully designed test of critical thinking used in research on liberal education is made up of multiple-choice items that involve reasoning. Correct choices are *believed* to depend on critical thinking (as in the hypothetical account of what presumably happens in the mind of the test taker, according to Dressel and Mayhew, 1954, p. 51), but the actual critical thinking process and results are not themselves recorded directly as they would be, for example, in essay responses to set questions (for example, "Compare and contrast the Renaissance and the Reformation"). Other taxonomies of cognitive objectives (Bloom, 1956) and emotional growth (Krathwohl, Bloom, and Masia, 1964) are also assessed by traditional "objective" questions instead of being measured directly.

Are these two procedures equivalent? The distinction is analogous to the difference between "objective" and "essay" examination questions. In survey research, a similar distinction is made between close-ended and open-ended questions; in psychology, the terms *respondent* and *operant* are often used.[3] By now there is considerable evidence that operant and respondent measures of the presumed "same" variable are in fact quite different, do not correlate highly, and obey different laws (Skinner, 1938, 1953; de Charms and others, 1955; McClelland, 1958, 1966, 1972, 1980; see also Table 7 in Chapter Four).

Many researchers are nevertheless uncomfortable with operant or open-ended measures. Some believe that they are "immature," at best a prelude to developing respondent measures (despite the considerable evidence of divergence in validity). Others doubt the reliability of operant measures or the objectivity with which they are coded. (See Winter and Stewart, 1977b, and McClelland, 1980, for discussion of the reliability issue with operant measures.) These doubts are unfortunate vestiges of the atomistic level of analysis and the emphasis upon experimental manipulation and control that have pervaded so much social science research and have prevented the fullest scientific scrutiny of complex and subtle phenomena, such as liberal education. In fact, highly objective procedures can be devised for coding operant data (see Winter, 1973, chap. 3, for an example). The real issue is the amount of constraint the researcher wants to impose on the subject. Respondent measures involve high constraint and have low tabulation and analysis costs. Operant measures involve low subject constraint, but their costs of analysis make them expensive for large-scale surveys.

Most of the presumed effects of liberal education, as outlined in the previous list, are operant behaviors. That is, they are *processes for operating on and using information* rather than mere knowledge of facts or information. As such, they should show up only when subjects have to *do something* with data, and they should be most fully manifest in a *record of what the subjects do*. Multiple-choice questions based on the outcomes of these processes could, then, give only the dimmest reflection of the processes themselves. As measures of processes that are subtle and show up best under conditions of low constraint, they would be inadequate. Thus it follows that *the most fruitful measures of the distinctive effects of liberal arts education are likely to be operant measures.* In the study that led to this book, therefore, developing innovative operant measures that do greater justice than heretofore to the goals previously outlined was a first priority. These new measures will be introduced in the next chapter.

Notes

1. Stokes (1959) documents the connection between Utilitarianism and an authoritarian streak in the administration of British India. McClelland and his colleagues (McClelland and others, 1958; McClelland, 1964) noted the linkage between rational striving and an authoritarian political cynicism in Germany. In his diaries, Albert Speer (1970, 1976) expressed this same relationship in more personal terms.

2. The Oakland Financial Group, for example, estimated

in 1976 that the total four-year cost to parents of private college education for a child born in 1975 would be $82,830, which would require yearly savings of $2,750 from 1975 on. Of course, these figures do not reckon with the much higher inflation rates (and even greater rates of increase in college costs) since 1976. They also do not include the costs that are paid by endowment income or grants from governments and foundations, which are at least as great as the costs paid by students' families.

3. Skinner (1938, pp. 19-21) first formulated clearly the distinction between operants and respondents. In his usage, *operants* (or emitted behaviors) have originating forces that are not in the environment, are not under the control of eliciting stimuli, and have no stimuli consistently correlated with their occurrence. *Respondents* (or elicited behaviors) are opposite in each respect. Our use of these terms is analogous but not identical to Skinner's distinction. By *operant*, we mean behavior that is not highly defined and controlled, as to nature and direction, by the alternatives presented by the investigator (the "stimuli"). Such behaviors are therefore less related to specific stimuli and have originating forces relatively more within the person than within the task itself. Respondent behaviors, in our usage, are responses the nature and direction of which are more closely under the control of external stimuli provided by the investigator. It is certainly true that writing stories to pictures in the Thematic Apperception Test (a typical operant in our sense) is technically a respondent in Skinner's terms, since there are identifiable stimuli and people rarely emit such behavior spontaneously. The nature of the story (content, style, and so forth), however, is much less controlled by the text instruction stimuli than is the nature of a multiple-choice response. We believe that our focus on the issue of *relative* control of behavior by external stimuli preserves much of Skinner's original meaning.

TWO

Measuring Cognitive, Motivational, and Emotional Outcomes

Because research on the effects of liberal education has been hampered by test instruments and measurement procedures inadequate to demonstrate the kinds of effects that educators believe liberal education ought to have, we have assembled a battery of tests that we believe does justice to the claims of liberal education and makes possible a fair test of whether it has any distinctive effects. These measures of liberal arts competence—"competence" simply being a collective term for all these effects—include adaptations of a few instruments that had shown promise in earlier psychological research as well as some completely new procedures to measure particular kinds of effects where we felt there were major gaps in coverage.

Two main principles guided us in selecting and developing these measures. First, we wanted to cover as many as possible of the skills and qualities of mind that educators have claimed as goals and outcomes of education in the liberal arts, as shown in the list in the previous chapter. Second, we wanted to break new ground with measures that involve using knowledge, operating on facts, or generating responses—operant measures—rather than the more traditional objective tests that ask for choices and involve mere knowledge of facts.

Two New Measures of Intellectual Abilities

Many tests exist to measure such widely used but vaguely defined intellectual or cognitive goals of education as "critical thinking," "intellectual flexibility," and "effective argument." But as discussed in Chapter One, we felt that most of these measures had defects or problems that made them unsuitable for our purposes. Many of them seemed at best to be only pale reflections of what liberal educators meant and at worst to be completely irrelevant. Many of the best-intentioned tests are in an objective-choice format better suited to measuring factual knowledge or the outcomes instead of the processes of sophisticated cognitive functioning. Finally, none of these existing measures has been conspicuously successful in showing distinctive effects of liberal education. Thus if a case for the liberal arts can be made, it will have to be made with a fresh approach and new measures. Two that we developed are the Test of Thematic Analysis and the Analysis of Argument test.

Critical Thinking and the Test of Thematic Analysis. Critical thinking is perhaps the most general term for the intellectual abilities that are supposed to be characteristic of the liberally educated person. Some of the many aspects and nuances of this term are indicated in the list in Chapter One. Taken together, these elaborations describe a skill of *advanced concept formation*—the ability to form complex concepts that discriminate among abstractions and then to communicate these concepts in clear language. To the liberally educated person, the environment furnishes "data," whether from doing a scientific experiment, observing social and economic activity, viewing a painting, or simply living everyday life. As presented, these data are chaotic, confusing, and seemingly random; sometimes they may even be labeled with wrong or useless concepts. The liberally educated person, it is argued, is able to transform these data into intelligent and useful information by creating and using abstract *categories.* With good categories, the complex can be restated in terms of simple, ordered component parts so that coherent knowledge and intelligent action are possible (see Bruner, Goodnow, and Austin, 1956, chap. 1).

Here we are concerned with concept *formation* rather than concept *attainment.* *Concept attainment* is the ability to "pick up" and remember concepts that someone else (for example, the experimenter) has defined in advance. Concept attainment is thus much simpler than concept formation. Since much of the early research on human cognition involved concept attainment, usually with simple combinations of discrete elements (Hull, 1920; Heidbreder, 1946; Bruner, Goodnow, and Austin, 1956), it is not of much relevance to the more complex processes at work in liberal education.

We decided to make a fresh start, more closely related to what actually happens in a liberal arts college classroom. The result was the Test of Thematic Analysis. (See Winter and McClelland, 1978, for a full account of the development of this measure.) Consider a typical liberal arts final examination question: "Compare and contrast the Renaissance and the Reformation." This question calls for the integration of an enormous amount of confusing and conflicting material from lectures, primary source readings, and other analyses. Of course, a good answer requires knowledge of a wide range of historical facts; but there is no single "correct" set of facts, and a good answer actually depends more on how the facts are selected, arranged, organized, and interpreted than on the facts themselves. Probably all educators would agree that even controlling for factual knowledge, liberal arts education should enable students to write better answers to questions of this sort. This particular question, however, would not be a fair general test because it gives an advantage (presumably) to the history (or theology or art) major. We sought to preserve the format of the question while using material not drawn from any particular discipline yet complex enough to allow us to construct an adequate measure of the effects of liberal education. As used in this research, the Test of Thematic Analysis presents a person with two different groups of brief, imaginative Thematic Apperception Test stories, four in each group. The two groups of stories had been written under different testing conditions and were therefore different in content and style. (Although one might suppose that either literature or psychology majors might have a special advantage on this version of the test, they do not in fact score better than do other students.) Persons taking the test are given the two groups of stories and are instructed to formulate and describe the difference between them, in whatever terms and at whatever level and length they wish. Typically, they are given thirty minutes for this task. Any two groups of stories, or two contrasting sets of material, can be used. The following stories are typical of those used in this research.They are reproduced here to give the reader a feel for the test.

Group A Story

A business office—head of business sitting at desk surrounded by his executive staff. News has been received that business has failed. Head of business has been cheating and swindling and the letter he is holding has brought it out into open. The others are horrified, but at the same time they like their "boss" and want to help him, as well as them, so that news doesn't leak out and ruin firm, their boss, and their jobs. How will it be covered up? An impossible situation. No matter how they cover up, boss and firm can't be saved.

Group B Story

Five men—the speaker is attempting to improve his speech and the four men are helping to give him advice. This man is a public official who has been asked to express his views on a controversial topic. He is taking great care to be prepared. The man looks like he's thought for a moment, hoping the other men could possibly help him with

advice. The problem will be resolved—by his work
and his associates the speech will be given in clear
and accurate form.

In order to maximize the test's capacity to measure the
effects of liberal education, the scoring system was designed on
the basis of a pilot study of freshmen and seniors at Ivy College.
(This pilot research was completely separate from the main
study reported in this book and was in fact carried out several
months before it, with subjects from completely different college classes.) On the basis of a comparison of half the responses
of each group, nine categories were developed to differentiate
the freshmen and seniors. These nine categories were then cross-
validated on the rest of the responses of each group, mixed together and scored blind (without knowledge of college class).
This procedure ensures that the categories as defined will maximize the differences between the two groups and yet be objective. Six categories appeared more often in the seniors' responses and so are scored +1:[1]

1. *Parallel Comparison:* Some element is ascribed to one group
   of stories, and in the other group, *either* it is explicitly not ascribed *or* a contrasting element is ascribed.
2. *Exceptions or Qualifications* to any ascription.
3. *Examples* are used to illustrate an ascription.
4. *Overarching Issues:* Similar to category 1 except that an
   overarching issue that unifies the two contrasting ascriptions
   is mentioned.
5. *Redefinition:* Redefining an element in order to improve
   coverage.
6. *Subsuming Alternatives:* Defining an element disjunctively,
   with nonsynonymous but functionally equivalent options. An
   example is a "strike" in baseball, which can be a missed
   swing, a pitch in the strike zone, or a foul hit.

Three categories were more common in the responses of the
freshmen, and so are scored −1:

7. *"Apples and Oranges" Nonparallel Comparison:* Comparison between groups using two elements that are unrelated ("John is tall and Jerry is smart.")
8. *Affective Reaction:* Comparison based on emotions.
9. *Subjective Reaction:* Comparison based on the writer's subjective reaction, using first-person singular pronoun.

These nine categories, then, are taken as the measure of students' critical thinking ability. The range of possible scores is from −3 to +6. In order to give readers a further sense of how these categories actually occur in responses to the test, we reproduce a typical high-scoring response and a typical low-scoring response:

> *High-Scoring Response*
> In each of the stories, there are two major relationships: that among the figures described and (usually implicitly [*qualification,* scored +1]) that between the group in the picture and the writer of the story [*overarching issue,* followed by a *parallel comparison* between the two groups, both scored +1]. In Group A, each writer feels that self-interest divides the figures from one another and that what they are doing is either criminal—hence to his own disadvantage—or at least not helpful to him. In Group B, each writer conceives of a cooperative relationship among the figures in the picture and thinks of them as performing a service that may benefit him (for example, medical progress, newscasting [*examples,* scored +1]) or is at least in itself worthwhile [*subsuming alternatives,* scored +1]—thoughtful speaking on controversial issues, leadership for those who feel they need it. [Total score = +4]

> *Low-Scoring Response*
> It seems to be that in the stories in Group A, in every case, each story makes the reader have a bad feeling [*affective reaction,* scored −1]. The

people in the higher positions, such as lawyers or
politicians, are generally men who should be re-
spected. In the stories, however, they come across
as cheaters, liars, and men out to better themselves
and cheat the people. The people who trust them
and are more or less considered "good people,"
who come out of the stories in a disillusioned way
but also appear as the ones who the reader should
"root" for to win at the end.

In Group B stories, there is an element of to-
getherness and cooperation of the people in the
stories ["apples and oranges," *nonparallel comparison* with Group A, scored −1]. I as the reader
came out of these stories with an easier feeling and
with more respect for the people involved [*subjective reaction,* scored −1]. [Total score = −3]

The whole scoring system is objective in that two trained scorers working independently on the same material reached over
85 percent category agreement on the presence of the categories. On the basis of the pilot study, therefore, it appears
that liberal education increases the precision, parallel structure,
breadth of coverage, and objective emotional neutrality of comparisons involving complex concepts. In simpler terms, most
professors would probably recognize these categories as what
distinguishes a "good" essay answer from a "bad" one, controlling for the amount of factual knowledge. In the next chapter,
we report how the thematic analysis categories hold up in the
larger study.

Intellectual Flexibility in Analysis of Argument. Under
many different names, disciplined flexibility in analytical thinking is usually thought of as a hallmark of the liberally educated
person. Sometimes it is called relativism of judgment or commitment to one position while understanding diverse views
(Perry, 1970). Sometimes it is simply called reasoning ability. In
any case, it involves the ability to keep cool and see the elements
of truth in all sides of a heated controversy, to analyze arguments and construct coherent ways of evaluating them. This
disciplined analytical flexibility is what makes liberal education

an object of such scorn and attack to the totalitarian or authoritarian mind. People's real intellectual skill in this area could be shown only by putting them "under fire," by involving them in an argument that tempts their own emotions. For this reason, it is a hard quality to elicit and measure with standardized procedures in a laboratory setting, although it could easily be observed in any college dormitory "rap session."

We designed the Analysis of Argument test to duplicate as much as possible the familiar situation in which a complex, potentially emotional issue is being discussed. (See Stewart, 1977a, for a full account of the development of this measure.) Subjects are first given a brief quotation (three hundred to four hundred words) that expresses a strong, extreme position on a controversial and emotional issue. In this research, we used excerpts of a 1968 sermon by Norman Vincent Peale, strongly attacking the "permissive" childrearing advice of Dr. Benjamin Spock and linking this advice to moral laxity, race riots, crime, and opposition to the Vietnam War. Peale's views were certainly controversial and, in the early 1970s, could be expected to arouse a strong negative reaction in most college students. (More recent forms of Analysis of Argument use extreme statements on nuclear power or abortion.) After reading the article, subjects are given five minutes to write a response: "Assume that you are to argue against it. Your response can be of whatever form and nature that you think are most satisfactory and appropriate." After writing their responses, without any prior mention, subjects are then told to turn the page, where the next instruction reads as follows: "Write a defense of the article—including, if you wish, argument against your criticism that you have just written. Again, your defending response can be of whatever form and nature that you think are most satisfactory and appropriate." Thus the test demands that the person actually produce arguments on both sides of a controversial issue, while under pressures of time, emotion, and perhaps also consistency.

Again, in order to maximize the test's capacity to measure the effects of liberal education, the scoring system was designed on the basis of freshmen and seniors at Ivy College. (This was the same pilot study sample used to develop the thematic analysis scoring system; the derivation and cross-validation were done in exactly the same way.) Five categories, three for the attack and two for the defense, appeared more often in the seniors' responses and so are scored +1:[2]

Attack
  1. *Central Organizing Principle* of the criticism.
  2. *Focus on Logic* and logical errors of the statement.
  3. *Proposing Distinctions and Exposing Contradictions* among elements of the statement, some of which may be accepted while others of which are rejected.
Defense
  4. *Modified Endorsement:* Reworking or delimiting the original statement so as to defend it.
  5. *Acceptance of Particular Arguments:* Singling out of some elements (rather than all) of the original statement for defense.

Five categories were more common among the freshmen and so are scored −1:

Attack
  6. *String of Criticisms:* A series of criticisms that are not organized around a central principle, insight, or focus.
  7. *Focus of Attack on Facts:* Debate about whether the contents of the statement are true.
  8. *Proposing Counter-Facts:* Opposing arguments are given, but without evidence or other support.
Defense
  9. *Total Endorsement:* Simple reversal from previous criticism to a fairly global endorsement (without regard for any inconsistencies thereby created).
  10. *Proposing New Arguments:* Introduction of new arguments not even given in the original statement.

Two trained scorers working independently on the same material reached 94 percent category agreement for these categories. The range of possible scores is from −4 to +6.

Intellectual flexibility in analysis, defined by these categories, involves differentiation among the separate elements of a controversial position, a generic or abstract organization of elements into an overall argument, and limits instead of absolutes. Superficially, it might seem that liberal education makes students better able to argue any side of any question—intellectual harlotry, as it were. Actually, this is more characteristic of the freshman arguments, which switch from strong attack to strong endorsement. The seniors show greater concern for overall consistency: They distinguish among elements in both attack and defense; so their defense is by no means a repudiation of their prior attack. In establishing their initial position, they take serious account of the opposite point of view, even though at that time they do not know they will be called upon to defend it later. In the next chapter, we report how these Analysis of Argument scoring categories hold up in the larger study. Meanwhile, to give readers a feel for the test, we reproduce a typical high-scoring response and a typical low-scoring response:

High-Scoring Response
    Attack: In response to the absolutely reactionary article about modern society, I think that Dr. Peale is overlooking a great deal of reality in associating the events of modern society to Spock's permissiveness. Certainly there are problems in society today, yet it is important to realize that [*proposing distinctions,* scored +1] the youth are not causing the problems but rather reacting to them [*focus on logic,* scored +1]. We can't view all of society's problems so simply; there are many interrelationships to be drawn. Each of these factors must be considered in its own light—none stands alone and it is very narrow-minded to trace virtually all activity to one phenomenon [*central organizing principle,* scored +1].
    Defense: I feel that several of the points in Dr. Peale's discussion have been very well taken. I agree with his belief that we are living in probably the most undisciplined sort of age in history [*accepts particular argument,* scored +1]. Yet the

mere fact that society is undisciplined is not an evil in itself, however [*modified endorsement,* scored +1]. I feel that the problems of society are of a much more serious nature, with more significant causes. [Total score = +5]

Low-Scoring Response

   Attack: Dr. Peale is quite wrong in a number of ways in this article. First, to place so much blame on Dr. Spock is totally wrong. Second, there is still a great deal of moral laxity in the American home [example of *focus on facts,* scored −1]. To link lack of discipline to students' expressing their own opinions is terrible. Doesn't Dr. Peale think students should express their opinion? Lastly, there have been many other ages of less discipline. [*string of criticisms,* scored −1]

   Defense: As Dr. Peale says, children aren't disciplined today as much as they should be. Just look at all the freedom with sex they have nowadays [*proposes new argument,* scored −1]. This is partly due to Dr. Spock and his teaching. Young people just don't have the same moral standards they once had. It is all due to the lack of discipline in the American home today. [*total endorsement,* scored −1] [Total score = −4]

Adapted Traditional Measures of Intellectual Ability

   While these two new measures are the major source of results about intellectual abilities to be discussed in the next chapter, we also adapted some more traditional measures of intellectual performance and cognitive style. Since these measures are more familiar in educational research, our discussion of them here will be brief.

   Concept Attainment. In discussing the Test of Thematic Analysis, we argued that most of the existing research on concept formation actually involved the attainment (and not the formation) of rather simple concepts or categories. Concept attainment measured in this way seems so basic and elementary an ability that (perhaps like grammar or simple addition) it is an educational preface to the liberal arts rather than being directly affected by them. Nevertheless, to test whether a simple concept attainment of this kind does increase as a result of liberal education, we included a modification of Heidbreder's (1946) test. Subjects are given five trials. On each trial, they are presented with nine objects, each of which embodies one of three concepts (number, spatial arrangement, or concrete object class) and is labeled with one of three nonsense syllables corresponding to the concept. (While using nonsense syllables in this way might seem to be a remote and inadequate test of liberal education—and we believe it is—the technique has a venerable history in concept-attainment research.) Each trial presents new objects embodying the three concepts, and subjects are asked to label each object. The score for each trial is the number of correct labelings on the trial; in this study, we used the number correct on the final two trials.

While the Test of Thematic Analysis was designed to measure the generation of complex, abstract concepts, it can also be used in two ways to study concept attainment. The two groups of stories used in this study were drawn from one group in which power concerns had been especially aroused (see Winter, 1973, chap. 3) and one group that was in a neutral state of arousal. As a result, power themes or images are more common in the "aroused" group than in the "neutral" one. Therefore, any Test of Thematic Analysis response that referred to power as a differentiating element between the two groups of stories would be in some sense correct. The number of power themes mentioned as elements in the thematic analysis response was taken as a rough measure, then, of whether the student had attained a concept that was in fact the major difference between the two groups. (This is analogous to the difference between a "good" exam answer that may not be "correct" and a "correct" answer that may not be "good." Of course, power themes may not be the only difference between the two groups of stories.)

After completing the Test of Thematic Analysis, some students were also given four more stories and asked to classify them according to which of the two groups they came from.

(Two stories came from each group.) The number of stories correctly placed is another measure of whether any of the concepts that "really" differentiated the two groups had been attained, regardless of whether they had been explicitly mentioned in the response or whether the response itself was "good."

Divergent Thinking. While there has been considerable debate about the number and kinds of separate skills included in the concept of intelligence, the distinction drawn by Getzels and Jackson (1962) between creativity and intelligence is most relevant to the question of liberal education. Hudson (1966, 1968) has elaborated this distinction into "divergent thinking" and "convergent thinking," respectively, as two different styles or kinds of intelligence. Convergers have orderly, systematic minds and perform well on the usual kinds of intelligence tests; divergers are more creative, innovative, original, and fluent in self-expression. Hudson originally based the distinction on the differential aptitudes of humanities and science students (although the distinction has much wider ramifications; see Hudson, 1975). This suggests that divergence/convergence may have more to do with choosing particular fields of study than it does with liberal education as a whole. Creativity does not explicitly appear in the list of goals in Chapter One; and while most liberal educators would stress originality and independence of thought, they would also distinguish the liberally educated person from the creative artist—the former should be able to appreciate and *comprehend* what the latter *expresses.* Divergence, then, may not be an overriding goal of liberal education, although it is certainly an important goal of some institutions. We thought it worthwhile to include divergence in the battery of tests, partly to see whether it was in fact unaffected by liberal arts education and partly to test some critics' claims that curiosity and originality are actually lowered in the liberal arts college (see Chapter One).

Hudson measures divergence with two tests originally introduced by Getzels and Jackson (1962): the "Uses of Objects" and the "Meanings of Words." In the first test, people are given a list of common objects (such as a paper clip or a blanket) and asked to think up as many uses as possible in fifteen minutes.

Here are examples of some unusual uses suggested for a blanket: "To make smoke signals with. As a sail for a boat. As a substitute for a towel. As a target for shooting practice for near-sighted people. Dog's basket. A modern sculpture. As a thing to catch people jumping out of burning buildings. For making blanket statements" (Hudson, 1966, p. 46). On the second test, people are given a list of common words that have multiple meanings (such as bit, fair, or port) and asked to think up as many meanings as possible in fifteen minutes. Hudson subtracts the combined scores on these two tests from scores on a standard intelligence test (which measures convergent thinking) to get a measure of relative divergence. We simply used the two separate divergence measures.

Sensitivity. According to some theorists, empathy is a goal of liberal education. While this kind of empathy is usually elaborated in cognitive terms—to understand the logical structure of other peoples' arguments, as in Analysis of Argument—it can also imply intuitive or emotional sensitivity. To measure empathy in this latter sense, one can use part of the Profile of Nonverbal Sensitivity (PONS) developed by Rosenthal and others (1979). Subjects listen to a tape recording of a woman's voice as she expresses a series of different emotions, and in each case, they attempt to decide which of two emotions is being expressed. In the "intuitive" section of the PONS, the tape has been altered by screening out certain frequencies so that the words cannot be understood. The content is effectively filtered out; so the listener must rely on an intuitive understanding of the speaker's tone of voice. In the "analytical" section of the PONS, the tape has been altered by cutting it into small bits and splicing the bits back together in a random fashion. Thus the listener might hear the end of a word before its beginning and so has to analyze and mentally reassemble the bits and pieces into something he or she can understand.

Learning New Material. A presumed outcome of all higher education is the ability to learn new material more quickly, both because of general familiarization with the content area ("transfer of training," in technical terms) and because of improvement in what might be called "learning how to learn." We believe that the latter skill is, to some extent, reflected in the Test of Thematic Analysis. To test the former skill, traditional instruments can be employed that involve actual learning of new material in different broad fields of science, social science, and humanities in order to see whether majors in a particular group of fields are able to learn new material in that area more quickly and fully than are majors in other areas. In retrospect, our use of these instruments was not really successful, since even the science material was actually verbal material about science rather than science itself. Yet had we used scientific and mathematical symbols and notations, the real language of science, we would have obtained effects that would have been spurious, since physics majors can obviously learn a calculus formula more quickly than can mathematically illiterate art majors. The test materials used can be classified by modes—written, aurally presented, and programmed instruction—as used in higher education.

In the written mode of the test, subjects read brief articles on three topics: the "bright spot" technique for finding oil, the retraining of older workers, and the literary styles of a nineteenth-century French novelist. After each passage, they turned the page and filled in several blanks in sentences, drawing on information in the previous passage. The score was simply the number of blanks correctly filled in. This test is probably the measure that is most similar to existing tests, but since the material was new to all students, it does measure a simple ability to learn after one brief exposure, rather than measuring prior general knowledge.

In the aural mode, students listened to a biographical excerpt about a scientist and a discussion of historical theory. After each passage, they filled in the blanks, as on the written version just described. However, in this test, they then listened to each tape and filled in each blank a second time; so there are both final scores from the second trial and also gain scores from the first trial.

In the programmed instruction mode, students first answered true-false questions drawn from the three passages used for the written version previously described. Then they were

given correct answers, new questions and then answers, and finally all items a second time, yielding both total final scores and
gain scores from first to second trial. This test was designed to
reflect in a simple way the kind of skill useful in programmed
instruction, a teaching mode more and more widely used in
higher education.

Measuring Qualities of Mind

One of the oldest and most widely used ways in which
psychologists have gathered operant data is the Thematic Apperception Test or TAT, first developed by Murray and his associates (Morgan and Murray, 1935). Subjects are shown a series
of vague or ambiguous pictures and are asked to make up a brief,
imaginative story about each picture. The basic assumption of
the test is that the stories people tell are a sample of their inner
thoughts, wishes, or mental dynamics.[3] At first, the TAT was
individually administered by clinicians who interpreted the
stories in complex, subjective ways after having had lengthy
training and clinical experience. Later modifications permitted
subjects to write stories in group administration (often in a format called Test of Imagination or Picture Interpretation Exercise to get away from the connotations of the psychology clinic).
Several objective scoring systems for motives and other psychological variables were derived on the basis of experimental
manipulation of the motive to be measured or other empirical
procedures. (See Atkinson, 1958, and Winter, 1973, pp. 37-40
and chap. 3, for an account of the strategy of empirical derivation.) Many of these later scoring systems have acquired a good
deal of construct validity—that is, they predict a wide variety of
behaviors that are both important in real life and also relevant to
liberal arts educational goals. At the same time, the TAT measures are sensitive to situation and personality change; so they
would be able to pick up changes due to education. (Indeed,
their very sensitivity has sometimes been used to criticize their
test-retest reliability.)[4] For example, one study of the effects of
an advanced studies summer school program on its talented student participants used both the TAT and several specially de-

signed objective questionnaires of the usual type. From before to after the program, TAT stories changed toward program goals and emphases, but the questionnaire responses showed little change (Winter, Alpert, and McClelland, 1963). This demonstrated superiority in detecting education-induced change is, then, a good reason for including the TAT in the test battery.

The TAT is also efficient, in that several different measures or variables can be coded from the same set of stories (which take about one half hour for subjects to write). Another related advantage is that while researchers can never go back in time to administer a new questionnaire or ask another interview question, they can easily preserve TAT stories and at some future time apply new coding systems to them. In rather metaphorical terms, then, the TAT can be used to collect and "freeze" samples of thought for future analysis by coding systems yet to be developed. (In fact, any sample of thought or writing that is at least partly imaginative can be used in this way, although there are methodological problems; see Winter and Stewart, 1977a). In the main research reported in this book, students wrote five-minute stories to the following four pictures: a ship captain talking to a man, which elicits stories dealing with authority; a man and a woman in a nightclub, which elicits stories about personal relationships; two women scientists working in a laboratory, which elicits stories about working relationships and success; and a man and a woman performing on a trapeze, which elicits stories about work, fame, and interpersonal relationships.

We used five measures based on the TAT. Each measure has a scoring system that is objective in the sense that after brief training, two coders working independently on the same material will have at least 85 percent category agreement with each other and with expert scorers (see Winter, 1973, p. 248). This was the standard of interscorer reliability for TAT measures we used throughout the research we describe in this book.

Achievement Motivation. The achievement motive (or *n* Achievement) is a measure of people's concern with excellence —doing well at some task or accomplishing something that is unique. While such a motive might seem to be relevant to academic success and achievement, research studies have consistently found it to be unrelated to grades or any other measure of school performance. (See Birney, 1968; but see also Atkinson and Raynor, 1974, chaps. 7-10, for some qualifications to this conclusion.) These results do not exhaust the possible interest of n Achievement for our purposes, however. What the achievement motive measure does predict is achievement of an important and quite different kind: successful performance as an entrepreneur or business innovator (McClelland, 1961; McClelland and Winter, 1969)—through taking moderate (versus extreme) risks and setting moderate goals, modifying performance on the basis of results, getting task help from experts rather than friends, and having a restless and energetic personal style.

Do these behaviors have anything to do with the liberal arts? They are important in their own right, and they are related to at least some of the presumed goals of liberal education described in Chapter One. Nevertheless, many people believe that the liberal arts and worldly economic success are irreconcilably opposed (except that many colleges were originally endowed by high n Achievement businessmen!). Perhaps, one might argue, contempt for business success (or *lowered* n Achievement) should have been included in the Chapter One list, at least as an implicit or even unintended outcome of liberal education. There is, after all, disdain for business among the graduates of Oxford and Cambridge (and many American liberal arts colleges as well), a disdain that can be plausibly connected to the continuing troubles of the British economy. However, the style of raising children that makes them high in n Achievement—setting high goals but giving freedom and scope to accomplish these goals without specific directions—is a lot like the image that many liberal educators have of what they are and how they teach. Taken together, all these contradictory findings and speculations suggest some paradoxical and complicated connections between n Achievement and the liberal arts. Maybe there is no consistent and enduring pattern. Since the waxing and waning of the achievement motive does seem to play a major part in the growth and decline of cultures, however, we think that the question of how this motive is affected by the liberal arts is an important one, no matter what the answer. In terms of the explicitly mentioned effects of liberal education listed in Chapter One, an increase in achievement motivation would appear to be most closely associated with the goal of independence of thought.

Leadership Motive Pattern. The same TAT technique has been adapted to measure other important human social motives. McClelland has developed a measure of the leadership motive pattern, which reflects an interest in expressing controlled power. Managers with this pattern generate exceptionally high morale in their subordinates, who see them as promoting individual responsibility, clarity of organizational structure and goals, and team spirit while avoiding or at least not emphasizing conformity (McClelland and Burnham, 1976). Such managers also advance more rapidly in large corporations (McClelland and Boyatzis, 1980). Among other individuals, this pattern predicts involvement in organizational power and authority, discipline and self-control, altruism, and concern for justice. Among societies, the pattern predicts mobilizing resources for overall system capability and war instead of for individual consumption—hence the alternative label of "imperial" motive pattern (McClelland, 1975). Finally, recent research suggests that men with this motive pattern are more vulnerable to high blood pressure (see McClelland, 1979).

Taking all these findings together, the pattern seems to involve *organization building* or the mobilization and coordination of resources and collective psychic energy toward consciously defined goals. Whether in particular instances this is called "empire building" probably depends on one's values, interests, and hindsight. Whatever the label, however, this combination of discipline, organization, altruism, and justice certainly touches on many of the presumed goals of liberal arts education listed in Chapter One (especially goals 5 and 6), so that the leadership motive pattern is an important part of the test battery.

The pattern is defined as "present" if there is the following configuration of separate scores: (1) power motivation in at least the top 70 percent of the distribution, (2) power motivation greater than affiliation motivation (when both are expressed in standardized terms), and (3) activity inhibition score above the median. The power motive (n Power) is a concern for impact, control, influence, and prestige. It predicts liking vigorous and personally challenging experiences, getting formal social power and prestige, and (among men) exploitative sexual behavior and difficulties in intimate relationships with the opposite sex. When combined with low activity inhibition, it also leads to unsocialized forms of power: gambling, taking high risks, liquor, and drugs (see Winter, 1973; Winter and Stewart, 1978). The affiliation motive (n Affiliation) is a concern for friendship, love, nurturance, and companionate activity. It predicts warm sociable activity (when the person is comfortable and at ease), getting help on a task from friends rather than from experts, and reacting to disagreement with dislike (see Boyatzis, 1973). Finally, activity inhibition, measured by the frequency of use of "not," strongly affects how motives such as power and affiliation are expressed (see McClelland and others, 1972).

Fear of Success and the Education of Women. Fear of success is also a TAT-based motive variable but it really also introduces the wider issue of the education of women, about which we shall have more to say in later chapters. Fear of success certainly does not appear in the list in Chapter One, and no educator would claim it is even an outcome, much less a goal, of liberal education. It is nonetheless an important variable when we consider possible differences in the effects of liberal education on men and on women.

Access to higher education itself is a good measure of one aspect of women's status (see Stewart and Winter, 1977). From the time of Plato down to the late nineteenth century, the Western ideal of liberal arts education was exclusively a male ideal—education of men, by men, for the benefit of male-dominated social institutions (church, government, military, economy, intelligentsia). Nowadays the formal barriers to women's education are mostly down, and in the United States, the proportions of female and male students in liberal arts colleges are nearly equal. This does not mean, however, that the effects of this education are always equal for both sexes. With considerable support from research, the women's movement argues there are sex differences in *evaluation* of academic performance (the work of male students is graded higher than that of female students; see, for example, Pheterson, Kiesler, and Goldberg, 1971) and in *guidance and encouragement* (men are tracked to become empire builders, scientists, and theorists and women are tracked to be "helpers" and "culture bearers"). Some even go so far as to assert that the whole liberal arts tradition is a tradition of "male knowledge," in contrast to other, more "female" modes of knowing. This distinction resembles the *Erkenntnis/Erlebnis* issue discussed in Chapter One. While it is not easy to determine how to test such a claim, it is obvious that, at least until recently, women in a liberal arts college like the male-oriented Ivy College encountered very few female faculty role models, many subtle forms of discouragement, and little guidance in relating their education to the same kinds of later careers that men have.

The fear of success measure was designed to capture the psychological aspects of just these kinds of social pressures educated women face. Thus Horner (1969, 1972) originally found, in a sample of college women, that fear of success in women predicted a performance *decrement* when competing with males at an academic task, as compared to competing with other females. That is, women high on fear of success seem to be especially aware of role prescriptions and social pressures that shape, restrict, and inhibit their ambitions. While subsequent research on fear of success has produced some conflicting results (see, for example, Tresemer, 1977), two general trends do seem clear (see Fleming, 1977). In most women, fear of success is associated with avoidance of success. For example, Hoffman (1977) found that women high in fear of success tended to become pregnant and withdraw from careers just when they were about to become successful—more successful, often, than their husbands were. But in women from backgrounds stressing achievement and educational values, fear of success predicts *conflict* rather than outright avoidance. Thus Roth-Walsh and Stewart (1976) found that female doctors who were high in fear of success tended to cluster in pediatrics and psychiatry, the two specialties with the highest proportion of women. In other research, Stewart (1975) found that women of this same background who were high in fear of success tended to show a paradoxical pattern of career success under the most difficult conditions (with young children) but not under easier conditions (without children).

Thus fear of success is an important measure, at least for the women college students in this study, not because it reflects a conscious goal of liberal education but because it may reflect the psychological aspects of subtle discrimination (or at least pressures) against women liberal arts students and because it may reflect the psychological residue of centuries of male dominance in higher education generally.

Self-Definition and Maturity of Adaptation. In recent years, Stewart has developed TAT-based measures for two other qualities of mind: Self-definition and Stages of Psychological Adaptation to the Environment (reflecting maturity of adaptation). Research done to date on these variables suggests that they both involve characteristics and behaviors that are important to liberal education.

Stewart and Winter (1974) originally developed the Self-definition measure to distinguish the TAT stories of college women who planned full-time careers after college from the stories of women who planned only marriage and family, without an outside career. Stewart (1980) later confirmed that for women in a college emphasizing female career aspirations, Self-definition also predicted whether women actually either had careers or did free-lance work some fourteen years later. Stories with explicit causal relationships, and actions that happen for reasons, are scored for Self-definition. Stories that lack causality or involve ineffective characters are negatively scored for Self-definition—they reflect, in other words, social definition. Because Self-definition involves viewing the world in causal terms, it involves a dimension of cognitive maturity or instrumentality. At the same time, the behavioral correlates of Self-definition suggest an instrumental style of action: independence of ascribed roles, nonegocentric perceptions of others and the world in general, and effective coping with problems and stress (Stewart, 1978). Thus there are good grounds for believing that Self-definition is a quality of mind that is relevant not only to college women's future careers and plans but also to many of the broad goals of liberal education.

Stewart (1977b, in press) developed the TAT-based Stages of Adaptation measure in order to validate a theory about stages of adaptation to the environment. The measure draws on the stage theories of social-emotional development of Freud ([1940] 1964, chap. 3) and Erikson (1950, 1959), but it also assumes repeated renegotiation of the stage sequence in adult life. There are four stages of adaptation to the environment, each more "mature" than the one before it. In the first "receptive" stage, people see authority as benevolent, wishes as immediately gratified, and themselves as passively feeling loss and confusion. At the second "autonomous" stage, people see authority as criticizing, wishes as not gratified, and the self as acting incompetently to clear away disorder and confusion. Next is the "assertive" stage, where people oppose authority, run from other people, and yet see themselves as failing. In the final "integrative" stage, a sense of balance pervades each of these issues: Authority is seen as limited and not monolithic; feelings are differentiated and ambivalent; and the person feels work and interpersonal involvement. Each of these four stages has its own independent score, and there are also various ways of combining the separate scores into one summary measure of the maturity of psychological adaptation, as discussed in general terms by Rest (1976). The measure used throughout this book is of "modal stage," the stage of the person's highest score. In case of ties, the higher stage is always used as the modal stage.

In a study of one large company, McClelland and Burnham (1976) found that the more effective managers showed higher scores (higher levels of maturity of adaptation) than did the less effective managers. The authors' description of these mature managers gives a good sense of the behavior and style reflected in the stages measure. They "can be most simply described as less egotistic. . . . They are less defensive, more willing to seek advice from experts, and have a longer range view. . . . It is as if they have awakened to the fact that they are not going to live forever and have lost some of the feeling that their own personal future is all that important" (McClelland and Burnham, 1976, p. 106).

McClelland (1975, chap. 2) also found that Stage of Adaptation had an important influence or moderator effect on the ways the power motive is expressed in action. For example, high *n* Power plus a "receptive" orientation leads to a concern with *vicarious power* in thought, fantasy, and dreaming—perhaps the "omnipotence of thought" stage of immaturity described by Freud ([1930] 1961, chap. 1). Combined with the "assertive" stage, power motivation leads to aggressive and assertive showing off. Finally, in the "integrative" person at the fourth stage, the power motive is expressed in more institutional and even altruistic ways. Power is the goal throughout the sequence; but the level of adaptation or maturity has a decisive effect on the particular kinds of power sought and the particular ways it is pursued.

While the Stages of Psychological Adaptation measure is new, it has obvious relevance to several of the goals of liberal education, both on the basis of the original conceptualization and derivation of the measure and on the basis of its demonstrated action correlates.

Self-Rated Skills

Implicit in the whole history of liberal education is the goal of increased self-knowledge: that students come to see themselves, their strengths and their weaknesses, accurately and to appraise their relationship to the rest of the world accurately. While it is difficult to know whether students see themselves accurately, it is easy to measure how they see themselves and their skills. Therefore we asked all students simply to rate how they view their abilities in the following sixteen areas. Each skill was rated on a five-point scale from "outstanding" (scored 5) to "do not possess this skill" (scored 1).

supervising	sticking to a task
analyzing	negotiating
analytical writing	teaching
creative writing	persuading
public speaking	quick learning
working alone	organizing and presenting ideas
working in a group	accepting criticism
respecting diversity	conceptualizing

Measures and Goals of Liberal Education

Table 2 summarizes the major goals of liberal arts education, listed in Chapter One, showing where each test, variable,

Table 2. Goals of Liberal Arts Education and Measures
Used in This Study

Presumed Effect (see Chapter One)	Measures Used in This Study
1. Critical thinking; broad analytical skill	Test of Thematic Analysis Analysis of Argument Concept Attainment Test
2. Learning how to learn	Learning new material (three modes)
3. Independence of thought	Self-definition Divergent thinking Achievement motivation
4. Empathy; seeing all sides of an issue	Analysis of Argument Profile of Nonverbal Sensitivity
5. Self-control for broader loyal-	Leadership motive pattern
6. Self-assurance in leadership ability	Leadership motive pattern (low) Fear of success Self-ratings
7. Mature social-emotional judgment; personal integration	Stages of Psychological Adaptation
8. Equalitarian, liberal values	Self-ratings
9. Participation in and enjoyment of cultural experience	—

or procedure described in this chapter fits in terms of these goals. Overall, we have covered most of the nine major goal areas, usually with more than one measure for each. "Participation and enjoyment in cultural experience" is not directly measured, but this should be easy to evaluate by simple everyday questions about books read, concerts and galleries attended, cultural forms understood, and so forth. Nor did we attempt to measure directly the increase in democratic or equalitarian values, largely because previous research has demonstrated that such an increase occurred in many institutions of higher learning (see Feldman and Newcomb, 1969). While some of our new measures may seem unusual, when taken together, they constitute a serious effort to cover what educators have felt is important and distinctive about education in the liberal arts. Whether they are successful in showing gains, of course, depends on the research results to be presented in the next chapter. The research to be reported in this book is therefore a kind of "bootstraps" operation, with two separate but related concerns. On the one hand, we are trying to discover the distinctive effects of liberal arts education through the use of a battery of innovative measures. Accomplishing this goal, on the other hand, will also expand the validity and therefore usefulness of the new measures.

Notes

1. These brief descriptions are not adequate for scoring purposes. Full copies of the test and further information can be obtained from McBer & Company, as discussed in Resource A. Other aspects of conceptual style could also be scored from these responses, for example, differentiation (Bieri, 1961, 1966) or integrative complexity (Schroder, Driver, and Streufert, 1967).

2. These brief descriptions are not adequate for scoring purposes. Full copies of the test and scoring manual can be obtained from McBer & Company, as discussed in Resource A.

3. The TAT is sometimes called a "projective" test and is said to measure apperception (the process of assigning meaning to the physical stimulus), but whether it involves projection in the strict psychoanalytical sense is not important to this discussion (see Winter, 1973, pp. 33-36).

4. The issue of TAT reliability is actually complex (see Winter, 1973, pp. 86-93). A recent study by Winter and Stewart (1977b) suggests that the rather low test-retest correlations often obtained with the TAT may be largely artifacts of the test instructions to "be creative" rather than evidence of inherent low reliability.

THREE

Testing the Impact of Liberal Education at "Ivy College"

The research reported in this chapter was designed to establish the distinctive effects of liberal arts education by comparing the performance of freshman and final-year students at three colleges on the instruments described in the last chapter. But what exactly is a liberal arts education? Is it the study of certain core disciplines or bodies of knowledge—courses such as Western Civilization, Modern Literature, or a particular set of great books? (Most students take at least a few such courses during their college years.) Is it *any* course that is consciously and deliberately interdisciplinary or multidisciplinary, such as Freedom and Authority in the Modern Novel, or Science and Responsibility? Or is it how learning occurs rather than what is learned—concepts rather than facts, independent inquiry rather than rote learning? Finally, some educators see the liberal arts as simply a kind of residual category, including every course that is not of obvious practical use or vocational relevance (especially if it is esoteric or trendy, such as The Don Juan Theme in Literature and Society, or Ancient Icelandic Sagas).

We began with one institution that has undoubted liberal arts credentials by any of the above definitions; in addition, it has fame, wealth, and prestige. We shall call this institution "Ivy" College. What is an appropriate comparison or control institution? Another liberal arts college? Such a comparison would make it impossible to distinguish the (presumably many) effects common to both institutions from the effects of simple maturation; so the research would be reduced to a confirmation (or disconfirmation) of the "small differences" that are so dear to the narcissism of graduates and faculty of particular colleges. It would clearly not capture the general effects of liberal education. The best way to establish these effects is to compare Ivy College to other colleges that offer very different kinds of education—for example, vocational training or junior college education. We chose two other institutions from among these types, a four-year state teachers college and a two-year community college. While both offer some liberal arts courses (in the narrow sense of the first definition previously quoted), they are very different from Ivy College in terms of their total orientation, institutional structure, curriculum, climate, values, and priorities. If these comparisons show differences in effects, we can conclude that Ivy College does have distinctive effects on its students. Then further research could determine whether these special effects hold up for other liberal arts colleges or whether they are specific to Ivy College and identify the probable causes —curricular, institutional, or other—of these effects.

The advantage of this strategy is that it maximizes the chance that meaningful differences will be found at this initial stage. Given the present status and prestige of the liberal arts, this seems a wise first goal. It is the major purpose of this book.

A Research Strategy

For reasons of time, we shall focus for the most part on a cross sectional study in which freshmen and seniors at each institution were tested at the same time. Testing the same students at entry and exit—the longitudinal design Feldman and Newcomb (1969, pp. 52-53) prefer—is much more time-consuming, since a full "cycle" takes at least four years plus time for data analysis. It is therefore of much less use in guiding educational policy. In addition to being quicker, the cross sectional design controls for the effects of history and retesting effects, which the longitudinal design does not do. However, since we found important freshman-senior differences at the liberal arts Ivy College, we did retest some of the Ivy College freshmen sample in their senior year to see whether these same effects occurred over time.

For each institution, the differences between freshman and senior responses are an estimate of the change effects of that institution. The crucial comparison, for present purposes, is between the freshman-senior differences at Ivy College and those at the other two institutions. Changes common to all three colleges could be either a generalized effect of any higher education or else the effect of simple maturation. Changes at Ivy College that are unique, or that are significantly greater than corresponding changes at State Teachers and Community colleges, can be taken as a unique effect of the education Ivy College offers.

What are the problems with this design? The three colleges recruit and select very different kinds of students, as reflected in differences among the three groups of freshmen. Since we cannot control selection and assignment of students to the three colleges, our research becomes (in the words of Campbell and Stanley, 1963) a "quasi-experimental" study with nonequivalent control groups. As such, it is subject to three main kinds of error or alternative interpretations. The first is *change in the basis of recruitment or selection.* If any of the three institutions changed the criteria according to which they select students between the years that the seniors and the freshmen were admitted, or if the nature of the applicant pool changed during that time, then the former (now discontinued) selection criteria will appear as spurious change effects while the new criteria will appear, spuriously, as variables that are lowered by the college. There is, however, no evidence of any change of this sort at any of the three institutions during the time of the present study. At Ivy College, there is an additional control for this possibility since we also retested the same students in freshman and senior year.

The second is *attrition from freshman to senior year.* Some students drop out of college along the way. If those who do remain (at one college) are different in any characteristic, then this characteristic will appear as a spurious change effect of that college. In the present research, we have concluded that differences in attrition rates actually work *against* the hypothesis of distinctive liberal arts effects, if they have any effect at all. First, the freshman-to-graduation attrition rate at Ivy College is low—about 8 percent, compared to 45 percent at State Teachers College and 40 percent (freshman-to-sophomore) at Community College. If one assumes that the students who do drop out, compared to those who stay, are either lower or at least not higher in whatever abilities or characteristics are affected by college (reasonable assumptions, according to Feldman and Newcomb, 1969, pp. 290 and 306, and Ellison and Simon, 1973, pp. 48-50), then the higher attrition rates at State Teachers and Community colleges will make them appear relatively more effective in changing students than Ivy College. To rephrase the point: Compared to Ivy College, the other two institutions might look more effective than they really are because only the best of their students were still around to be tested; at Ivy, a far greater proportion of the original freshmen remains. Thus while attrition effects might bias the study of a single institution, in this case, the differential rates should work against finding any special effects at Ivy College.

The third kind of error or alternative interpretation is *interaction of selection differences with maturation* (or history). As discussed, the critical comparison is of freshman-senior *differences* at Ivy College with those at the other two institutions. Any direct effects of selection and recruitment differences are thus taken into account and ruled out as a source of error. However, these differences could *interact* with maturation (or history) to produce spurious estimates of greater change at Ivy College. In other words, Ivy College may pick the students who will show greater growth as well as a higher initial level. Whether a greater freshman-to-senior difference among Ivy College students is due to the effects of Ivy College depends on the levels of the relevant characteristic before entry. If Ivy students also scored about the same in secondary school as they do as freshmen, then we could conclude that Ivy College did appear to have change effects of its own, even though they were initially higher than the students at the comparison college. But if Ivy freshmen scored lower before college than as freshmen, the proper conclusion is simply that Ivy College recruited and/ or selected students who were going to change in this way—indeed, who had already started to develop the characteristic in question.

This selection-by-maturation interaction is very difficult to rule out completely in any quasi-experimental design, especially without prefreshman data. (It is worth noting that longitudinal testing of the same students in freshman and senior years does not help to solve this problem.) However, two further kinds of information can be used to reduce the likelihood that apparent changes are due to this kind of interaction effect. First, if the Ivy students and the comparison students did not differ on the characteristic at the time of the freshman year testing, then the interaction effect is less likely as an explanation of the different freshman-senior changes, because in such a case the Ivy students would have scored *below* the comparison students before college or else the interaction effect would have taken place exactly and only during the college years. Both these possibilities appear unlikely, although of course they are by no means impossible. The second kind of information that can be used to rule out interaction effects is the correlations of the hypothetical characteristic with other variables that are known to be different at entry—notably intelligence and social class—among the pooled group of all students tested in the freshman year, before any institutional change effects have taken place. If the characteristic is uncorrelated with these obvious "selection" variables, then interaction of selection and maturation is less likely, though not impossible. (These correlations are given in the Statistical Supplement, available as indicated in the Preface.)

As long as researchers cannot assign students at random to different colleges, it will be impossible to rule out interaction effects of this kind, involving selection variables. In the research reported in this book, we have taken what precautions were possible, and we present what further data are available and useful in order to minimize the likelihood of spurious effects of this sort.

Three Colleges

Ivy College is a well-endowed private liberal arts college with a long tradition of scholarly excellence, an eminent faculty, and great prestige. It is located in a large metropolitan area in the Eastern United States but draws a diverse group of students from the entire country and from abroad. Admissions standards are rated as "most competitive"; and 20 percent (two thirds men, one third women) of those who apply are accepted. Over 90 percent of freshmen graduate and about three quarters of the graduates go on to further education. Most students live in dormitories. The student-faculty ratio is about eight to one. The curriculum emphasizes traditional liberal arts courses, including both broad interdisciplinary surveys and advanced individualized scholarship. Ivy College has a long tradition of excellence, individuality, and autonomy; but as a consequence, some students feel abandoned to their own resources. As a total institution, Ivy College is very different from the two comparison colleges.

State Teachers College is a state-controlled institution founded specifically as a teachers' college, but it has gradually expanded its course offerings in the direction of general and career programs (law enforcement, health professions, and so forth), although about half the students are preparing to teach. It is located in a large metropolitan area, from which it draws most of its students. Its admissions standards are rated as "moderately competitive"; about half (equal proportions of men and women) of those who apply are accepted. About half of the entering freshmen graduate, and 40 percent of those go on to further education. There are no dormitories; so all students are commuters. The student-faculty ratio is about fifteen to one.

State Teachers College emphasizes vocational preparation for teaching and more generally for service-related careers.

Community College is a publicly controlled two-year institution. It is located near a large metropolitan area and draws mostly from nearby suburbs. It has a very liberal admissions policy, taking about 70 percent (three fifths men, two fifths women) of those who apply. About 60 percent of the entering freshmen finish the second year, and 40 percent of those go on to higher education. Students live off campus. The student-faculty ratio is about ten to one. The curriculum emphasizes career programs (data processing, nursing, electronics, secretarial technology), business administration, and a general transfer program.

Sampling, Subjects, and Model of Analysis

The basic design called for testing first-year and final-year students, male and female, at all three colleges during the autumn of the 1974-75 academic year. Since we wanted to examine various subgroups within the Ivy College sample (as reported in Chapter Five), our goal was to recruit at least 125 freshmen and 125 seniors. The State Teachers College and Community College samples are used primarily as a baseline to control for the effects of maturation and having had any postsecondary education at all; so smaller samples (30 from each class at each college) seemed adequate. At each institution, subjects from each class were selected randomly within the quota groups defined by sex, SAT scores (high/low), and broad area of major or intended major. Those selected were sent letters from the college administration asking them to attend one of several three-hour testing sessions that had been scheduled and offering $12 for their participation. Additional samples were drawn where necessary to meet the approximate sampling goals. At Ivy College, the response rate was around 70 percent; it was slightly lower at the other two colleges. Obviously, these procedures depart from the laboratory ideal of completely random selection and total participation of all students first contacted; but they are probably as good as can be expected in educational research of this kind. The comparability of freshman and senior samples, within each college, on key background and ability variables is the most important single requirement of our design, and the data we present suggest we achieved this goal in our study. The details of testing procedures are presented in Resource B.

In the spring of 1978, we recontacted as many as possible of the Ivy College students we had tested as freshmen three years earlier. We were able to recruit ninety of these students for further testing (about 70 percent of those students in the original freshman sample who were still at Ivy College and could be located). Eighty of these students had continued at Ivy College without major interruption and were scheduled to graduate that spring. These eighty students, then, constitute the longitudinal Ivy College sample. To make sure they are representative of the entire original group of Ivy College class of 1978 students, we compared their freshman scores to those of the rest of the sample on all variables. There were significant differences on only one or two variables, which will be mentioned where appropriate in the analyses that follow.

For the retesting, we paid students $15 for about five hours of testing in two different sessions. The test battery included the Thematic Apperception Test (given first, with the same four pictures used in the earlier testing), the Test of Thematic Analysis, and the Analysis of Argument test. Several other tests, given for other purposes and not analyzed in this research, were given in the second testing session. For the second administration of the TAT, we used the instructions Winter and Stewart (1977b, p. 438) recommend for removing biasing self-instructional sets and maximizing test-retest reliability: "Do not worry about whether your stories are similar to or different from any stories you may have written before. Write whatever stories you wish." In order to ensure scoring objectivity, the freshman and senior responses of the entire longitudinal sample were pooled and scored (or rescored, as the case may be) by scorers who did not know the college, class, or identity of the students.

Table 3 describes the characteristics of the total samples tested at each college. As it turned out, the Ivy seniors had

Table 3. Background and Ability Characteristics of All Student Samples

| | Years of Education | | Level of Father's Occupation[a] | Working Mothers | Plans to Teach | SAT Scores | | | | |
| | | | | | | Total Sample | | Matched Sample | | |
Group	Father	Mother				Verbal	Math	N	Verbal	Math
Ivy College										
Freshmen (N = 146)										
(71 men, 75 women)	17.1	15.8	2.93	66%	19%	677	687	(123)	690	695
Seniors (N = 118)										
(69 men, 49 women)	17.3	15.5	2.90	75%	21%	703	698	(101)	690	697
State Teachers College										
Freshmen (N = 32)										
(15 men, 17 women)	13.8	12.9	2.37	52%	41%	463	474			
Seniors (N = 38)										
(17 men, 21 women)	12.8	12.5	2.65	49%	34%	473	468			
Community College										
Freshmen (N = 30)										
(6 men, 24 women)	13.8	12.9	2.33	59%	4%	441	482			
Final Year (N = 32)										
(14 men, 18 women)	13.8	13.0	2.19	69%	8%	448	454			

[a]On a scale of 1 = unskilled or semiskilled worker, 2 = skilled worker, 3 = white collar, professional, or executive.

higher average Scholastic Aptitude Test (SAT) scores than did the Ivy freshmen. (There were no differences in SAT scores, however, between the entire classes of 1975 and 1978 at Ivy College.) On tests correlated with SAT scores such a difference could produce a spurious "gain" tendency for that test at Ivy College. In such cases, therefore, we constructed subsamples of Ivy freshmen and seniors matched on SAT scores by randomly discarding some of the high-scoring seniors and low-scoring freshmen. Apart from this, there were no significant differences between freshmen and final-year students at the same college on any of the variables in Table 3. This means that differences in average scores between freshmen and final-year students cannot be attributed to differences in intelligence or social-class background but may instead be attributed to the effect of attending that institution, assuming that other possible influences on test scores have remained more or less constant.

The data in Table 3 confirm the differences in the characteristics of the institutions already presented. Ivy College is highly selective, with average SAT scores in the top 2-3 percent of those taking the test, whereas the mean SAT scores at the other two colleges are slightly below the national average of about 500. The students at Ivy also come more often from highly educated families in which the father is a professional or executive. In line with tradition, those attending State Teachers College are more often planning to teach.

These differences in background of students attending the three colleges will make it difficult to interpret changes in average scores between freshman and senior year if a measure is associated with these background variables. For instance, if a measure is correlated with SAT scores, Ivy freshmen will score higher on it; and if Ivy seniors score still higher on the same measure, it could be argued that they have gained more because they are more intelligent. This is the familiar selection-by-maturation problem previously discussed. Fortunately, most of our new measures did not turn out to be significantly correlated with academic intelligence (SAT scores) or with parents' educational background. (A table in the Statistical Supplement presents these correlations.) However, the "traditional" test measures are rather highly correlated both with each other and with intelligence and social class, suggesting that they reflect a single general ability or "middle-class" factor. Perhaps this is one reason measures of this type do not show much change as a result of higher education. Of course, alternative explanations can never be completely ruled out in a quasi-experimental field research design, but the fact that most of our new measures are not related to the two main dimensions along which the college populations differ—intelligence and social class—gives us confidence that we may be able to isolate some of the effects of Ivy College.

Details of the procedures for reduction and analysis of the data are presented in Resource B. In brief, freshman-senior differences at each college were examined, tested for significance, and compared. We were guided by a three-way analysis of variance (with college, class, and sex as independent variables), paying special attention to the college by class interactions; but we did not follow this mode of analysis slavishly because of the large differences in cell sizes, due to the small numbers of students tested at State Teachers College and Community College. The results to be presented did not differ for men and women, with the single exception of fear of success, which will be discussed. In the rest of this chapter, we present the results in ordinary language, with a minimum of statistical notation. The more important findings are also presented in upcoming figures. For those readers who are interested in all of the actual numbers, we present descriptive and inferential statistics in the Statistical Supplement.

Critical Thinking and Analysis

In terms of the goal of critical thinking discussed in Chapter One, do the Ivy College seniors show greater skill than the freshmen in forming sophisticated, complex concepts about the differences between two groups of stories on the Test of Thematic Analysis? As Figure 1 shows, they did perform much better than did the Ivy College freshmen. Longitudinal results confirmed the finding. The retested group gained significantly (p

Figure 1. Average Thematic Analysis Scores in Freshman and
Final Years at Three Colleges

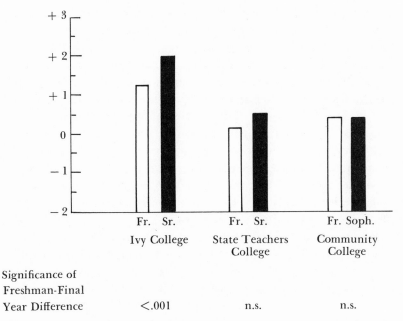

<.01) in thematic analysis scores between freshman and senior year. At the other colleges, freshman-senior differences were smaller and insignificant. Of course, the Ivy seniors in the longitudinal design were taking the same test again; so their gains might be due to practice, but this could not be the explanation for the higher score of the Ivy seniors relative to the Ivy freshmen in the cross sectional design.

The Ivy College seniors were not, however, more successful than freshmen at concept attainment—assigning new stories correctly to one or the other of the two groups. Perhaps this is because both groups did so well at the task. On the average, the Ivy freshmen correctly classified 7.8 of the additional 10 stories, while the seniors averaged 7.9 correct. Both scores may be near the ceiling of possible correct choices.

The reader may still wonder whether the "better" thematic analysis responses of the Ivy seniors were also more likely to be accurate—that is, to have correct elements, issues, and dichotomies. After all, every teacher knows the difference between a "good" answer that is not correct ("bull") and a correct answer that is poorly articulated. As discussed in Chapter Two, since the two groups of studies used for the Test of Thematic Analysis in this study were drawn from "power-aroused" and "neutral" groups, the number of power themes introduced in the response is, in a limited way, a measure of accuracy.

The Ivy seniors did mention power themes significantly more often as distinguishing the two sets of stories (average of 2.20 versus 1.87 for the freshmen, $t = 2.20$, $p < .05$). No significant differences between first- and final-year scores on this variable appeared for the other two colleges (respective averages were 1.63 and 1.24 for State Teachers College and 1.38 and 1.44 for Community College). Overall, seniors at Ivy College appear to have improved markedly in their ability to form abstract conceptualizations that are both well formed and also accurate.

However, it is not unambiguously clear that this gain is entirely due to their exposure to Ivy College because even as freshmen, Ivy students score higher on thematic analysis than the others, and among the pooled freshmen, there are small though significant correlations between thematic analysis score and intelligence (r with SAT = .18, $p < .05$) and social class (r with father's education = .22, $p < .01$). Thus it is possible that Ivy College seniors show a greater gain than other final-year students because they are more academically "intelligent" to start with and would therefore tend to show greater gains whatever institution they attended. The most likely interpretation is that the improvement is due to some kind of interaction between ability and the type of education at Ivy. This is suggested by the fact that the correlation between SAT score and thematic analysis among freshmen at Ivy is negligible ($r = .05$), whereas among seniors, it is quite significant ($r = .29$, $p < .01$). This suggests that the more intelligent students, even at these very high levels of ability, have been stimulated by their education to learn even better how to think critically, how to create complex categories. Furthermore, among freshmen, thematic analysis is not correlated with correctly mentioning power themes as distinguishing the two groups of stories (r = —.05), whereas it is among seniors (r = .34, p < .001). This suggests that the students at Ivy—because of their higher natural ability, their education, or both—gain not only in formal analytical skill and in correct conceptualization, but also in fusing these two component skills. Whatever the reason for the changes in these aspects of critical thinking, there is solid evidence that freshman and senior students at Ivy College show differences in it, differences greater than those shown by students at other colleges.

Analysis of Argument. The results of the Analysis of Argument test, illustrated in Figure 2, are even more striking.

Figure 2. Average Analysis of Argument Subscores in Freshman and Final Years at Three Colleges

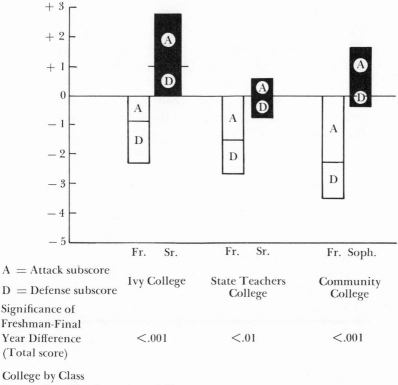

A = Attack subscore

D = Defense subscore

	Ivy College	State Teachers College	Community College
Significance of Freshman-Final Year Difference (Total score)	<.001	<.01	<.001

College by Class Interaction (Total score) p <.01

For one thing, the Ivy College students start out at nearly the same levels as students in the other colleges. In fact, they are actually somewhat lower on the "defense" score—the ability to be both flexible and consistent while arguing the reverse of their previous position in defending an unpopular position. Scores are higher in the final year than in freshman year at all colleges, but the differences are significantly greater at Ivy College. (Thus the college by class interaction is significant.) The Ivy College freshman-senior difference in the defense subscore is especially marked, being twice as large as that at Community College and six times greater than at State Teachers College. The longitudinal results for Ivy show a similar confirming pattern: When retested as seniors, the Ivy College students show significant gains from freshman year in both total score and defense subscore (p < .05 in each case).

It is unlikely that these results are due to artifacts such as the higher SAT scores of Ivy College students or practice effects. First, the defense subscore actually has a negative correlation with combined SAT scores (r = −.16). Second, freshman-year scores are about the same at all three colleges. Finally, in 1978, we tested two additional small samples of Ivy College freshmen and seniors with the Analysis of Argument test, using both the familiar "Peale" form and a new experimental form in which a professor strongly advocated nuclear power as a cheap source of electricity (an unpopular position at Ivy College). In both cases, seniors scored higher than freshmen (one-tailed p's < .02 and < .10, respectively). The correlation of scores on the two forms, moreover, was highly significant (r = +.51, p < .001), suggesting that the Analysis of Argument test reflects a generalized ability to reason well in a variety of controversial, emotional situations. Thus although higher education greatly improves the quality of students' ability to analyze arguments, the educational impact of Ivy College improves it even more, particularly when this analysis involves the intellectual flexibility of defending an unpopular position in a way that is consistent with one's initial attack on the position.

Since previous research studies of skills such as "reasoning ability" have failed to show freshman-senior differences in detecting logical errors, fallacies, and the like, why were our results so striking? We believe our results are due to the operant nature of the Analysis of Argument test. Instead of asking students in an "objective" way to choose the best of several arguments or to decide which argument embodies which logical fallacy, the Analysis of Argument test engages the reasoning and dialectical processes in ways that are much more vivid, *and much more like the real world of controversy and argument,* than the more traditional tests. For this reason, the results of the Analysis of Argument test are all the more impressive.

Concept Attainment. The remaining measure of critical thinking was the rather traditional, highly structured Concept of Attainment Test devised by Heidbreder (1946). Our findings with it are very similar to those reported by other investigators; that is, we too are unable to demonstrate that higher education has any effects. As with most respondent or highly structured tests, speed of concept attainment is highly correlated with academic intelligence ($r = .33$, $p < .001$) and social class as measured by father's education ($r = .37$, $p < .001$). As a result, Ivy freshmen already score higher on the test than freshmen at other institutions; but even so, attendance at Ivy College does not appear to improve their ability to perform on this test more than does attendance at other institutions. For the spatial and numerical concepts, at least, final-year students tend to do slightly better than freshmen toward the end of the test, but there are no significant differences among institutions.

These results give some support to our general position that operant measures are likely to be sensitive to variations in the impact of higher education, while more structured respondent measures are likely to reflect differences in academic intelligence. In any case, the Heidbreder Concept Attainment Test seems to involve something quite different from high-level conceptual and articulation abilities—in short, from critical thinking —and it is in fact not very highly correlated with either the Test of Thematic Analysis ($r = .22$) or Analysis of Argument ($r = .03$).

Learning How to Learn

As we pointed out in Chapter Two, one widely held belief about higher education is that it sharpens the mind, as it were, so that college graduates can absorb information faster. More technically, college graduates are said to have developed frames of reference that make it easier for them to understand and remember new material. We designed three types of tests that measured the speed and accuracy with which freshmen and seniors could learn new material drawn from the humanities, the social sciences, and the natural sciences. None of these measures demonstrated that final-year students could learn faster than freshmen at any of the three colleges. The measures were highly structured in the sense that the student, after reading or listening to some new information, had either to answer some true-false questions or fill in the blanks in response to questions about the information. We had expected that performance on this type of test might be related to academic intelligence, and it was. We also thought, however, that at least gains from one trial to the next might be greater for seniors, particularly at Ivy College. They were not.

A further reason for including these tests was to see if exposure to a particular major field in college improved the ability to absorb new material in that general area. Thus we thought that humanities majors might do relatively better on the passage on literary criticism than on the other passages, that social science majors would do better on the items about unemployment, and that natural science majors would improve more on the passage that described a new method of geological investigation. Again, we were disappointed. Seniors at Ivy College who had concentrated in one of these three areas were not better at picking up new information on a selected topic than were freshmen who intended to concentrate in these areas. Either content specialization does not facilitate absorbing new facts in that area, which seems unlikely, or else our methods of measurement were either too crude and general (for example, an item about geology does not adequately represent all science majors) or too structured to show the impact of education.

Independence of Thought

At the cognitive level, our key measure of being able to think for one's self is the Self-definition score, obtained from the TAT stories. This score measures the extent to which characters in the story are active rather than passive and, even more significantly, the extent to which events in the stories are described as being caused. In other words, the person who scores high in Self-definition thinks of the world in terms of cause and effect and imagines people as acting in ways that have effects. In contrast, in the stories of students low in Self-definition, things just "happen."

As Figure 3 shows, Self-definition is higher in the final

Figure 3. Average Self-Definition Scores in Freshman and
Final Years at Three Colleges

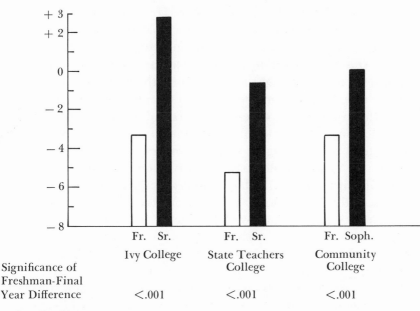

	Fr. Sr.	Fr. Sr.	Fr. Soph.
	Ivy College	State Teachers College	Community College
Significance of Freshman-Final Year Difference	<.001	<.001	<.001
College by Class Interaction	p <.01		

Note: Although raw scores are presented in this figure, analysis was done on scores corrected for length of protocol and standardized, as explained in Resource B.

year at all three colleges, as a result either of maturation or of exposure to any kind of higher education. Advanced students at all three colleges think of the world more in cause and effect terms. Nevertheless, at Ivy College, the difference is significantly greater than at the other colleges. This result is further supported by the longitudinal study, where Ivy freshmen tested as seniors showed a significant gain in Self-definition scores (p < .05). The cross sectional results cannot be dismissed as the result of higher intelligence among the Ivy students, since self-definition does not correlate with combined SAT scores (r = .05) and freshmen in all colleges start out at about the same level of Self-definition. Furthermore, the longitudinal gain from freshman to senior year at Ivy cannot be attributed to intelligence because the same students were involved. These results, then, support the belief that higher education promotes a sense that people act in ways that have effects in a lawful universe, that actions have consequences. The effect of education at Ivy College is to increase this type of causal thinking even more than does higher education at other institutions.

Divergent Thinking. A different approach to measuring independence of thought is provided by the measures of creativity or divergent thinking described in Chapter Two—the number of different uses for a series of objects and the number of different meanings for a series of words. Final-year students at all colleges tend to score higher in the number of different meanings of words. There was no comparable difference in the number of uses of objects listed. In fact, the Ivy freshmen are slightly better than the Ivy seniors at this latter task. These small effects are, however, overshadowed by the great superiority of Ivy freshmen over other freshmen at both tasks, which is not surprising since both are highly correlated with combined SAT score (r = .42, p < .001 for Uses of Objects, and r = .72, p < .001 for Meanings of Words). Even with covariance adjustments for academic intelligence and social class, these same effects occur—initial college differences but no greater freshman-senior difference at Ivy College. It seems safe, then, to conclude that Ivy College does not increase creativity or divergent thinking, as compared to other colleges, at least in the ways we have measured these characteristics.

Such results are not surprising. Consistent with its aura of tradition, Ivy College has historically made a strong commitment to analysis and interpretation as modes of intellectual functioning rather than creation, innovation, or the kind of spontaneous, almost playful recombination of elements that is the mark of divergent thinking at its best (see Getzels and Jackson, 1962; Hudson, 1966, 1975). In the arts, for example, Ivy College stresses the critical-interpretive or historical side rather than the creative or performing side. Such an orientation is probably a feature of Ivy College's particular tradition rather than an intrinsic aspect of liberal education. Some other liberal arts colleges do stress performance and creativity, either specifically in the arts (Bennington, for example, as noted in Chapter One) or in more general ways (as in the "innovative" programs and colleges that sprang up in the 1960s, see Grant and Riesman, 1978). One might expect that students at institutions of this kind would show gains in the divergent thinking measures.

Achievement Motivation. Another aspect of independence of thought involves innovation, resistance to conformity, and the use of feedback to improve outcomes. These are characteristics of people high in the achievement motive (McClelland, 1961; Heckhausen, 1967), although achievement motivation has many other correlates as well. Does higher education increase the need to achieve? The answer is a clear negative. Average n Achievement scores of freshmen and final-year students at the three colleges, when adjusted for length of the stories they wrote, are practically identical. The only sign of a possible change occurs in comparing the retest scores of the Ivy College seniors in 1978 with their earlier scores as freshmen in 1974. The decline (from 2.62 to 1.61) is highly significant ($p < .001$), but in the absence of any other evidence, it would be unwise to draw any general conclusions from it. (See also Chapter Six on achievement motivation in years past at Ivy College.) It seems more likely that motive levels are not so much influenced by higher education as such as they are by general atmosphere or social climate of the country and by early experiences in the life of the individual (McClelland, 1961).

In conclusion, Ivy College promotes independence of thought in the generic sense of thinking in causal, ordered, and instrumental ways but not in the sense of being able to think creative or unusual thoughts or in the sense of innovative, "entrepreneurial" achievement motivation.

Empathy

The Analysis of Argument results already presented demonstrate that education at Ivy College in particular enables students to take a point of view different from their own and defend it with logic and consistency. This certainly represents one kind of empathy, at least in the intellectual sense.

There is also emotional empathy—the capacity for *mitfühlen* or "feeling with" another. Is that increased by higher education? The relevant measure is provided by the Profile of Nonverbal Sensitivity or PONS measure (Rosenthal and others, 1979). Students were asked what emotions were being expressed in taped speech segments where the words could not be understood. Average scores obtained by final-year students on the two subscores of this test did not differ significantly from scores obtained by freshmen at any of the colleges. College effects were also minor, although there was a significant tendency ($p < .05$) for Ivy students to score higher on the analytical subscore, in which the task is to "reassemble" speech segments into the right sequence so as to understand what is being said.

One must conclude that the empathy promoted by Ivy College is primarily cognitive empathy—understanding intellectually a different point of view as measured by Analysis of Argument—rather than emotional empathy. This is not to say, however, that some other forms of education and even some other liberal arts colleges might not increase emotional sensitivity. Referring again to Chapter One, we might expect colleges like Springfield or Wesleyan, with their emphasis on service and community, to increase students' PONS scores.

Self-Control for Broader Loyalties

As noted in Chapter Two, the leadership motive pattern is associated with organizational leadership. This pattern consists of a strong concern for influence (high power motivation), which is greater than the concern for being liked (low affiliation motivation), and high self-control (high activity inhibition score). If higher education increases self-control in the interest of broader loyalties, it might well increase this leadership motive pattern. So far as its components of n Power, n Affiliation, or activity inhibition are concerned, the mean scores of first- and final-year students do not differ significantly at any of the three colleges. The only significant college effect is that students at Ivy tend to be low in affiliation motivation (the concern for being friendly with others and liked by them), but this difference is already true of the Ivy freshmen and is not influenced by the experience at Ivy College. Thus higher education has no significant general effects on separate motives such as n Power, n Affiliation, n Achievement, or activity inhibition.

However, the leadership motive pattern or *combination* of these component scores is more common in senior than freshman year at Ivy College, as shown in Figure 4. The differ-

**Figure 4. Percent Showing Leadership Motive Pattern in
Freshman and Final Years at Three Colleges**

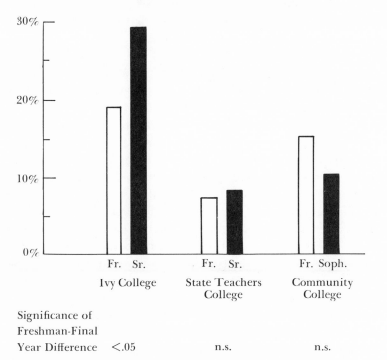

ences occur among both men (24 percent among freshmen versus 35 percent among seniors) and women (14 percent versus 20 percent) at Ivy College. There are no significant differences at State Teachers College and Community College. The Ivy College longitudinal sample, however, shows only a small and not significant increase in the leadership motive pattern from freshman to senior year. Some special characteristics of this sample may be relevant to this discrepancy in results. The seniors (especially the men) who came to the retesting had more often shown the pattern originally as freshmen than had the seniors who were not retested. One reason the percentage of students who showed the leadership motive pattern did not increase in the longitudinal sample, then, may be that it was already quite high in this group as freshmen. We could, of course, dismiss the results in Figure 4 as due to chance fluctuations, except that an earlier cross sectional study of Ivy College students showed the same significant increase in the leadership motive pattern from freshman to senior year (see Chapter Six). The safest conclusion seems to be that Ivy College has instilled the leadership motive pattern in its students in the past but that this effect may have been a little uncertain in recent years.

To the extent that the leadership motive pattern is an enduring effect of Ivy College, it means that students did not become more interested in power, less interested in affiliation, or more inhibited as such, but rather that these three separate elements were drawn together or fused into the characteristic leadership pattern. In other words, an existing level of power drive was tempered, controlled, or "socialized" in the direction of disciplined leadership or morale building rather than, for example, dissipating itself in unsocialized or profligate impulsivity (see Winter and Stewart, 1978). Such a change would support the connection between liberal arts education and training for leadership roles in society, a connection that can be traced throughout the tradition of educational writing, as discussed in Chapter One. Both Plato and the critics of the 1960s were perhaps right: Institutions like Ivy College do increase students' desire to rule. In a time of empire, they therefore support imperialism, as Cecil Rhodes recognized in his will establishing scholarships to Oxford. In other times and under other philosophies, however, they may support other goals. In this way, liberal arts education may be the servant of the society in which it takes place. By increasing the leadership motive pattern, Ivy College may tend to produce leaders who can marshal resources, morale, and self-discipline toward the attainment of whatever goals society holds to be important.

Self-Assurance in Leadership Ability

Self-assured leadership is another presumed effect of higher education that is demonstrated in part by the shift in the leadership motive pattern, but it can also be checked with other measures. A key indicator of lack of self-assurance, particularly in women, is the fear of success score obtained from the TAT. When male and female scores from the three colleges are considered separately, a slight trend emerges: Fear of success is lower in senior than freshman year for the men at Ivy College and for women at the other two colleges. However, among Ivy College women, seniors score about the same on fear of success as freshmen. That is, the Ivy college women do not show the same lower scores in fear of success that women at other colleges show, leading to a not quite significant class by college interaction among women only (p < .10). However, before we conclude that Ivy College fails to decrease fear of success in women the way the other two colleges do, we should note that the freshman women at Ivy already start out lower in fear of success than women at the other two colleges; so they have less opportunity to "improve." The Ivy longitudinal data also fail to show any sex differences. From the freshman to the senior testing, both men and women drop very slightly and insignificantly in fear of success. We are therefore not sure exactly what effect Ivy College has on women's fear of success. Perhaps the safest conclusion is that it *may* hurt women by "maintaining" their fear of success, but we really need more research to be sure.

Other measures of self-assurance obtained from the self-rated skills show an interesting pattern of results. In the cross sectional comparison, Ivy seniors rate themselves higher than Ivy freshmen on such strictly intellectual skills as analyzing and writing analytically (p < .10), trends even more strongly confirmed in the longitudinal testing. In the longitudinal comparison only, seniors also rate themselves higher than they did as freshmen in other areas having to do with work (working in groups, sticking to a task, quick learning; p < .01 in each case). In both the longitudinal and especially the cross sectional comparisons, in contrast, Ivy seniors appear to have somewhat less self-confidence in other, less intellectual areas than Ivy freshmen, tending to rate themselves lower on more general skills, such as creative writing (p < .05), public speaking (p < .10), persuading (p < .01), and accepting criticism (p < .01). The same apparent loss in self-esteem does not occur at the other colleges.

How are we to interpret what seems at first to be an erosion of self-confidence at Ivy College? As freshmen, Ivy students rate themselves higher on most scales than do the other freshmen, probably because they know they are a highly selected group. Once at Ivy College, however, they meet other highly selected students; so over time, their changing frame of reference causes them to lower their self-ratings. In the extreme case, the dismayed Ivy College freshman discovers that most of the freshman class seems to have been valedictorians, student council presidents, newspaper editors, varsity athletes, and prize winners.

The shifts in self-ratings are not simply lowered self-esteem, however. The level of the highest-rated skill—that is, the maximum of the sixteen skill ratings—shows no freshman-senior difference at Ivy College or either of the other colleges. However, the range of skills, or difference between highest-rated and lowest-rated skill, is significantly larger for Ivy seniors than for Ivy freshmen, while it is either the same or smaller at the other colleges. In other words, at Ivy College, seniors spread out the ratings of their abilities more than do freshmen (p < .01). They still rate their best skills highly, but they no longer rate themselves as good at everything. This suggests that their self-perceptions have become more differentiated and possibly more realistic. This is surely an important aspect of self-knowledge.

Finally, Ivy College seniors show a significantly lower self-rated ability to "accept criticism" than do freshmen, both in the cross sectional and longitudinal comparisons. This effect is not found at the other colleges. Perhaps Ivy seniors feel more insecure, having learned that they are not as smart as they thought they were as freshmen. Or this effect may really give some validity to the common stereotype of Ivy College graduates as impervious to criticism, arrogantly believing they know all the answers. Such self-assurance, grown slightly abrasive, may be an unintended effect of liberal education—the dark imperial or imperious side of the leadership motive pattern and Cecil Rhodes's "instinct for leadership" or what Senator Fulbright (1967) called the arrogance of power.

Maturity of Adaptation and Personal Integration

Maturity of adaptation, as measured by modal Stage of Adaptation to the Environment, showed large and significant differences from freshman to final years at all three colleges, as shown in Figure 5. Freshmen at State Teachers College score somewhat higher than freshmen at the other two colleges, perhaps because they were somewhat older when they entered college. At all three colleges, final-year students score higher than do freshmen, suggesting either that the experience of all three institutions increases maturity of adaptation (see Healy, 1979) or that increasing age exerts a maturational effect. However, the Ivy College students show an increase in maturity of adaptation that is significantly greater than the other gains, which suggests a special Ivy College effect in addition to the general effects of college.

Longitudinal findings at Ivy College are more complex. When retested as seniors, Ivy students scored slightly but not significantly higher on the maturity of adaptation measure than they did when tested as freshmen. Within the longitudinal sample, however, the women showed an almost significant gain (one-tailed p = .06). Among the men, there was actually a very slight loss. One explanation for this curious effect is that these men (available and willing to participate in the senior-year retesting) had scored higher in maturity of adaptation as freshmen

Figure 5. Average Modal Stage of Adaptation Scores in Freshman and Final Years at Three Colleges

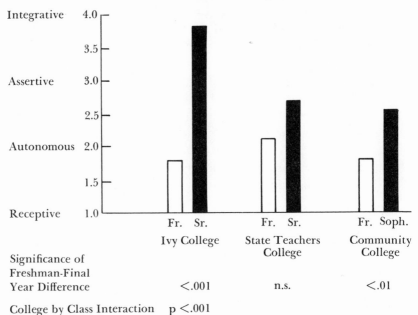

than did the men who were either unavailable or unwilling to be tested again as seniors. Because they scored higher originally, they may have had less chance to show gains. (The same effect and explanation apply to the leadership motive pattern, as previously noted.)

In terms of the actual stages (Stewart, in press), Ivy College students in the cross sectional study could be said to move, on the average, from low stage II (autonomy) to a point between stages III (assertion) and IV (integration). Thus we could say that Ivy College moves students along from being concerned to exert willpower to break dependence on others, beyond rebellion and self-assertion, toward a more mature stance in which they can accept and even identify with authority. Students at the other two colleges show growth, but only from a concern with establishing autonomy to a somewhat greater interest in self-expression or self-assertion. In terms of the categories of the scoring system, students enter all three colleges focused on issues of authority being critical, lack of gratification, incompetence, and the need to impose order on disorder. Some development toward self-expression and assertion occurs naturally (or at least at any of the three colleges), but by the time Ivy College students are seniors, they appear to have moved beyond these concerns to issues of rebellion and opposition and then further to being more integrated with others and less self-centered. As seniors, more Ivy students than students at the other colleges see authority as limited, objects as differentiated, and people as involved in work. The measure of maturity is relatively new, but it is based on a sound theory of development, and the changes cannot be attributed to differences in intelligence or social class of students at the three colleges. These background variables are, if anything, negatively related to the maturity of adaptation score ($r = -.11$ and $-.13$, respectively). On the whole, this measure yields striking results very much in line with educators' claims that college, and particularly the residential liberal arts college, contributes in a major way to the development of personal maturity. In the long run, Ivy College's greatest impact on its students may be that they learn to adapt to the environment in more mature ways—learning the limits of authority, dealing consciously with ambivalent feelings, and taking pleasure in work and other people.

Equalitarian Liberal Values

The effect of liberal education on equalitarian liberal values has been amply documented by other researchers. The one relevant result from our study is that in both the cross sectional and longitudinal studies, self-rated respect for diversity, already high among freshmen, is significantly higher among Ivy seniors. It also tends to be higher for final-year than for first-year students at the other two institutions. Thus, there is no overall college-class effect that approaches significance. This liberal acceptance of views other than one's own appears to be a general effect of attending any institution of higher education or simply of growing older and not a specific effect of Ivy College.

Summary

Within the limits of the sampling procedures and data analysis techniques employed in this study, the results presented in this chapter establish a strong case that education at Ivy College (at least during the time of this study) has substantial and important effects on students. For the most part, these effects appear to be over and above whatever changes one would expect from maturation, from simply any kind of higher education, or from the selectivity of Ivy College.

Education at Ivy College has *cognitive* effects. It increases students' abilities to form and articulate complex concepts to order and arrange confusing impressions and data. It increases intellectual flexibility and consistency—the ability to deal in rational and sophisticated ways with conflicting arguments on both sides of controversial issues.

Education at Ivy College has *motivational and emotional* effects. It increases the leadership motive pattern—at least it did in the past, though perhaps not so much recently. This means it tends to produce students who can discipline and temper their power drives; so they can mobilize resources and work for the goals of a larger society rather than pursue a profligate path of individual potency. Ivy College also increases both maturity of adaptation and Self-definition, the tendency to think in terms of the effects of actions. In terms of prior research findings, this means that students become more integrated and instrumental in the emotional or "psychological" sphere as well as in the cognitive sphere. At the same time, however, in this habitually male-dominated institution, fear of success among women in 1974 did not decline as much as it apparently did among women in other institutions. Given the discussion of fear of success in Chapter Two, this finding may be intelligible even if it is not exactly expected by educators; and it raises both the specific question of how women are affected by education at Ivy College and the more general issue of losses and gains for particular groups.

Finally, education at Ivy College has effects on *self-knowledge*. Students seem to develop a more realistic, differentiated sense of their own strengths and weaknesses in the course of liberal arts education.

In terms of the results of this study, Ivy College appears to have no measurable effects on creativity or emotional sensitivity. This may not necessarily hold for all liberal arts institutions, although it is worth noting that these two goals are relatively less prominent than the more "cognitive" ones in most of the statements of goals reviewed in Chpater One. Nor is there any apparent effect on such basic-level skills as quick learning of particular facts about an unfamiliar topic. This latter finding pinpoints the distinctive contribution of Ivy College as increasing the *ability to think*—to articulate, arrange, and analyze facts into broader abstract categories—rather than improving the ability to retain the facts themselves.

Table 4 summarizes the results of the present study in terms of the lists of goals presented in Chapter One and in Table 2. We were able to measure at least eight of these goals to some extent; and the results presented in this chapter show distinctive gains at Ivy College, on at least one relevant measure, for seven of them. The only exception is learning how to learn, and here our measures may have been at fault, although it is certainly arguable that liberal arts education could not be expected to increase this skill in a unique way. Thus this single exception does not seem very important.

The major conclusion that can be drawn from Table 4 is that our results do establish a strong case for the distinctive effects of at least one college. Traditional liberal education, at least at Ivy College at this time, does affect students and it does more or less the things that liberal arts educators have claimed it does. We could say that it strives toward Plato's goal of the philosopher-king: adept at conceptual articulation and imbued with mature and instrumental motives for leadership.

In reflecting on our main results, we realized that they fit rather well into the categories Parsons (1952) originally suggested for the functional analysis of social systems and Parsons and Platt (1973) applied to the educational subsystem of American society. In the most general sense, Parsons argues that any system, from society as a whole down to the subsystems of the

Table 4. Summary of Effects of Liberal Education at Ivy College

Hypothesized Effect (from Chapter One)	Measure Used	Evidence about Effect of Ivy College
1. Critical thinking; broad analytical skill	Test of Thematic Analysis	Significantly increased
	Analysis of Argument	Significantly increased
	Concept attainment	No effect
2. Learning how to learn	Learning new material	No effect
3. Independence of thought	Self-definition	Significantly increased
	Divergent thinking	No effect
	Achievement motive	No effect
4. Empathy; seeing all sides of an issue	Analysis of Argument	Significantly increased
	PONS (emotional empathy)	No effect
5. Self-control for broader loyalties	Leadership motivation pattern	Significantly greater among seniors in 1974 but not 1978
6. Self-assurance in leadership ability	Leadership motivation pattern	Significantly greater among seniors in 1974 but not 1978
	Fear of success (low)	Decline among women seniors less than expected in 1974 and 1978; no significant effect among men
7. Mature social-emotional judgment; personal integration	Self-rated abilities	More realistic self-appraisal
	Stages of Psychological Adaptation to the Environment	Significantly increased
8. Equalitarian, liberal values	Self-rated value	
9. Participation and enjoyment in cultural experience	(not directly measured)	Increased respect for diversity

human body, has an internal-external dimension and an instrumental-consummatory dimension. To take an example from the physiological systems of the human body, certain systems (such as circulation) help to maintain the integrity of the body and its functions (its internal-consummatory aspect), and other systems (such as the brain and musculature) act on the environment to fulfill human goals (its external-instrumental aspect). In an analogous manner, students in a liberal arts college may be conceived as developing certain internal functions that maintain them as viable persons or units within the larger social system and also as developing certain adaptive skills vis-à-vis the external world that lead them to attainment of goals within it. Table 5 illustrates the four system functions as they apply to a liberal

Table 5. Major Changes in Ivy College Students Classified by System Function

Relation to Environment	*Function*	
	Instrumental	*Consummatory*
External	*Adaptation* Generalization of adaptive capacity: providing basic resources and skills to deal with the external environment *Measured by* Test of Thematic Analysis (conceptual skills) and Analysis of Argument (reasoning skills)	*Goal Attainment* Establishing specific system-environment relationships, for example, vocational choice, and roles in society, activity in organizations, and so forth *Measured by* leadership motive pattern
Internal	*Latent Pattern Maintenance* Defining and maintaining the self as distinct from its environments *Measured by* Self-definition	*Integration* Organizing differentiated and conflicting internal processes *Measured by* Stage of Psychological Adaptation to the Environment

arts student and classifies the main changes we found at Ivy College. The overall fit appears to be quite good. Organizing our results in this way demonstrates that the traditional "laundry lists" of liberal education goals, when translated into actual observed effects, can be expressed in the broader, more abstract terms used by a general theory of social systems. In short, the study of higher education can be integrated with more general theories of action. In the long run, this integration should produce clearer conceptions of the relationships between the liberal education system and the personal systems of individual students, on the one hand, and the social system of the larger society, on the other. More sophisticated conceptions of this type should improve educational theory, research, and policy. (In Chapter Six, we shall use this same fourfold table principle in extending our results to other institutions.)

Liberal arts students at Ivy College learn adaptive conceptual and reasoning skills that prepare them for better instrumental functioning in the external world. They develop a goal or direction toward roles in which these skills can make important contributions to society. At the same time, their sharpened sense of self (or self-definition) serves an internal-instrumental or pattern maintenance function. Their increased maturity of adaptation helps to integrate or regulate all these personal subsystems so they can better perform their own internal or external functions. Whether one accepts these Parsonian categories as definitive in terms of systems theory, they certainly do help to illustrate the presumed goals of liberal arts education and to summarize the effects of the liberal education at Ivy College in developing students both as people and as useful, contributing members of society.

Why has the research presented in this chapter shown results that are both positive and encouraging, in contrast to the usual run of disappointing research results reviewed in Chapter One? For one thing, we selected the three institutions so as to maximize the likelihood of getting results. In later chapters, we try to isolate how and why these distinctive changes actually occur at Ivy College. We believe that the major reason for our results, however, is our measures—both because they were carefully designed to reflect the goals of liberal education and because they use an operant format. Still, these measures and these results immediately raise further questions:

So what? Are the abilities and characteristics measured by these new tests important in the real world of adult life after college? (Chapter Four)

What aspects of Ivy College caused these changes? Do they have anything to do with its liberal arts education rather than with its other institutional characteristics? (Chapter Five)

To what extent are the results generalizable to other colleges? (Chapter Six)

What are the implications of this research for the liberal arts college? For education and society? For future research on higher education? (Chapter Seven)

FOUR

Importance of Liberal Arts Education in Adult Life

Although the effects of Ivy College on liberal arts competence may be well established by the freshman-senior differences presented in the last chapter, the reader may still wonder how important these effects are for students' adult lives. Does it really matter that a student scores higher on Self-definition or on the leadership motive pattern after four years at Ivy College? Will a higher Stage of Psychological Adaptation score in college really lead an Ivy graduate to a more mature adaptation in later career and family roles? Demonstrated relevance to later life performance is an important standard for evaluating measures of educational outcomes, as we shall argue in Chapter Seven. How well do our new measures of liberal arts competence meet this standard? We gave some answers to this question in Chapter Two, where we discussed the previously established validity of each measure.

Accepting the prior empirical credentials of these measures, the reader may still wonder whether they would hold up in such a highly selected group. Even if they do hold for Ivy College graduates, how important are the dimensions of liberal arts competence compared to other student characteristics and experiences? Are they, for example, more important than intelligence, than college grades, or than independent work on a senior honors thesis? Recently there has been a good deal of dispute about the importance of scores on standardized intelligence tests such as the SAT (see Duncan, Featherman, and Duncan, 1972; Jencks and others, 1979; National Public Interest Research Group, 1979). A skeptical review of the evidence (McClelland, 1973) suggests that test scores and college grades have surprisingly little relationship to any measurable outcome or achievement in later adult life. Even more sympathetic discussions (for example, Brody and Brody, 1976, pp. 91-109) suggest that their predictive relevance declines sharply above a certain threshold.

Are gains in liberal arts competence more important than family background and social-class position? The Coleman report (Coleman and others, 1966) emphasized the importance of home and family. Domhoff (1967) argued the importance of class—that liberal arts colleges are really an elaborately stratified sorting system designed to perpetuate the power of elite groups while co-opting talented and willing members of the middle class. Both perspectives suggest that an elite liberal arts college such as Ivy really functions as a "way station" along life paths already defined by the social position of the student's family (albeit a somewhat raised path for students of precocious intelligence and ability). Any changes during college, both arguments conclude, are of much less consequence for students' adult lives than are their initial family situation and social-class position.

In this chapter, we will answer some of these questions

about the importance of liberal arts competence in adult life. We will present results of further research on Ivy College graduates showing that some of the liberal arts competence measures have relationships to important life outcomes, relationships that are still significant when the effects of family social class, intelligence, and college grades are also taken into account. In some cases, the predictive power of the liberal arts competence measures, taken together, is greater than that of social class, intelligence, and college grades combined. In short, liberal arts competence is important. By promoting growth and change on these measures, colleges can have a demonstrable effect on the later lives and performances of their students.

A Longitudinal Study of Ivy College Class of 1964 Graduates

The best way to demonstrate the relevance of liberal arts competence to real life is to follow college graduates through time, observing whether scores on the measures discussed in this book (or better yet, gains in these scores during college) are related to life outcomes several years later. The major problem with this kind of longitudinal research plan is that it takes time. If we assume that the true dimensions of adult life emerge at the earliest only by the age of thirty-five or forty, then we would have to wait until the 1990s to follow up properly any of the students we studied.[1]

As a substitute for such a long-range project, we have reanalyzed some longitudinal data originally collected for other purposes. Here we were most fortunate because students from the Ivy College class of 1964 had been thoroughly studied during their college years. Some of the data collected in this study were made available to us so that we could follow up the class of 1964 graduates in the 1970s. As a part of this study, TATs had been given to a sample of about one third of the class (240 men, 244 women) at the beginning of their freshman year in the autumn of 1960. Some information on background characteristics and college performance was available from the larger study or from other sources such as the class yearbook or alumni/

alumnae reports. Finally, in 1974, all students originally tested in 1960 were sent a "Life Patterns Questionnaire" as part of a study of Ivy College graduates. This questionnaire asked about postcollege education, career, approximate income, marriage and children, spouse's career, and leisure activities. Two hundred four of the questionnaires were returned by people who had written scorable TATs as freshmen (88 men, 116 women). This 42 percent rate of return was high, since the addresses available for some graduates were doubtless neither accurate nor up-to-date.

Some problems and limits of these data should be discussed at the outset. First, only those measures of liberal arts competence that are based on the TAT (achievement motivation, leadership motive pattern, Self-definition, and Stages of Adaptation) could be used in this study, since the Analysis of Argument test and the Test of Thematic Analysis were not developed until the 1970s.

Second, the studies of men and women had been carried out for the most part separately; so the male and female data, both in the original study and in the 1974 follow-up, do not cover exactly the same topics and therefore are not always directly comparable.

Finally, the scores on the TAT-based measures were from freshman year, before the presumed gains in these very measures brought about by Ivy College. We certainly could have made a more precise estimate of the later-life effects of these aspects of liberal arts competence if we had had TATs from senior year (or better yet, TATs from both freshman and senior years, from which we could derive change scores, as in Chapter Five). As in all longitudinal studies, however, only what has been collected is available; it is not possible to go back and collect the best possible data. Both these problems actually work in a conservative direction, leading us, if anything, to *underestimate* the adult life effects of liberal arts competence. We have available only some of the measures of that competence; if Analysis of Argument and Test of Thematic Analysis scores had been available, the aggregate contribution to adult life outcomes could only be greater than what we estimate from our research.

We must therefore distinguish the scientific importance of our findings from their number or magnitude. The absolute number of significant longitudinal relationships between the TAT-based liberal arts competence variables and the later-life outcomes is not great, although it certainly exceeds what would be expected by chance. But we would not expect every relationship to be significant. The point is that the liberal arts competence variables predict the particular life outcomes that we would expect them to, on the basis of theory and prior research. (For example, maturity of adaptation predicts satisfaction, and the leadership motive pattern predicts office holding, but not the other way around.) Even where significant, these relationships only explain a small amount of variation in adult life outcomes. Such small (but positive) magnitudes are to be expected, however, since the course of adult life obviously is affected by many things besides personal qualities as measured fourteen years before.

Liberal Arts Competence and Men's Life Outcomes

As a first step in analyzing the data from the men of the Ivy College class of 1964, we defined, measured and grouped fourteen important life outcomes from information in the 1974 follow-up questionnaire as follows:

Career Outcomes
   Income
   Early success: Achieving great success within ten years after college, according to separate criteria for professors, doctors, lawyers, and business executives. (These four careers included 60 percent of the male sample; the rest were not scored on this outcome.)
   Entrepreneur: Starting or running one's own business.
   Publications: Weighted index of number of books and articles published.
   Career satisfaction: Positive feelings about one's career, measured by nine questions.

Family Outcomes
    Dual-career family: Spouse has a full-time career.
    Children

Voluntary Organizations
    Membership: Number of voluntary organizations listed.
    Office holding: Number of offices held in voluntary organizations.

Personal Feelings
    Happiness: Four-item scale of recent mood states.
    Unhappiness: Three-item scale of recent mood states. (Research by Bradburn, 1969, chap. 4, shows that happiness and unhappiness, defined in these ways, are not opposites but are instead unrelated to each other.)

Positive Self-Image
    Focused: Self-description as focused, responsible, orderly, careful, and traditional.
    Energetic: Self-description as hard-driving, hectic, tense.

One additional outcome, having ever been married, was not significantly related to any predictor variable and is therefore omitted. In addition, a final composite attainment outcome was defined as a combination of income, early success, career fulfillment, membership, office holding, happiness, and low unhappiness—each weighted equally. (Dual-career family and having children were not included in this index because we wanted to see whether they predicted composite attainment scores.) While these fourteen variables cannot do full justice to the complexity of any individual adult life, they do include many important accomplishments and benchmarks applicable to young adult years up to about the time of the onset of the mid-life crisis.

The relationships of the four TAT-based liberal arts competence scores, social class of parents, intelligence (SAT scores), level of honors at graduation, and two aspects of current life situation (dual-career family and having children) to each outcome were then evaluated through multiple-regression analysis. This enabled us to consider the independent effect of each of these predictor variables on a given life outcome while holding constant statistically the effects of all other predictor variables. (See Kerlinger, 1973, pp. 603-658, for an introduction to multiple-regression analysis.) We use dual-career family and having children as both life outcomes and also aspects of current life situations that may affect other life outcomes. (Strictly speaking, in this latter case, "predict" should be understood in its statistical rather than temporal sense. Also, of course, these two variables were not used to predict themselves.) We use dual-career family and having children as predictors in a deliberate attempt to counteract a bias in most previous research. In the study of *women's* adult life patterns, the importance of marriage, spouse's career, and children for the outcomes of a woman's own career and personal feelings has long been obvious (see Weil, 1961; Ginzberg, 1966; Astin, 1967; Hoffman and Nye, 1974, as well as the study of Ivy College women reported later in this chapter). When researchers study *men,* in contrast, they usually do not examine the effects of spouse's career and having children. (Veroff and Feld, 1970, are a notable exception.) Yet more recent studies suggest that men's lives and emotions are by no means unaffected by marriage, spouse's career, or children.

We are thus considering the combined effects of four kinds of variables on adult life outcomes: liberal arts competence (or personal qualities), ability and educational achievement, social class, and current life situation. We believe that this multiple approach is a conceptual and methodological advance over earlier research strategies, which tended to focus on variables from only one class at a time.[2]

Results and Discussion. We used simultaneous multiple regressions to analyze the relationships between all predictor variables and each life outcome. (See Cohen and Cohen, 1975, pp. 97-104, for further discussion of this procedure.) Table 6 summarizes the results, with the fourteen life outcomes as columns and the predictor variables as rows. Where a predictor variable has a significant positive or negative relationship ($p <$ .05) to an outcome, taking into account the effects of all other predictor variables (that is, a significant beta weight), a plus or

Table 6. Predicting Male Life Outcomes after Fourteen Years from Liberal Arts Competence Measures and Other Variables

Predictor Variable	Career				Career Satisfaction	Family		Organizations		Personal		Self-Image		Composite Attainment
	Income	Early Success	Entre-preneur	Publica-tions		Dual-Career Family	Chil-dren	Member-ship	Office Holding	Happi-ness	Unhap-piness	Fo-cused	Ener-getic	
Liberal Arts Competence														
Self-definition								(+)				<u>+</u>	<u>+</u>	
Achievement motivation			<u>(+)</u>	(+)										
Leadership motive pattern									<u>+</u>					
Modal Stage of Adaptation					++					+		++		+
Background														
Parents' social class		(-)												
SAT scores		+												
College Honors						+		(-)						
Current Situation														
Dual-career family				(+)	(+)	X	X							
Children	+			+	++	X	X	(+)			-		-	(+)
[Professor][a]														

[a]Used to predict "publications" only.   X: not used to predict.

Note: +, ++, and +++: significance of beta weight < .05, < .01, or < .001, respectively. Beta weights significant at < .10 are in parentheses. -: negative beta weight. Double-underlined relationships were predicted and tested with one-tailed tests.

minus sign appears in the relevant cell. Less-significant trends (p < .10) are shown in parentheses. In four cases, as noted in the table, explicit directional predictions were based on one-tailed tests of significance. (See Rosenthal, 1980, for a discussion of probability levels when directional hypotheses are tested.)

Are the measures of liberal arts competence from freshman year related to outcomes fourteen years later? When the effects of background, college honors, and current life situation are taken into account, do the TAT-based variables still predict the kinds of things they have predicted in other research? Careful study of Table 6 suggests affirmative answers to both questions. Among the liberal arts competence measures, ten relationships (18 percent) are significant at the .10 level or less, which is almost double the number expected by chance. This statement must be tempered by the fact that, as expected, the relationships are not as strong as they usually are in laboratory studies.

Self-definition tends to be associated with the two "focused" and "energy" clusters of adjectives that graduates checked as describing themselves. It also predicts active membership in voluntary organizations. These results are consistent with previous findings that Self-definition predicts an energetic, instrumental style of action, especially under stress (see Stewart, 1978). Thus self-defining people not only act energetically and effectively, but they also feel energetic and effective to themselves.

Self-definition was also significantly correlated with dual-career family—that is, with a wife who had a career outside the home—(r = +.19, p < .05 one-tailed), although the relationship was weaker in the regression analysis. This trend suggests that among men, Self-definition is associated with a general independence from ascribed roles and specifically with a belief in careers for women, just as previous research has shown it to be among women (Stewart and Winter, 1974). But we must carefully distinguish a married woman with a career from a married *mother* with a career. The latter was certainly more counter than the former to the ascribed role norms that the class of 1964 learned while growing up in the era of the feminine mystique (Friedan, 1963). In fact, Self-definition is significantly associated with dual-career families only among men with children ($r = +.23$, $p < .05$), just as we should expect from the previous research. Among men without children, where career wives were far more common and less sanctioned by traditional sex-role norms, there was no relationship.

Achievement motivation is significantly related to having an entrepreneurial career, just as McClelland (1965) found in another longitudinal study of liberal arts graduates. Achievement motivation also predicts having a lot of publications, even when being a professor is included (for this outcome only) as a predictor variable. Professors do publish more than other people, but that relationship is only a little stronger than the relationship of publications to achievement motivation. Among people with careers that generally use their highly developed verbal skills, therefore, it appears that publications function like profits—giving a sense of concrete, measurable results.

The leadership motive pattern is associated with holding office in voluntary organizations, again as expected on the basis of prior research (Winter, 1973, chap. 4; McClelland, 1975, chaps. 7-8).

The maturity of adaptation measure is significantly related to many adult life outcomes, in each case supporting previous findings. Among these graduates, the higher the modal Stage of Adaptation in freshman year, the greater their sense of career satisfaction, personal happiness, and self-image of being "focused." Maturity of adaptation also has a significant relationship to the composite attainment measure. In terms of the strength and breadth of relationships to later life, the *maturity of adaptation measure is, for men, the single most relevant aspect of these four dimensions of liberal arts competence.* The themes of the integrative stage—perceiving authority as limited, acknowledging feelings as ambivalent, and focusing on work and mutual sharing as sources of pleasure—are associated with future happiness, career satisfaction, and effective investment of energy in one's surrounding environment. Another way of looking at these results is to say that the men who adapted quickly and effectively to Ivy College as freshmen (higher scores in freshman year testing) also adapt more effectively to life.

From Table 6, then, we can conclude that the four TAT-based liberal arts competence measures predict several important life outcomes ten years after college and that these predictions still hold up when a variety of other background and current situation factors are introduced and controlled. *Since Ivy College increases scores on at least three of these four measures, we conclude that it is having important and enduring effects on students.*

A Comparison: The Predictive Value of Traditional Measures. Turning now to the other predictor variables in Table 6, we find that social class has very little relationship to any of the life outcomes. Since Ivy College admittedly draws its students from the upper middle class and above, such a conclusion may be true for only this very limited range. Ivy College does, however, draw at least some of its students from just those "ruling-class" groups whose elite backgrounds might be thought to make a real difference in life outcome, if Domhoff's (1967) analysis is accurate.

SAT scores and level of honors at college graduation are two of the most popular and widely used measures of presumed general competence. The rise of the merit principle focused the attention of college admissions officers on SAT scores because they purported to predict academic performance in college. College performances, in turn, are presumed by some educators to predict all kinds of successful outcomes in later life. Thus at the commencement exercises of an academically oriented college like Ivy, the *summa cum laude* graduates are honored, in the minds of the faculty at least, as the best and brightest. They have learned the most that the college can teach, therefore they are headed for the best that life can give. Even many of those who reject academic values still have the nagging belief that people who are that clever will have some kind of an edge in later life. In agreement with Hoyt's (1965) classic critique, however, our Ivy College results suggest once again that these beliefs are greatly exaggerated, if not absolutely wrong. SAT scores actually predict negatively to our early success measure. Level of honors predicts early success and dual-career family and shows a significant simple correlation with unhappiness ($r = +.26$, $p < .05$), which is weaker in the regression analysis.

Table 7 illustrates a direct comparison of one of the most promising of the new operant measures (the modal Stage of

Table 7. Comparative Predictions from Stage of Psychological Adaptation to the Environment Score and from Combined SAT Scores

	Relationship to Outcome Measure		
	Levels of Honors at Graduation (respondent; in college)	Composite Attainment (operant; in life)	
Predictor	Correlation	Correlation	Regression beta weight
Modal Stage of Psychological Adaptation to the Environment (operant measure)	−.13 (N = 181)	+.25[+] (N = 49)	.35*
Combined SAT scores (respondent measure)	+.26*** (N = 299)	−.26* (N = 54)	−.20

[+]p < .10

*p < .05

***p < .001

Note: This table differs slightly from that reported in McClelland (1980), which used a modal Stage of Psychological adaptation score with standardized individual stage scores.

Adaptation score) with combined SAT scores, one of the most popular traditional respondent measures. As would be expected, SAT scores significantly predict level of honors achieved in college among the class of 1964 men, but the Stage of Adaptation score shows no such relationship. When we consider later-life outcomes, however, the pattern reverses dramatically. Taking the composite attainment measure as the best overall summary of the men's life outcomes, we find a nearly significant positive correlation to maturity of adaptation (as measured back in freshman year), a relationship that is even stronger in the multiple-regression analysis, and a significant *negative* relationship to SAT scores. (Both SAT relationships are very similar to what Heath, 1977, found in a longitudinal study of Haverford College students.) While these results illustrate the superiority of the Stage of Psychological Adaptation measure over SAT scores for predicting life outcomes (at least in our highly selected sample), they also suggest a broader methodological conclusion. As McClelland (1958, 1966, 1980) has suggested, operant outcomes and behaviors are generally predicted best by operant measures of personal qualities, while respondent measures tend to give their best predictions to respondent outcomes (such as academic achievement).

Overall, how do the liberal arts competence variables compare to SAT scores and level of honors? Which information is more important in predicting the course of later life? The data at hand, drawn from one time period at one institution, can provide only a partial answer to such a general question; but even this partial answer is of interest because it contradicts conventional wisdom about the importance of SAT scores and college performances. Table 8 summarizes additional statistical data from the findings presented in Table 6 to answer the question of comparative predictive power. If we add up the percent variance uniquely explained[3] by all predictor variables in a given category (for example, the four TAT-based liberal arts competence measures) over all life outcomes in a given group, we can compare the explanatory or predictive power of liberal arts competence, ability, parents' social class, and current situation both within the different domains of adult life and also overall, across all domains. (The summation is carried out over all relationships, including nonsignificant ones, though of course the significant relationships contribute the most to the totals.)

In some cases, variables predict to life outcomes in a negative direction, as shown by a negative sign in Table 6. Sometimes this negative prediction is contrary to what one would expect or desire—for example, level of honors predicts *not* being a member of organizations, and SAT scores predict *not* being an early success. In these cases, we also show the total of variance predicted positively, or in the "desired" direction, in parentheses underneath the total predicted variance. (For unhappiness, of course, the desired direction is negative.) The two right-hand columns of Table 8 give for each group of predictors,

Table 8. Comparison of the Predictive Power of Liberal Arts Competence Measures and of Other Factors

Group of Predictor Variables	Unique Variance[a] Accounted for in Area of					Total	Total Predicted in Desired Direction
	Career	Family	Organizations	Personal	Self-Image		
Liberal Arts Competence	29.3 (27.2)	8.3 (2.0)	18.2 (18.2)	12.8 (12.1)	16.4 (14.9)	85.0	74.4
Social Class	3.8	0.9	0.1	1.1	0.9	6.8	1.1
SAT Scores and Honors	18.8 (9.1)	8.9 (6.1)	7.0 (2.3)	3.4 (0.0)	2.8 (2.0)	40.9	19.5
Current Life Situation	36.1 (35.9)	X X	6.2 (5.7)	5.7 (5.7)	8.6 (0.6)	56.6	47.9

[a]Sum of unique variance predicted (semipartial correlation coefficient) across all outcomes in the group, for all predictor variables in the class; see text. XX: Predictor variables not used in predicting outcomes in this area.

Note: Figures in parentheses are unique variance predicted in the "desired" direction for each area of outcome; see text.

respectively, the overall total variance explained across all areas and the overall total variance explained in the desired direction across all areas.

Read Table 8 cautiously. The absolute numbers and the column totals at the bottom are not too important, since they depend partly on the number of outcomes in each group. The important comparisons are those among the different groups of predictor variables, both overall and within each group of life outcomes. Thus, for example, liberal arts competence predicts, in positive directions, more variance in career outcomes (27.2) than do SAT scores and levels of honors (9.1) but less than the two current situations variables (35.9). (Divide these numbers by five to get the average percent variance uniquely explained per individual career outcome.) Liberal arts competence is by far the most important predictor of organizational activity and the subjective areas of personal feelings and positive self-image.

The final column at the right of Table 8 gives comparative totals of variance predicted in the "desired" direction by each group of predictor variables, added together across all five groups of life outcome. Taken together, the liberal arts competence measures have more than three times the predictive power that SAT scores and level of honors combined have and almost twice the predictive power of the two current situation variables. Even if these totals are divided by the number of predictor variables in each group, the liberal arts competence measures perform comparatively well. Obviously such a conclusion needs to be drawn with great caution, because these results depend very much on the particular subjects, predictor variables, and life outcomes used in this study. These results do, however, establish a strong case for the *importance and relevance of the liberal arts competence measures in real life, especially compared to other more traditional measures of competence.*

It is not surprising that current situation in general has important effects on men's life outcomes, but it is certainly interesting that the two aspects of situation used here—dual-career family (that is, wife's career) and especially children—are so important. Ever since Freud's late and controversial writings on female personality (Freud, [1925] 1961, especially), many psychologists have argued that having children is somehow necessary to women's ultimate destiny or complete fulfillment. Many researchers have also reported the enormous difference having children makes in predicting women's life outcomes. Table 6 suggests that children may be equally important for the life outcomes and personal fulfillment of men. As the results indicate, whether a man has children is an important predictor of his composite attainment and his sense of career satisfaction. It also predicts publications and avoidance of unhappiness. (Are the books "baby-substitutes," to reverse the spirit of Freud's argument about what babies symbolize?) Having children even predicts income level, although the causal direction may be reversed to imply that only the rich can afford to have children. This seems unlikely in the present case, however, since most of the Ivy graduates had income sufficient to support the two to three children typical of families in this sample.

Another interesting finding is that men whose wives have full-time careers feel more satisfaction about their own careers and are more likely to be members of voluntary organizations. This suggests that the dual-career family, for all the complexity of life and the compromises of partners' needs that it involves (see Winter, Stewart, and McClelland, 1977), is good for husbands as well as for wives.

Other Correlates of Liberal Arts Competence Measures. We have presented the major results of the longitudinal study in the multiple-regression analyses, but there were some interesting findings that were not especially predicted in advance. These can be brought together here as an addendum to the study.

Self-definition is negatively correlated with both systolic and diastolic blood pressure as measured in freshman year (r's = −.14, p < .05 in each case). While the correlations are small, they are statistically significant and also consistent with other research (Stewart, 1978), suggesting that Self-definition predicts effective management of personal problems and stress. This finding is all the more striking because blood pressure was measured in freshman year (at about age eighteen), when the range of blood pressures was not nearly as great as it would be ten or twenty years later. The role of Self-definition as a psychological

factor of physical health and well-being deserves to be explored
in further research (see McClelland, 1979).

Self-definition is also associated with later self-ratings, in
adulthood, of political moderation versus either left or right ex-
tremes (r = .33, p < .001). Finally, on the 1974 questionnaire,
all graduates were asked their opinion about the long-range effects of Ivy College. They were asked to rate on a five-point
scale how strongly their experience at Ivy had affected eleven
different aspects of their present lives, ranging from occupational choice to moral and ethical perspectives. The overall average of these eleven ratings was significantly correlated with Self-
definition (r = .22, p < .05), suggesting that men scoring high in
Self-definition are more affected, or at least in retrospect see
themselves as more affected, by the Ivy College experience.
Perhaps by being more open to new experience, they can adapt
to stress more effectively.

Stage of Adaptation scores, in contrast, are negatively
correlated with this self-rated average estimated effect of Ivy
College (r = −.23, p = .05). This seems paradoxical, since maturity of adaptation should involve openness to new experience. A
closer examination of the results reveals that maturity of adaptation is only negatively related to estimated Ivy effects on such
social-emotional qualities as getting along with others, circle of
friends, and political, religious, and moral-ethical perspectives.
Maturity of adaptation is unrelated to estimated Ivy effects on
occupational choice, cultural interests, or verbal expression and
is positively related to seeing Ivy College as broadening (r = .33,
p < .01) and contributing to cognitive growth (r = .26, p < .05).
What does this pattern mean? Perhaps because they already
start out at a more mature level, men scoring high in maturity
of adaptation are less swayed in their social and moral senti-
ments by the experience of four years at Ivy College. They may
be more resistant to the "brainwashing" effects of total institutions in general (see Goffman, 1961; Lifton, 1961; Schein,
1961) while remaining open to the intellectual and cultural dimensions of Ivy College. This conclusion is certainly consistent
with our ordinary ideas of maturity and deserves to be followed
up in further research with the Stages of Psychological Adaptation measure.

Finally, in 1974, the 1964 graduates were asked to evaluate their current job with respect to twelve dimensions, on four-point scales. The maturity of adaptation measure from 1964 is related to high ratings on three of these dimensions: "You have sufficient authority to do your job properly" ($r = .36$, $p < .01$), "Your supervision is competent" ($r = .22$, $p < .10$), and "You have all the freedom you need to do your job well" ($r = .25$, $p < .05$). The results are not an artifact of income or being in a particular career, such as doctor or professor, since maturity of adaptation is not significantly related to any of these factors. This pattern is striking because reconciling one's own freedom and authority with competent supervision by others is not an easy task. It is a problem at the root of many human relations difficulties in corporations, families, and society at large. Combining these potentially conflicting demands for freedom and authority is often described as an essential part of mature citizenship, and these results demonstrate the validity and integrity of this combination.

Achievement motivation is positively correlated with senior-year grade-point average ($r = .16$, $p < .05$), which is consistent with previous findings of a positive but low relationship between achievement motivation and academic performance (see Atkinson and Raynor, 1974, chap. 2). Achievement motivation is also correlated with becoming a doctor ($r = .22$, $p < .01$), as well as the previously mentioned relationship to becoming an entrepreneur. At Ivy College in the 1960s, medicine (more than most careers) was perceived to involve competition with others against standards of excellence, which is the actual scoring definition of achievement motivation. For the upper-middle-class Ivy College students, moreover, it may also represent greater upward mobility—another characteristic of achievement motivation—than would a business career (see McClelland, 1961, pp. 249-251).

Like Self-definition, the leadership motive pattern is associated with political moderation ($r = .23$, $p < .05$). It also predicts feeling that one's job takes too much time and involves too much pressure ($r = .30$, $p < .05$), a finding consistent with the known tendency of men with this pattern to have cardiovascular problems (McClelland, 1979). Finally, the pattern is associated with identifying the turning points in one's life as choosing a career (r = .29, p < .05), serving in the Peace Corps or VISTA (r = .26, p < .05), or a public event such as the assassination of President Kennedy or the Vietnam War. This last finding suggests that people who are concerned with expressing controlled power may also tend to see their lives as lived out on a world stage.

Liberal Arts Competence and Women's Life Outcomes[4]

The four liberal arts competence measures show a few direct relationships to adult life outcomes among the class of 1964 Ivy College women, but the results are complicated by whether the women have children. Still, the overall pattern is intelligible; indeed, having children affects the adult life expression of liberal arts competence for both men and women.

Our analysis of women's adult lives differs from that of men not only because of differences in the amount and kind of available data but also and more important because the life patterns of women are different from those of men. Almost all the men had careers, for example, but among the women, only 53 percent had full-time careers as of the 1974 follow-up. Most of the other career-related variables shown in Table 6 and on which we have data for women are, among the women, represented by very small numbers (for example, being an entrepreneur). From the available information, we defined the following four life outcomes:

Higher degree: Any further educational degree above the A.B. level.

Full-time career: Being active in a full-time career or actively preparing for such a career (for example, getting a Ph.D. to become an academic or going to law school to become a lawyer).

Spouse in executive career: Husband is a business executive, a bureaucrat, or a lawyer (category developed by Birnbaum, 1975).

Happiness: Questionnaire scale developed by Zung (1965) to measure depression, scored in the reverse direction.

Three additional outcomes—office holding, being married, and having children—were not significantly related to any of the predictor variables and are therefore omitted.

In addition to the liberal arts competence measures, we used social class of parents, level of honors at graduation, husband in executive career, and having children as predictor variables.

The regression results are summarized in Table 9 in a

Table 9. Predicting Female Life Outcomes after Fourteen Years from Liberal Arts Competence Measures and Other Variables

	Life Outcome			
Predictor Variable	Higher Degree	Full-time Career	Executive Spouse	Happiness
Liberal Arts Competence				
Self-definition	+	$\overset{+}{=}$		
Achievement motivation				(+)
Leadership motive pattern			(+)	
Modal Stage of Psychological Adaptation to the Environment				
Parents' Social Class				
College Honors	+			
Current Situation			—	
Executive spouse		— —	X	
Children		— — —	X	(+)

Note: Symbols in this table are the same as in Table 6.

form parallel to that of Table 6 for men. On the whole, the direct relationships between liberal arts competence and later life outcomes are not as strong for women as they are for men (although the liberal arts competence measures do predict well compared to social class and level of college honors, as they did with men). Since we found no tendency for women to change more than men in the cross sectional and longitudinal studies at Ivy College, these results cannot be explained by any presumed greater changeability or instability in the women's freshman-year scores. Perhaps women's life outcomes are too variable for this kind of analysis, or perhaps we have simply not looked at the right outcomes. Some readers might even conclude that the liberal arts competence measures, along with personal qualities and preferences in general, have less of an effect on women's lives than they do on men's lives. Certainly, many classic social theories and a good deal of social science research seems to dwell on an image of woman as the passive product of historical, social, and situational forces beyond personal control or modification (see Stewart, 1975, chap. 1). But such an easy and sweeping conclusion is scarcely justified before taking a closer and more careful look at the data.

Self-definition is significantly related to getting a higher degree after college and, as predicted from previous research, to having a full-time career in 1974. Actually, these two outcomes are closely related. For most professional careers, a higher degree is a prerequisite. In addition, going to graduate school right after college apparently gives women a kind of "inoculation" against later dropping out of a career, while going to work right after college is associated with being a housewife ten years later. (The correlations between immediate graduate school and immediate work and an uninterrupted later career path are +.31, p < .001, and −.18, p = n.s., respectively.)

The leadership motive pattern is associated with having an executive husband. Perhaps this reflects a desire for controlled power expressed both vicariously (through the husband's power and status) and indirectly (as the "power behind the throne"), two kinds of power that have been traditionally available to women. Achievement motivation tends to predict later happiness. Maturity of adaptation scores do not have any direct relationship to these four outcomes.

The most striking results in Table 9 are the very strong negative relationships between two predictor variables—having children and having an executive husband—and whether a woman has a full-time career. Both findings are consistent with previous research. The retarding effects on women's careers that children (especially pre-school-age children) exert have been documented by a host of researchers (Bryan and Boring, 1947; Ginzberg and others, 1966; Astin, 1969; Bailyn, 1974; Bernard, 1974). The importance of the husband's characteristics is also well established. Birnbaum (1975) found that even highly educated women were less likely to work if their husbands were executives, bureaucrats, or lawyers. Bernard (1974) has stressed the importance of the "iron law of husband cooperation" as a factor in wives' careers, a law illustrated by both the data of Weil (1961) and the case experience of Seidenberg (1975). In another analysis of the Ivy College data on men, Winter, Stewart, and McClelland (1977) showed that male executive career and having children were both negatively associated with the career level of the wives of the Ivy College men.

Because having children is by far the single most important predictor variable, especially of whether women have full-time careers, we decided to carry out a more complex analysis in order to understand how liberal arts competence may *interact* with having children in shaping women's adult life outcomes. We therefore divided the sample into women who had children as of 1974 (N = 68) and women who did not (N = 48) in order to explore the predictive power of the liberal arts competence measures separately within each group. (Present marital status was ignored here because it is less important in affecting careers than is the presence of young children; see Stewart, 1975.) We are treating the presence of children as a *moderator variable*: a catalyst, transforming the longitudinal effects of other variables, rather than just adding its own effects to them, as is assumed in ordinary (linear) regression. Table 10 shows the relationships of Self-definition, achievement motivation, and the leadership motive pattern to selected adult life outcomes (beyond the four outcomes presented in Table 9) for each of these two groups separately. (We did not find that having children affected the correlates of maturity of adaptation scores.)

Self-definition shows a significant positive relationship to higher degrees and having a career among women who do not have children and no relationship among those who do. The self-defining women with children are, however, far from inactive. They are involved in free-lance activity, for profit, carried out in their homes. Examples of such free-lance activity include writing articles or poetry for publication, giving music or cooking lessons for money, and opening up a home-based craft store. These women are active in a way that is consistent with

Table 10. Relationships of Liberal Arts Competence Measures to
Selected Life Outcomes for Women with and without Children

Liberal Arts Competence Measure	Life Outcome	Correlation with Life Outcome Among Women with	
		Children (N = 68)	No Children (N = 48)
Self-definition	Higher degree	.04	.45**
	Career	.12	.35*
	Free-lance activity in the home	.39***	−.20
Achievement motivation	Higher degree	.01	.38*
	Career persistence[a]	.02	.28+
	College professor	−.01	.31*
	Executive husband	.26*	−.15
Leadership motive pattern	Office holding	.18	−.09
	Organizational involvement[b]	.25*	−.24
	Personal skill development[c]	−.01	.50***
	Husband's occupational status[d]	−.02	.43*
	Happiness	.16	−.22
	Discontent[e]	−.10	.35*

[a]Measure used by Baruch (1967) and modified by Stewart (1975).

[b]Office holding, political activity, and volunteer work, each weighted equally.

[c]Time spent on development of skills in tennis, music, macrame, dance, and so forth.

[d]Coded on a Hollingshead-Redlich scale.

[e]Present/absent coding from entire 1974 questionnaire.

+$p < .10$

*$p < .05$

**$p < .01$

***$p < .001$

their family situation. As their children grow up, we would expect them to expand their free-lance activity or develop it into a full-time career outside the home, perhaps in conjunction with further education. Thus Self-definition is significantly related to adult career outcomes over a fourteen-year time span.

Dividing the sample of women in this way also brings out

several significant relationships between women's achievement motivation and life outcomes. Among the women with no children, achievement motivation predicts getting a higher degree, persisting in a career,[5] and being a college professor. Perhaps for these women, an academic career (rather than being an entrepreneur or executive) is one of the few professional careers openly available to women that involves the kind of moderate risks and aspirations that are attractive to those with high achievement motivation. Among women with children, achievement motivation predicts having an executive husband (as it does for all women with the leadership motive pattern, as previously shown). In this case, the achievement desire may be displaced on to the husband and satisfied vicariously.

The split also brings out some surprising life outcomes associated with the leadership motive pattern. Among women with children, this pattern shows the customary relationships to office holding and organizational involvement (office holding, volunteer work, and political activity). Among women with no children, however, the leadership motive pattern is *negatively* related to these expected outcomes. Instead, it predicts having a husband with a high-status occupation and spending a lot of time on the development of such personal skills as music and dance, tennis, macrame, or running. (These are consumption activities, as contrasted with the "productive" activities of free-lance work previously described.) Finally, among these childless women, the leadership motive pattern is negatively associated with the happiness scale and positively associated with a generalized mood of discontent coded from the overall tone of the follow-up questionnaire.

While the results for Self-definition and achievement motivation suggest that having children constrains (or at least channels) the later expression of women's liberal arts competence, these last results suggest that children facilitate the realization of controlled power drives, even in extrafamilial areas. Why should this be? For these women, it appears that the presence of children acts to channel controlled power *motives* into responsible, organized power *behavior*. Without children, these same power concerns are free to pursue status tinged with self-indulgence—the "jet-set" style or, in Parsons's (1954) terms, the "glamor pattern." (Parsons used "glamour pattern" to indicate one of the restricted status options open to women in the "traditional" sex-role structure of American society, a structure that was still strong during the years in which these women grew up.) After ten years, however, this pattern apparently breeds discontent among women who want power. For women, then, children apparently play an important role in channeling power concerns.

Do children have the same effect on men's controlled power concerns? Table 11 splits the Ivy College male sample

Table 11. Relationship of Leadership Motive Pattern to Selected
Life Outcomes for Men with and without Children

| | Correlation of Leadership Motive Pattern with Life Outcome among Men with | |
Life Outcome	Children (N = 49)	No Children (N = 37)
Organizational memberships	.29	−.16
Offices held	.32*	.07
Early success	.17	−.39*
Publications	.29	−.23
Career frustration[a]	−.17	.21
Self-Image[b]		
Settled	.15	−.01
Focused	.03	−.26
Responsible	−.03	−.36*
Relaxed	−.02	.35*
In flux	−.07	.55***

[a]Answer to the question "Overall, how frustrating is your present job?" on a five-point scale.

[b]From a list of twenty-one adjectives, of which four were to be checked as best characterizing "your current life-style."

*p < .05

***p < .001

into the same two groups and shows the different outcomes related to the leadership motive pattern in each group. The overall pattern is quite similar. The leadership motive pattern predicts organizational membership and office holding only among men with children. Within this group, it also is related to achieving early success, having a self-image of being "settled," and even having many publications. Among the men without children, however, the pattern predicts *not* being an early success, feeling career frustration, and having a self-image that is relaxed but with strong overtones of drift. *Thus with men as with women, children seem to have the effect of channeling power concerns from drifting and discontented self-indulgence into responsible, organized, and effective leadership behavior.* For power and leadership motivation, at least, children are apparently an essential aspect of maturity in both sexes.

Other Correlates of Self-Definition. Stewart (1978) has reported other results from the study of Ivy College women that further illustrate the importance of Self-definition in women's adult lives. Fifty-seven of the women who returned the 1974 follow-up questionnaire were randomly selected and given fifteen- to thirty-minute tape-recorded telephone interviews about stressful experiences. After initially establishing rapport, the interviewer asked each woman "to describe the period in your life that you think of as the most unhappy or upsetting time you've lived through. . . . A time when . . . things really seemed to go badly." Where appropriate, the interviewer probed for the factors that led up to the situation, what actually happened, and how it all ended. The interviews were later coded for a variety of categories, such as clarity, number and locus of cause(s), and problem content. Coders had no knowledge of the interviewee's TAT scores.

Self-definition, as measured fourteen years earlier in freshman year, significantly predicts the clarity with which a woman formulates and describes both the problem and its causes (r's = .64 and .73, respectively, p < .001 in each case). Women who had scored high in Self-definition cited more causes to the problem. They located the causes of the problem in the environment but the solutions to the problem within themselves, thus establishing the cognitive basis for effective coping. ("The problem wasn't my fault, but my actions can make a difference.") In fact, they responded to the problem by doing something rather than doing nothing, and what they did was often something instrumental rather than an irrelevant action. In other words, Self-definition is associated with an effective and instrumental approach to personal problems and stress. Because of the way they perceive the world and themselves, self-defining women are better able to mobilize themselves in response to difficulty and unhappiness. In terms of causal attribution theory, self-defining women attribute causes of problems and solutions in ways that reduce helplessness and increase mastery (see Weiner, 1980, pp. 380-406). By increasing Self-definition, then, liberal arts education would increase people's capacity to think and act effectively in dealing with stress. Perhaps that is why Self-definition is related to low blood pressure in the Ivy College male sample. (We did not have blood pressure data for the women.)

Interestingly enough, among the Ivy College women, Self-definition predicts the kinds of power-related careers, such as executive, teacher, psychologist, and other helping professions ($r = .33$, $p < .001$), that are usually associated with power motivation in men (see Winter, 1973, chap. 4). Adding this result to the previous findings about higher degrees and careers in general leads us to a broader speculation about women's status and their responses to social suppression. Previous research at the cross-national level (Stewart and Winter, 1977) has established that female status and power relative to men has two independent dimensions: social-educational and economic. At the individual level, we now find that Self-definition predicts advancement along both dimensions, as well as getting established in a power-related career. Perhaps, then, the key psychological characteristic for women's own advance in status and power is not so much wanting power or even (as we shall see) wanting controlled power, but rather developing the instrumentality of thought and action that transforms these wants into effective results. *If this is true, then for women, Self-definition may be the single most important dimension of liberal arts competence.* Growth in Self-definition would therefore be the single most important psychological benefit of liberal arts education for women. In Chapters Five and Six, we shall explore what aspects of liberal education, both at Ivy College and elsewhere, raise Self-definition.

Further Correlates of the Other Measures. In addition to the findings moderated by having children, there are two other interesting later-life correlates of achievement motivation. Ivy College women who as freshmen score high in achievement motivation later marry men with about the same (versus more) education as themselves (r = .25, p < .05). They are also more likely to report in 1974 that marriage has been a "high point" of their lives (r = .36, p < .001). If these two results go together, it might suggest that women's achievement motivation leads them to satisfying, companionate (rather than traditional) marriages, although it could also suggest that for this group of women, marriage still functioned as an "achievement." More research would be required to interpret these two findings fully.

The only additional interesting correlate of the leadership motive pattern actually involves its relationship to background factors rather than to adult life outcomes. Although the pattern is not related to parents' social class or education, it is related to attending a private school (r = .24, p < .05), especially a girls' (private) school (r = .31, p < .001). This suggests that a "special" education, made possible by parental sacrifice and effort rather than wealth, may be one important antecedent of women's controlled power concerns. (We shall return to this theme of specialness in our discussion of the leadership motive pattern in the next two chapters.) But it may also indicate that the male-dominated atmosphere of the typical coeducational American high school may impair women's development of leadership motivation.

Our additional findings about the maturity of adaptation measure are at first glance frankly perplexing and in considerable contrast to the positive career and happiness relationships for men, as previously reported. Women with higher modal Stage of Psychological Adaptation scores as freshmen show signs of later unhappiness. In looking back over the years since college, they list fewer high points and more low points (r = −.22, p < .05, with net number of high points), especially concerning their careers (r = .23, p < .05, with career as a low point). While not reporting explicit symptoms of depression, they also mention that it is hard to get up in the morning (r = .24, p < .05). Finally, they are more often involved in communes or other alternative living arrangements ($r = .21$, $p <$ .05), perhaps as a way to overcome this vague unhappiness.

Why should maturity of adaptation scores predict such an apparently unhappy pattern of life outcomes? An existentialist might argue, with Sartre, that a truly mature adaptation to life "begins on the other side of despair," but as a universal truth, this view is clearly refuted by the male data. Why are the results so different for women?

Phrasing the question in slightly different terms may suggest an answer. When will more mature persons be less happy and effective than less mature persons? One obvious possibility is when their opportunities for combining (in Freud's words) love and work are limited, either by external factors in the world or internal factors in the family. Without a career, for example, it is difficult to experience work as a truly autonomous calling. Within a traditional male-dominated marriage, moreover, it is difficult to give and receive mature love. Given Bernard's (1974) discussion and our own research (Winter, Stewart, and McClelland, 1977), we believe that the external and internal factors may simply be different ways of viewing the same kind of life situation that frustrates mature adaptation in women. External barriers gain much of their frustrating effect from a husband's discouragement. In *A Doll's House,* Ibsen vividly portrays this kind of marriage. To Helmer, his wife Nora is a "sweet little twittering lark," "my own bewildered helpless little darling," whom "I've done nothing but pamper and spoil." In the end, Nora leaves Helmer with the insight that "We have never exchanged so much as one serious word about serious things."

With the present data, we can test this explanation in at least a limited way. Women who have married and who have careers and children probably have the maximum opportunity to combine or integrate love and work. Their life situations are most like those of the Ivy College male graduates, virtually all of whom had careers and most of whom were married with children. For these women, therefore, maturity of adaptation scores should predict positive, energetic, and happy life outcomes, as they do among men. Even though having a career, marriage, and children may enhance women's opportunities for mature adaptation, they cannot completely eliminate the subtle forms of institutional and individual sexism; so even in this group, we would not expect the relationships of maturity of adaptation to positive life outcomes to be as clear or as strong as among the men. Married women without careers, however, should have much less opportunity to integrate love and work. For them, maturity of adaptation should predict an even stronger pattern of frustration than it does among the entire sample.

Table 12 presents the relationships between maturity of adaptation and life outcomes for these two groups and for the entire sample. While particular results are not always significant at usual levels, the overall pattern is consistent with our interpretation. Among married women with careers and children— women with a high opportunity for combining love and work— Stage of Psychological Adaptation scores are not associated with the various measures of unhappiness. But they do predict organizational involvement and a composite measure of career, family, and community attainment. (This measure is roughly equivalent to the male composite attainment measure discussed in the first part of this chapter.) Among women in the low-opportunity group, the tendency for maturity of adaptation to predict unhappiness and low attainment is stronger than for the entire sample.

For the present, we conclude that maturity of adaptation is a dimension of liberal arts competence that predicts success and satisfaction in later life for both men and women, *under conditions that give opportunity and scope to mature adaptation.* Under more constrained conditions, maturely adapted people may become frustrated and unhappy. (We have demonstrated this second conclusion with women; it could be further tested by research on men living in various situations of constraint, such as prisons, religious orders, or the military.) In Ibsen's vivid imagery, then, only an immature and dependent child could have stayed happy as Helmer's "doll-wife."

Summary

Despite the conceptual problems, methodological difficulties, and many gaps in the data regarding liberal arts compe-

Table 12. Life Outcomes Associated with Maturity of Adaptation
among Women With Differential Opportunity for Integrating
Love and Work

Life Outcome	All Women (N = 133)	Correlation with Modal Stage of Adaptation Scores Among	
		Women with High Opportunity to Integrate Love and Work (Married, with Career and Children) (N = 29)	Women with Low Opportunity to Integrate Love and Work (Married, with No Career) (N = 36)
Retrospective net high points[a]	−.22*	−.12	−.40*
Career as a high point	−.14	−.29	−.25
Career as a low point	.23*	.00	.42**
Happiness[b]	−.05	.30	−.02
"Hard to get up in the morning"	.24*	.00	.30[+]
Commune experience	.21*	.00	.37*
Organizational involvement[c]	.03	.50**	−.16
Overall attainment[d]	−.13	.39*[e]	−.24

[a]Number of high points minus number of low points mentioned overall.

[b]Zung depression scale reverse scored and dichotomized at the median.

[c]Office holding, political activity, and volunteer work weighted equally.

[d]Combination of career, children, office holding, and happiness. The career and children components are of course present for all women in the high-opportunity group, and the career component is absent for all women in the low-opportunity group. While this may reduce the intragroup variances, it should not systematically bias the intragroup correlations reported in this table.

[e]One-tailed test used, since this relationship was predicted.

[+]$p < .10$

*$p < .05$

**$p < .01$

***$p < .001$

tence measures, such as having scores on only four measures and those from freshman rather than senior year, our longitudinal study of the Ivy College class of 1964 has produced some important and encouraging results. These four liberal arts competence measures have significant and important relationships to later life outcomes, relationships that seem to be a good deal stronger than those we found for SAT scores and college honors, two of the most popular education-related predictors of academic performance and life outcomes. The number and magnitudes of the relationships are low, as would be expected in longitudinal research of this kind. Many of the effects are complicated by other factors, such as the presence of children. Still, the results are broadly what we would expect from theory and previous studies. They demonstrate that the four measures of liberal arts competence are significant and important in the postcollege worlds of working and living.

Notes

1. To facilitate such a study, we have deposited the data analyzed in Chapter Three with the Henry A. Murray Research Center of Radcliffe College, Cambridge, Massachusetts, where (with suitable precautions for preserving anonymity) they will be available for future scholars at that time.

2. The debate between "personality" (which includes the TAT-based measures of liberal arts competence) and "situational" explanations of behavior is classic. Some landmarks in the debate are Block (1977), Couch (1970), McClelland (1981), and Mischel (1968).

3. This is the increase in squared multiple correlation when a variable is added to all other predictor variables. It is also called the semipartial correlation coefficient (Cohen and Cohen, 1975, pp. 95-96).

4. This section draws heavily on research by Stewart (1975, 1980).

5. The measure of persistence is adapted from Baruch (1967), who found a strong relationship between achievement motivation and career persistence among women twenty or more years out of college but little relationship among women five to fifteen years out of college. The present results, originally reported by Stewart (1975, 1980), suggest that the presence of young children is probably the reason for this attenuation among Baruch's younger women.

FIVE

Understanding the Effects of "Ivy College": An Integrated Model

While the evidence presented in Chapters Three and Four establishes that at least one liberal arts college has substantial and significant effects, these results really raise more questions than they answer. Why does Ivy College have this distinctive impact? What causes the effects? Do they have anything to do with the liberal arts curriculum as such? Would the same thing happen at other liberal arts colleges or at other kinds of colleges?

Up to this point, we have assumed that the effects of Ivy College could be attributed to its liberal arts education. Yet such a deceptively simple phrase is hardly an explanation because "liberal arts" could mean almost anything. We might focus on teaching *style,* arguing that the essence of the liberal arts is not to be found in any particular course but rather in a certain special approach to the process of education. The formal curriculum is only one aspect of Ivy College, as it is of most other liberal arts colleges. Many other typical features of student experience and life have major effects on intellectual and personal development, even though they are extrinsic to the classical ideal of liberal education as described in Chapter One. This uncertainty about what is really essential, or even important, in a liberal arts college is nicely illustrated by two plausible but conflicting proverbs: "You could destroy all the other Harvard buildings [except the library] and still have a university" ("The Heart of Harvard's Greatness," 1968, p. 21). "A pine log, with the student at one end and Doctor [Mark] Hopkins at the other, would be a liberal education" (Wilson, 1938, p. 208). Taken together, these two kernels of educational wisdom offer little help to the educator who has to make increasingly difficult decisions about the allocation of scarce resources among libraries, faculty, pine logs, and a host of other eloquently and firmly defended features of the liberal arts college.

Any college, moreover, has a particular geographical and cultural setting, whether one of remote and isolated natural beauty that might induce meditative contemplation or (as at Ivy) one of urban diversity and opportunity that might promote cultural appreciation and sophistication. Many prospective students first focus on these geographical and cultural features when they begin choosing a college. At least for them, Ivy College is significant for *where* it is as much as for what it is.

It is even possible that for some students, Ivy College becomes important only after they leave. In common with other total institutions, such as mental hospitals, the military, and prisons (see Goffman, 1961), Ivy College embodies a cycle of withdrawal from the world, immersion in a new life, and finally, detachment from this new life and return to the world—the cycle of tests and trials through which the mythic hero must pass (Campbell, 1949). More recent empirical research (Stewart and others, 1980) has pinpointed how successive total transitions of this type build up the capacity for increased maturity of response to the environment, management of feelings and reactions to authority, and action. According to this paradoxical but plausible theory, the great disjunctivity between the liberal arts college and almost *any* future social role (except, perhaps, that of teaching in a liberal arts college) requires students to do major cognitive and emotional work as they try to adapt to their environment, building an identity between their inner selves and their outer world of social roles. If this theory is true, it follows that attempts to make college experiences relevant to the world or integrated with ordinary life (such as cooperative work study programs) would actually eliminate one of the most important features of the residential liberal arts college. According to this theory, then, one critical aspect of the liberal arts education offered at Ivy College is that it takes place in a total institution rather than anything about its curriculum, faculty, or resources. Thus the effects of Ivy College would be reduced at commuter colleges.

Finally, skeptical readers might argue that the distinctive effects of Ivy College have little to do with either the liberal arts curriculum or the nature of student life, but rather are largely the result of prestige suggestion. After all, Ivy College has wealth, prestige, facilities, tradition, and a reputation for excellence. When students enter Ivy College, therefore, they know that they are joining a highly selected, elite student body. They already have fairly clear expectations about Ivy College and the changes they are about to undergo at it. Thus prestige, reputation, and the expectations that they create may bring about many of the changes we discussed in Chapter Three as a kind of self-fulfilling prophecy. Let every feature of Ivy College be the same, this theory might assert; substitute only the shared student *belief* that this is a "third-rate" college filled with people who could not get into the institutions they really wanted to attend. When this is done, the skeptical argument concludes, then the unique effects of Ivy College will be effaced.

These, then, are some possible explanations for what happens at Ivy College. While each individual explanation may sound reasonable and any one of them might be valid, it is unlikely that all are true. In this chapter and the next, we shall evaluate some of these explanations, both with the data at hand and also with the results of some further studies. We shall try, in other words, to isolate and identify the efficacious principle(s) or active mechanism(s) of Ivy College. We seek this knowledge partly for reasons of scientific interest. Until we know the mechanisms or processes responsible for the results presented in Chapter Three, we cannot really understand them or even be sure they are true. Yet there are also urgent practical reasons for identifying these causes. If we can understand how and why Ivy College has the effects it has, then we can design educational and student life programs to replicate the effects of Ivy College elsewhere. Nowadays this kind of study is especially urgent. Even the most richly endowed colleges realize that their wealth is finite, especially in comparison to the dramatically increasing costs of all the things they would like to do and all the claims laid upon them as institutions by students, alumni, the public, or government. It is no longer possible for any college to justify and continue programs, styles of instruction, or features of student life with the old, familiar reasons—that the program has been done in the past, that some faculty members have faith it is good, or that some students say they like it. Even less are these criteria of tradition, faith, pressure, or consumer satisfaction adequate for evaluating and justifying the new programs and policies. Hard choices have to be made, and it is important that they be made on the basis of the best evidence available. If the liberal arts college should be preserved because it has effects that are important and worth preserving, then it becomes more and more important to identify exactly why and how these effects occur. That is an enormous and complex set of questions; all we can do now is begin finding some answers.

A Model for the Internal Study of Ivy College

The traditional laboratory way of answering questions about complex causality is to vary systematically all the elements presumed to be important and then to observe the differences in effects or outcome. Since colleges have to be studied as they exist out in the world and cannot be brought into the

laboratory, the ideal strategy of controlled variation obviously has to give way to more subtle, quasi-experimental techniques. Yet even the second-best alternative—replications of the present research at a large number of institutions that represent naturally occurring differences in levels and combinations of these variables—is also not feasible. The kinds of instruments we have used are, at this present experimental stage of development, simply too expensive and cumbersome to employ in large-scale studies of the kind undertaken by Astin (1977). Moreover, at the present stage of our knowledge, it would be difficult to select colleges for such a massive study. The number of ways colleges (even superficially similar liberal arts colleges) can differ is very large; so the number of potential variables that should be included is enormous. There is no certainty that the smaller number of general factors of college environments identified by previous research (Feldman and Newcomb, 1969) would necessarily be the critical variables for the more specialized and subtle effects with which we are concerned in this study.

In this chapter, we identify at least some of the active principles responsible for change at Ivy College through a further analysis of the results presented in Chapter Three. When freshmen and senior scores are compared, Ivy College appears to have several important effects, as summarized in Tables 4 and 5. These results are expressed in terms of group means: average senior scores minus average freshman scores in the cross sectional study, average change scores in the longitudinal study. While these average scores are appropriate for making group comparisons, they conceal great variation in the ways individual students actually change. For example, on the average, Ivy College students show significant gains in independence of thought as measured by Self-definition and in critical thinking as measured by the Test of Thematic Analysis; but some students gain more than others, and a few may actually go down from freshman to senior year. How did the college experiences of all these students differ? Did the students who showed the greatest gains do something or have some experience that the students with lesser gains or with losses did not do or have? For example, did they study harder, participate in more activities, or play on a varsity sports team? By examining the relationships between students' change scores and their college experiences, we can estimate the varying impact of different aspects of Ivy College and so test some of the previously discussed theories.

A few words about each of the three steps in the internal analysis will provide an overall view of what we did. The first task was to identify the major features of Ivy College experience, or at least those features that could be affected by educational policy and institutional goals. We asked Ivy College seniors about their activities and experiences in college. This background questionnaire covered topics such as major field, activities and interests, rated importance of different sources of learning at Ivy College, decisions and plans about a career, involvement in the arts and in sports, and the use of time in a typical week—over a hundred different variables in all.

The second task was to reduce these many isolated variables to a more manageable and meaningful set of broad, general aspects of Ivy College. We selected seventy important variables from the questionnaire and clustered them into the following seven aspects of college experience by means of a rotated factor analysis: academic involvement, extracurricular activity, dormitory-centered life, cultural participation, sports involvement, voluntary service, and science orientation. (See Kerlinger, 1973, pp. 659-692, for a brief introduction to factor analysis.) The 118 responses of the senior cross sectional sample from Chapter Three (pooling men and women) were used in this step to get the largest possible sample size and hence the greatest stability of results.

Finally, we examined the relationship between students' involvement in these seven aspects of Ivy College experience and their gains in liberal arts competence. Did students who were more active in extracurricular activities, for example, show greater gains in maturity of adaptation than did students who were less active? The best answer to questions of this sort requires us to isolate the unique effects of each aspect of college, independent of all the other aspects. We therefore used multiple-regression techniques to examine the relationship of scores for each aspect of Ivy College experience to gains in each aspect of liberal arts competence, while controlling statistically for the effects of all other aspects. Strictly speaking, of course, we can demonstrate only associations or correlations between aspects of college and growth in liberal arts competence. As in all science, causality (and its direction) is always an inference made from these associations. Causality can only be assumed and never proved. Since we are interested in the correlates of gains or change in scores, the most appropriate sample for this third step is the group of eighty students tested both as freshmen and as seniors—the longitudinal Ivy College sample from Chapter Three.

Seven Factors of Ivy College Experience

The seven factors of Ivy College experience that emerged from the factor analysis do not exhaust everything about Ivy College that might change students. They are only as comprehensive as the questionnaire from which they were derived. In fact, we shall look at other features of the institution later in this chapter. Still, these seven factors do suggest some of the most general and straightforward features of Ivy College. In the list that follows, we give the name and constituent variables for each factor. In the third step of this study, each factor was represented by its single most meaningful or typical variable, the one with the best statistical properties. These variables are technically known as "marker" variables and are italicized in the list.

1. Academic involvement

Great contribution to learning from thesis, seminars, tutorials, faculty contact

Had relatively great personal contact with faculty

Influence on vocational choice by course reading, contact and discussion with faculty, graduate teaching assistants in major, substantive enthusiasms and interests developed by studies

2. Extracurricular activity
- *Great contribution to learning from extracurricular activities*
- Influence on vocational choice by volunteer, emotional, and recreational experiences; extracurricular activities; leaves of absence
- College gave relatively great frustration

3. Dormitory-centered life
- *Great contribution to learning from college dorm experience* and dorm graduate student advisers
- College gave relatively great satisfaction
- *Not* in organizations outside Ivy College

4. Cultural participation
- *Relatively many hours spent participating in the creative arts*
- Member of arts activity outside Ivy College
- High participation in music, drama, plastic arts, crafts, and so forth
- Much attendance at art exhibitions, music, theater, and so forth
- Much reading
- Humanities major
- *Not* social science major

5. Sports involvement
- *Participated in a varsity sport*
- Relatively many hours spent participating in sports
- Influence on vocational choice by family

6. Voluntary service
- *Participated in tutoring and volunteer work*
- Great contribution to learning from fieldwork
- Influence on vocational choice by summer and volunteer work experiences, university counseling services

	(college career planning office), and preprofessional advisers

Participated in tutoring and volunteer work

7. Science
   orientation

Natural sciences major

Not humanities major

Great contribution to learning from laboratory experience

Not influenced in vocational choice by resident graduate teaching assistants

We shall review the constituents of each factor briefly in order to give a fuller sense of these dimensions. Factor 1 is labeled academic involvement because it reflects the experience of students for whom the university has been an academy: They feel they have learned through scholarly contact with the faculty; and this, together with the enthusiasm and interest they have developed toward their courses, has strongly affected their choice of career. These students are probably viewed by the faculty as ideal students, as the kind of student for whom Ivy College ought to exist. They are true proteges. Success at Ivy for this kind of student is graduating *summa cum laude,* writing a publishable thesis, and getting into a high-prestige Ph.D. program.

Factor 2, the extracurricular activity dimension of experience, seems to capture a no-less-traditional American variant on factor 1: Behind the academic surface, college is the chance to develop management and performance skills through participating in an activity such as a publication, a theatrical or arts group, or a political club. These experiences, together with other non-academic events and emotional factors, strongly affect career choice. As one might expect, these students feel frustrated by Ivy College, probably because they have to keep balancing their extracurricular interests with the college's academic demands. Success for this group would mean becoming an editor of the campus newspaper, having a lead role in a campus theatrical production, or perhaps being elected president of the Young Democrats.

Factor 3, labeled dormitory-centered life, requires some further explanation. Most students at Ivy College live in dormitories that are both living and dining quarters and also the basis for some organizations, intramural sports, and a good deal of informal social and intellectual life. Dormitory-based activities typically have a more informal, amateur style than do the collegewide organizations. In many ways, these dormitories resemble the colleges at Yale or the houses at Harvard (see Jencks and Riesman, 1962), both of which are in turn conscious imitations of the Oxford and Cambridge colleges. Students scoring high on this factor report great involvement and learning from dining hall conversations with the resident graduate student advisers, and they participate extensively in dorm organizations and activities (but not in collegewide organizations). They are very satisfied with Ivy College. Success for them would involve playing an important role in organizing dorm activities and perhaps knowing a lot of graduate student advisers.

The cultural participation factor, number 4, includes both participation in the arts (drama, music, visual and plastic arts) and appreciation or attendance at exhibitions and performances of others, both within Ivy College and in the larger community. This factor identifies those who have taken advantage of the many arts resources and facilities in the metropolitan area near Ivy College, as well as those who spend their college years reading (taking advantage of the library resources of Ivy). Success for these students would mean developing either some kind of performance niche within an arts organization at Ivy or in the city or at least a sense that they had developed a deep personal appreciation for the arts and their cultural tradition.

Factor 5, sports involvement, is readily understood. The main constituent variable is playing on a varsity team. Family influence on vocational choice is also a constituent of this factor. This is a curious finding and probably means that students heavily involved in sports simply continue the same career plans with which they entered Ivy College, attributing these early plans to the influence of their family. To them, success is obviously playing on a winning varsity team at Ivy in their chosen sport. (Being drafted by a professional team might be the highest form of success for this dimension of college experience, but that is only a distant goal for most Ivy College athletes.)

For the student high on factor 6, college is a base for voluntary service and, through that experience, a preprofessional training ground for later professional school in, for example, medicine, law, or business. These students learn most from fieldwork and are well served in career advice by the formal channels for preprofessional advice (career planning office, preprofessional advisers). They participate in tutoring and volunteer work, perhaps to secure experience in the area of their later career and perhaps also for its effect on their resumé. Success for them is, in the short run, helping others; in the longer run, it is perhaps getting into medical, law, or business school and entering the helping professions.

The science-oriented student, whose experience is largely reflected in factor 7, majors in a science and learns most from the laboratory. Dorm experience and graduate advisers are not important. Success is either making an original scientific discovery or getting into graduate school in science or medicine.

These factors or dimensions of the Ivy College experience seem to be coherent and consistent with the observations of others about the important aspects of liberal education at many colleges, although the factor structure of college experiences will vary from one institution to another. Readers should keep in mind that at least in this sample, the factors are *independent*: Whether a student is active or scores high on one factor is unrelated to what that student's activity or score is on any other factor. Thus students can score high on more than one factor.

The Sevenfold Impact of Ivy College

How do these seven aspects of college experience produce, moderate, or retard the characteristic impact of Ivy College on liberal arts competence? In other words, what unique contribution, intended or unintended, does each factor make to the results presented in Chapter Three? To answer this question, we first calculated freshman to senior change or growth scores for all students on each of the major measures of liberal arts competence discussed in Chapters Two and Three.[1] We then looked at how each of the variables representing an aspect of college experience was related to these growth scores when the other college experience variables had been held constant through multiple-regression analysis.[2] The results will tell us about the effects of each feature of Ivy College within the entire longitudinal sample. This is only part of the story, however, because we cannot assume that everything at Ivy College affects all students in the same way. For men and women, as an example, Ivy College is in many respects a different institution. Differences in sex-role expectations, as well as the (not inconsiderable) vestiges of direct sexism, create differences in the structure of norms, rewards, and sanctions men and women encounter. Over the years, many activities, such as athletics, have been male dominated; and even now the informal traditions, myths, and legends of Ivy College are populated largely with male characters. Women students find very few female role models among the Ivy College faculty, and after graduation, they have different career prospects and different problems integrating career and family roles. There are, then, good grounds for expecting many aspects of the Ivy College environment to affect men and women differently. To explore these differences, we divided the longitudinal sample by sex and calculated the regression results separately for the thirty-six men and the forty-four women.[3]

Secondary school background is another student characteristic that affects how students develop liberal arts competence. While schools vary in many ways, the private school versus public school distinction is likely to be especially important at Ivy College. In general, private school graduates have done more difficult and sophisticated academic work in a school environment that explicitly stresses college preparation and elite, upper-class values (McArthur, 1955, 1960). Often they have had more experience in living and working independently. Public school students, in contrast, usually enter college less well-prepared academically but with broader, more heterogeneous social experience and greater familiarity with mainstream middle-class American culture. As might be expected from these

considerations, previous studies of change in college have demonstrated the importance of the public/private distinction
(McArthur, 1954; Freedman, 1956). To explore how this dimension of secondary school experience affects the growth of
liberal arts competence at Ivy College, we also split the longitudinal sample into the forty-eight students who were graduated
from public high schools and the thirty-two students entering
college from private schools. We calculated the regressions separately for each group.

Table 13 presents the results of all five regression studies:
that of the entire sample, those of men and women separately,
and those of graduates of public and private schools separately.
The seven dimensions of college experience are the columns
(further broken down into the total sample and the different
subgroups), and the liberal arts competence measures are the
rows. In the table, a plus sign in a cell indicates that the particular aspect of college facilitates growth in the relevant component of liberal arts competence; a minus sign indicates that it
retards gains in that component. (On measures showing overall
gains at Ivy College, "retard" really means less of an increase.)
Whenever so many relationships are calculated, a certain number will appear as statistically significant merely because of
chance. Perhaps the reader's first question, therefore, is whether
our results exceed what would be expected by chance alone. If
we consider the five principal new operant measures of liberal
arts competence that show significant freshman-senior differences at Ivy College in Chapter Three (Test of Thematic Analysis, Analysis of Argument, Self-definition, leadership motive
pattern, and Stage of Psychological Adaptation) times the seven
aspects of college experience we use as predictors, calculated
five times for the five separate sets of regressions, then we are
examining 175 separate possible relationships. By chance alone,
about 9 should be significant at the 5 percent (.05) level or less.
In fact, we obtained 21 relationships (or 12 percent) significant
at this level, which is considerably higher than chance. Because
this research is exploratory, we have also presented some less-
significant trends (p less than .10 but not less than .05) in
parentheses in the table and some relationships to the more tra-

Table 13. Summary Chart of Effects of Seven Aspects of Ivy College Experience

Component of Liberal Arts Competence	Measured by	I. Academic Involvement	II. Extracurricular Activity	III. Dormitory-Centered Life	IV. Cultural Participation	V. Sports Involvement	VI. Voluntary Service	VII. Science Orientation
1. Critical thinking; broad analytical skill	Test of Thematic Analysis	−public		−all −men −private		+all +men +public		−private
3. Independence of thought	Self-definition			−private	−public	(+all) +women +private		
	Achievement motivation						(−all) (−women) −private	
4. Empathy; intellectual flexibility	Analysis of Argument							−private
5. Self-control for broader loyalties	Leadership motive pattern					(+women)		
6. Self-assurance in leadership ability	(lower) Fear of success			+public				
7. Maturity of judgment; personal integration	Maturity of adaptation		+all +men +public (+private)	−women −public	+men +public			−public
	Self-rated ability to accept criticism						(+all)	
	Range of self-rated abilities	+all +men						
8. Equalitarian liberal values	Self-rated ability to respect diversity			(+private)			(−private)	+all +men +public

ditionally measured components of liberal arts competence. We shall begin our discussion by reviewing the significant effects and trends associated with each factor of college experience in turn.

Academic Involvement. Academic involvement seems to have few effects on the growth of liberal arts competence other than spreading out the range that students (especially men) use when they estimate their own abilities. While the variable used to represent academic involvement—self-rated amount of faculty contact—is subjective and therefore open to a variety of distortions (see Nisbett and Wilson, 1977, especially pp. 246-253), using more objective measures such as grade-point average or level of graduation honors gives essentially the same result. Writing a senior honors thesis does show a positive (though nonsignificant) correlation with Self-definition gains, as would be expected from the independent thought and work a thesis involves, but it also tends to predict a decline in maturity of adaptation among men ($r = -.30$, $p < .10$ with gain in maturity of adaptation).[4]

In spite of these results, we cannot dismiss the academic aspect of Ivy College as wholly irrelevant to its effects on students. Academic activity and academic values permeate both the organized and the informal student culture of Ivy College, more than at most institutions and much more than at State Teachers College and Community College. Formal organizations like the college newspaper and informal dining table conversations display a conspicuously intellectual orientation. If intellectual activity and values cannot be shown to have an independent effect within the longitudinal sample of Ivy College students, they nevertheless are the very reason for the existence of everything else at Ivy College. Student culture, sports, the arts—all these other aspects of Ivy College are grounded in its intellectual orientation and would be very different without it.

Extracurricular Activity. Participation in formal, organized extracurricular activities seems to facilitate growth in maturity of adaptation for most students. For women, however, these gains are associated with joining extramural clubs ($r = .33$, $p < .05$) rather than being involved in Ivy College organizations ($r =$

.01). As we will suggest in connection with the dormitories, this difference may be caused by traditional male dominance of college organizations. In any case, these results lend further support to other researchers' conclusions about the importance of student culture and peer group influence (see, for example, Sanford, 1962, chaps. 13-15; Feldman and Newcomb, 1969, chap. 8).

Dormitory-Centered Life. Involvement in dormitory life, which we take to represent the informal side of student culture and peer group influences, seems to have preponderantly negative effects. Dormitory involvement is associated with less growth in critical thinking for almost all groups. Among private school graduates, it also leads to lesser gains in independence of thought as measured by Self-definition. Among both women and public school graduates, it also retards growth in maturity of adaptation. Because they are used to living away from home on their own, private school graduates may experience the dormitory structure of Ivy College as a constraint. For public school graduates, however, Ivy dormitories may have an infantilizing effect by prolonging the quasi-familial living atmosphere (resident faculty and graduate students *in loco parentis*). For women, the lesser growth in maturity of adaptation may be the result of male domination of dormitory life—in numbers, in traditions and atmosphere, and perhaps also in small-group interaction patterns (see Strodtbeck and Mann, 1956). Although the numbers are small, this retarded growth in maturity holds among women living in dormitories that had been all-women before the advent of mixed-sex living in the early 1970s as well as among women living in the formerly men's dormitories.

While involvement in dormitory life thus seems to work against many of the overall effects of Ivy College, we must remember that the causal direction of our results may actually be reversed. That is, students who find the impact of Ivy College to be beyond their abilities, desires, or comfort may turn instead to the less-pressured congeniality of dormitory life. On this alternate view, the dormitory structure would be more of a refuge than a counterforce in the liberal arts context of Ivy College.

On the positive side, dormitory involvement makes public school graduates more confident by reducing their fear of success and makes private school graduates more tolerant and respecting of (public school?) diversity. This last finding may reflect the growth of a liberal, equalitarian ethic; but given Ivy College's historical view of itself as training future national leaders, these two complementary growth processes may also reflect the psychological dynamics of co-optation and absorption of middle-class public school graduates into the future ruling classes (see Domhoff, 1967).

Cultural Participation. Time spent on creative writing and artistic activity is associated with greater gains in maturity of adaptation for men and for public school graduates, although it also retards growth on one measure of independence of thought for the latter group. These effects are confined to time spent on personal creative *production* and are unrelated to other cultural variables, such as attending concerts, visiting museums, and reading for pleasure, that measure what might be called creative "consumption."

Sports Involvement. The positive effects of playing varsity sports are substantial and even a little surprising. Among all groups (especially men and public school graduates), varsity sports predicts greater gains in critical thinking as measured by thematic analysis. Why should this be so? Varsity athletes did not score lower as freshmen; so any "catching up" (or regression toward the mean) explanation can be ruled out. Success in athletics does, however, require at least two qualities of mind: disciplined, thorough practice and adaptability to complex and rapidly changing circumstances. Applied to mental life, this practice and adaptability should enhance a person's ability to form and articulate abstract cognitive concepts to organize complex experience. (Thus coaches in many sports, for example, speak of a player's ability to diagnose or "read" the other team's intentions or the course of the game.) Among men, there is also a tendency (though not statistically significant) for varsity sports to be associated with gains in maturity of adaptation, probably also the result of disciplined practice and adaptability. For most groups, varsity sports predicts gains in instrumental independence of thought (Self-definition); among women athletes, there is also a trend toward greater gains in the leadership motive pattern. Taken together, these two results suggest that women gain a sense of confident instrumental assertion through sports, a conclusion that is certainly consistent with the claims of those who have argued for equality of female sports access and opportunities. The latter trend also fits with Riesman's (1976, p. xx) observation that for women, as for men, athletic participation teaches students to use power in cooperative ways —that "the road to the boardroom leads through the locker room."

At Ivy College, then, varsity sports build character or at least several components of liberal arts competence. In order to avoid any misunderstanding, we preface our discussion by some comments on the role of sports at Ivy College. Student athletes enjoy no special scholarships, dormitories, academic programs, or campus social prominence. While competition is keen at the varsity level, sports are certainly not emphasized as they are at many large universities. But most of the previously discussed findings are true only for varsity sports and do not hold true for Ivy College's more casually organized and extensive intramural sports program. Our results therefore have carefully restricted application. If college sports build character, they build it through the disciplined commitment of the varsity teams and not through mere casual physical activity, on the one hand, or heavily emphasized athletic programs, on the other.

Voluntary Service. Tutoring and other volunteer work have only a few strong effects, tending to reduce achievement motivation and to increase the range of self-rated abilities in most groups. Among private school graduates, there is a slight tendency for voluntary service to predict lesser gains in respect for diversity. Taken together, these findings may suggest a slight upper-class noblesse oblige tinge to voluntary service at Ivy College: broadening one's perspective through seeing the troubles of the rest of the world rather than energetically working to improve conditions.

Science Orientation. This aspect of Ivy College is represented by majoring in a natural science; so we could refer to the

effects of a particular group of major fields rather than of an aspect of the college as a whole. Among all students, majoring in
science increases self-rated respect for diversity. This seems to
be a straightforward case of students adopting one of the most
basic values of science. More surprising, however, is the evidence
that science seems to retard personal growth in different ways
among different groups. Majoring in science is associated with
smaller gains in maturity of adaptation for public school students and lower growth in independent instrumentality (as measured by Self-definition) among private school graduates.

Conversely, majoring in humanities has the opposite effect for each group: enhanced maturity of adaptation for public
school students and enhanced independence of thought among
private school graduates. Some humanists would seize upon
these results as confirming their stereotypes of the mad scientist
or the glazed countenance of the premedical grind, obsessively
focused on an ever more narrowly defined specialty (see, as an
example, Babbitt, 1908, and, as criticism, Snow, 1962). These
stereotypes do not necessarily reflect our results, for undergraduate science majors at Ivy College probably sample more evenly
and broadly from the entire range of the curriculum than do
humanities majors. (More science students take literature classes
than literature students take calculus or cell biology, for example.)

A more satisfactory explanation for the lesser personal
growth might be found by looking at some psychological and
sociological studies of science and scientists. McClelland (1964),
for example, cited several characteristics of creative natural
scientists that had been established in previous research: They
work unusually hard. They avoid complex interpersonal emotions. They are unconsciously attached to "nature" as a substitute for idealized persons. Snow (1962, p. 15) concluded that,
among scientists, "imaginative understanding is less than it could
be." Merton (1957) noted the close correspondence between
scientific values and the tenets of radical protestant theology,
especially in the tendency toward ascetic repression of impulse
life. In terms of the maturity of adaptation measure, each of
these aspects of science seems to be characteristic of earlier (or

lower) stages of adaptation to the environment (the stages of receptivity or autonomy) rather than of the later stages of assertion and integration. Without direct studies of career scientists, we can only tentatively conclude that natural science involves relatively lower levels of psychological or affective adaptation. If this conclusion holds, however, our results suggest it is a psychological characteristic that can be transmitted through college-level scientific training.

Testing a Skeptical Explanation

So far our analysis has focused on relating the observed effects of Ivy College to the formal and informal aspects of the institution itself, things that could conceivably be affected by educational policy. A more skeptical interpretation of our results, however, might argue that these effects have very little to do with Ivy College as such but rather are the result of some extraneous factor, ·such as students' images of themselves, their expectations about Ivy College, prestige suggestion, or perhaps peer norms. There is a good deal of evidence that these factors can have powerful change effects (see McClelland and Winter, 1969, chap. 2). In a commentary on an early summary of the results we presented in Chapter Three, Botstein (1977) has suggested that the presumed changes brought about by Ivy College are simply due to the expectations and perceptions students develop as a consequence of having been admitted to a prestigious, elite liberal arts college. One can argue, of course, that the prestige of Ivy College and the student expectations it generates are not extraneous but rather are real properties of Ivy College. Prestige and expectations, if they are to endure, must have some ultimate basis in institutional reality. Still, the skeptical interpretation deserves serious consideration as an alternative explanation.

While this alternative explanation cannot be tested fully and directly within the scope of the present study, we were able to assemble some relevant data from the Ivy College longitudinal sample. During the freshman testing, students were asked how much they expected to learn at Ivy College from each of thirteen different sources—for example, lectures, faculty contact, bull sessions, and dormitory life. The average expected contributions to learning from all thirteen sources is therefore a rough measure of how much students initially expected to learn simply as a function of being at Ivy College. This measure can be used to test whether the expectations students have when they enter Ivy College have any relationship to subsequent change. So far as they go, the results solidly refute the skeptical explanation. On only one measure, namely, reduced fear of success, did the students who as freshmen expected relatively more from Ivy College actually show greater gains in liberal arts competence during their college years. In fact, these same students also showed *less* growth in two personal components of liberal arts competence—independence of thought and maturity of adaptation. High initial expectations, then, actually tend to inhibit or reduce the changes we have observed at Ivy College.

We did find that some other aspects of initial freshman experience had interesting effects, of a very different kind. Freshmen were asked to rate how frustrating their Ivy College experience had been so far. Those students who found Ivy College more frustrating as freshmen later showed significantly larger increases in critical thinking (as measured by the Test of Thematic Analysis) and in the leadership motive pattern. (Greater initial frustration also tended to increase the range of women's self-rated abilities while decreasing the range of men's self-ratings.) Is this initial frustration an extraneous factor existing only in students' minds, or is it rather the subjective side of Ivy College's tradition of autonomy, a tradition so strong that to many it appears as a kind of institutional abandonment (see Stewart, 1975)? Perhaps the sense of frustration is the result of several factors, such as distance from home, heterogeneity of fellow students, new and more difficult kinds of academic work, impersonality, the remoteness (even arrogance) of faculty, and above all, the bewildering variety of unfamiliar stimuli.

Whatever the sources of this initial frustration, it does seem to spur the development of both conceptual ability or critical thinking and leadership concerns in all students. Perhaps these two effects are, respectively, the cognitive and the motivational ways to reimpose a sense of order upon the initial "blooming buzzing (and frustrating) confusion" that Ivy College presents to the entering freshman student. The struggle to create conceptual clarity out of this confusion thereby enhances critical thinking ability in general, while the necessity for disciplined assertion in a complex social environment develops leadership. In slightly different terms, perhaps both emerge from the sophisticated cognitive effort necessary to reduce dissonance and inconsistency: "Why did I choose to come to Ivy College if it is such a frustrating place? Perhaps I have been chosen for leadership. Perhaps these frustrations are an ordeal or test." Certainly the connection between early frustration and later growth in conceptual ability and leadership recurs in myth and practice from the ancient Greeks down to the present day. Plato argued that youth who show leadership promise should be removed from the secure satisfactions of their families in order to be trained as philosopher-kings. The myth of the hero who is removed from the land of his birth and subjected to deprivations, frustrations, hazards, and perils is one of the most ancient and enduring themes in world literature (see Campbell, 1949; Rank, [1910] 1959). In the nineteenth century, the future rulers of British India were sent to boarding schools and subjected to rigors and frustrations as an essential part of their preparation (see Woodruff, 1953). Winter, Alpert, and McClelland (1963) observed the analogous development of a sophisticated "classic personal style" among high school students who participated in a summer program at an elite American boarding school.

Thus while the explicit expectations that students have when they enter Ivy College may not be much of a factor in their later growth, the sense of frustration they experience early in college may be very significant for the development of many aspects of liberal arts competence. Yet there are risks and costs. Not all students respond to the early frustrations of Ivy College with counteractive assertion and conceptual effort. Some fail and leave, frightened perhaps by the seeming competence of the

faculty and of other students. Others fail in more subtle ways—
lost souls concealing their pain as they move numbly through
the rest of their college years.

Preliminary Conclusions

Up to this point, we have discussed the results of the
longitudinal study in terms of the different aspects of Ivy College, both as a way of explaining the findings of Chapter Three
and as an illustrative model of institutional evaluation research
using our new measures. It is now appropriate to focus on the
measures themselves. In a preliminary way, what have we
learned about the growth of these different components of liberal arts competence?

Cognitive Skills. Judging by the results presented in Table
13, growth in the cognitive aspects of liberal arts competence
(critical thinking, intellectual flexibility) seems to be an effect
of Ivy College as a whole, or at least of something other than
the seven institutional factors we have identified. All students at
Ivy College, for example, probably have exposure to different
intellectual points of view sufficient to develop intellectual flexibility. Nevertheless, some of the findings about critical thinking
we have discussed enable us to construct a model of how students learn critical thinking. Gains in the thematic analysis measure of critical thinking are associated with three factors of
college experience: high initial frustration levels, varsity sports,
and low involvement in dormitory life. We take the first to
mean immersion in a situation that is complex and confusing,
especially cognitively. At a considerable level of abstraction, we
take the latter two factors to mean a personal regimen of systematic and disciplined practice involving conceptual diagnosis
rather than less demanding and disciplined informal social conversation. In other words, according to this model, students develop critical thinking by applying systematic, disciplined cognitive effort to a conceptually confusing and complex situation.
While this process can take place in varsity sports, as we have
found, the most obvious place to look for it is in the curriculum. Unfortunately, we have not measured or recorded very

much about the actual courses students in the longitudinal sample took. Even course transcripts would be difficult to evaluate along these lines without a detailed knowledge of the nature, content, and style of each course and program at Ivy College.

Working from our preliminary model, however, we can frame the following hypothesis for further use in the next chapters and in future research: *Courses and course programs that present students with both complexity and confusion, on the one hand, and discipline and integration, on the other, will enhance the growth of critical thinking.* This hypothetical model immediately raises several further questions. Do the necessary complexity and confusion come from the diversity of separate courses a student takes at one time or over four years (that is, from a distribution requirement), or from individual courses that sweep broadly across several disciplines at once (that is, from some kind of integrated or interdisciplinary program), or from both? Does the necessary discipline only mean regular practice of the sort that is required in learning mathematics or a foreign language? Or can it also mean a demand to integrate disparate conceptual material, as might be raised by broad essay questions on final exams, integrative term paper assignments, or comprehensive exams? Answering these questions will require further research. Our own study of the joint humanities program at Cathedral College, discussed in Chapter Six, sheds some further light on how consciously cultivated diversity and discipline in the curriculum can increase students' critical thinking abilities.

Independence of Thought. Instrumental independence of thought, as measured by Self-definition, is increased among women and among private school graduates by varsity sports participation. For women, participating in sports at the varsity level goes a little beyond traditional sex-role prescriptions and stereotypes, or at least it did so in the mid 1970s. Since the Self-definition measure was developed to reflect defining one's self independent of social roles and others' expectations, it is not surprising that role-transcendent activity of this type should increase Self-definition scores.

Do other actions that transcend traditionally ascribed

roles have the same effect? While not statistically significant at usual levels, many other converging trends in the results suggest that they do. For example, Self-definition gains among women are also positively associated with majoring in mathematics or physics, with spending a lot of time in extracurricular activities, and with joining clubs that involve political or academic interests. To some extent, all these activities do not fit the traditional "co-ed" stereotype.[5] Women who joined extramural clubs involving the arts (for example, a musical chorus) or who spent a lot of time reading—both traditionally more "female" activities—showed trends toward relatively low gains. For men, in contrast, growth in Self-definition was associated with majoring in the humanities and with doing voluntary service work, both somewhat different from the male stereotype. To complete the picture, activities highly consistent with the traditional male stereotype, such as spending time on extracurricular activities and majoring in biology or chemistry, predicted lower Self-definition gains among men.

As a preliminary hypothesis, then, we suggest that participation in activities that transcend traditional role prescriptions will enhance the growth of independence of thought. Yet this raises a paradox: Independence of thought is increased by independence of action, but it may also be a prerequisite for that independent action. The two are probably dynamically related; so each reinforces and increases the other. At the institutional level, *opportunities for independent, role-transcending thought and activity of this kind should be greater at colleges that do not prescribe or promote tightly defined images of appropriate student conduct or intellectual inquiry,* whether the images are based on tradition, religion, public opinion, or legislative action. If future research confirms such a hypothesis, then it is easy to conclude that the overall growth in Self-definition at Ivy College reported in Chapter Three is due in large part to its strong heritage of individual freedom in thought and action. In terms of this independence of thought component, then, liberal education truly "liberates" students—from the confining constraints of prescribed roles and prescribed thoughts.

Leadership. Confident leadership is another component

of liberal arts competence that seems to be produced largely by the overall institution of Ivy College rather than by any of the seven particular aspects we studied. At the individual level, we did find, however, that a more intense feeling of early frustration in freshman year led to the growth of the leadership motive pattern or controlled power concerns. As we argued previously, this frustrating confusion may force students to learn controlled assertion in order to survive and be effective at Ivy College. At the emotional level, the experience of frustration and suffering may wound the student's pride or narcissism, thereby setting up a later demand for reparation. Emotionally, such a demand may emerge as a later feeling of being special, an exception to the scruples and constraints that apply to ordinary people. In action, it may show up as a claim to privilege and an unshakable confidence in one's right and ability to lead.[6] *A preliminary hypothesis, then, suggests that leadership comes from a sense of being special.* Such a feeling may be heightened by frustration and suffering in freshman year; presumably, it can also be fostered directly by an institution's vision of itself and its students. Ivy College seems to produce leaders in both ways: by widespread and intense early frustration and by fostering an explicit image of itself and its graduates as a special, elite group entitled to be leaders.

Personal Maturity. While Ivy College as an overall institution increases personal maturity, many of the seven aspects we studied also had effects in their own right on the maturity of adaptation scores of different groups of students. These effects can be subsumed by two broad principles. First, *exposure to new experiences appears to increase maturity of adaptation.* This principle also follows closely from Stewart's (in press) analysis of the course of affective adaptation, via the stages measure, to many different kinds of environmental changes. (Newness or unfamiliarity can be distinguished from both complexity or frustration and also role transcendence, both of which have slightly different effects, as previously discussed.) Thus men and public school graduates who were actively involved in artistic activity and cultural appreciation and showed relatively great gains. We assume here that precollege involvement in the arts is (in relative terms, at least) less frequent for both of these groups, although it is not necessarily confusing and frustrating, and certainly not role deviant. In contrast, many public school graduates enter Ivy College with relatively good science preparation because in their secondary schools, science was often the best (or only) way to express their academic abilities. Those who continue in this familiar path at Ivy College, by majoring in a natural science, show relatively *less* growth in maturity, as do women heavily involved in the (presumably familiar) informal social routines of dormitory living. Put another way: Women who strike out from a dormitory-based social life and public school graduates who strike out for the humanities and social sciences—relatively less familiar territory for both groups—show enhanced development of adaptive maturity.

Among all students, formal extracurricular activities, when experienced as a valuable contribution to learning, are associated with greater maturity gains. A second principle, then, is that *involvement in formal organized activities increases maturity.* For the moment, the scope of our data confines this principle to organizations in an academic setting, but it is consistent with the finding of McClelland and Burnham (1976) that in a large corporation, more effective managers scored higher on the Stage of Psychological Adaptation measure than did less effective managers. To the serious and committed participant, college activities both demand and foster the themes characteristic of the highest, integrated stage of the maturity of adaptation measure. (See Stewart, 1977b, for fuller details of the scoring system.) Thus formal organized activities depend upon *work and planning* instead of doing nothing or spending time in informal socializing (as around the dormitory dinner tables). Working with others in organizations requires *mutuality and sharing with others,* rather than isolation or exploitation of others, and the control of anger and other negative feelings by *balancing ambivalent and contrary emotions.* Finally, people who work in organizations quickly outgrow simplistic, global images of authority as either good or bad. Where *authority is diffuse and limited,* the only way to accomplish groups goals is to work with what effective authority there is. Neither idealization nor suspicion of authority gets the job done.

Toward an Integrative Model of Liberal Education

We have suggested several preliminary conclusions about how Ivy College increases the different components of liberal arts competence. Many of these conclusions are brought together in Figure 6 as an integrative model of the effects of Ivy College. This model has several purposes. First, by restating our results in broader, more abstract terms, it serves as a conceptual guide to understanding and integrating the Ivy College findings presented in Chapter Three and earlier in this chapter. In principle, Ivy College educators could use such a model to understand the complex relationships between institutional inputs and student growth outputs. With this kind of comprehensive understanding, they could make more informed decisions about institutional priorities and plans and identify particular groups of students at special benefit and special risk. Obviously, the present model is only a sketchy framework. It might not tell Ivy College educators anything they do not already know; and in any case, educators at other institutions may not be very interested in a model that applies only to Ivy College. With careful institutional research, however, a model of this kind could be further elaborated into a realistic tool for institutional assessment, planning, and decision making at Ivy College and other institutions.

Finally, this model is a first step toward developing a more general model of the effects of liberal arts education. It is based on only one institution, but the abstract conclusions to be drawn here suggest a more general framework that can be tested in later chapters and future research.

At the left of the figure are five institutional characteristics that appear to be especially important sources of the impact of Ivy College. Some of these characteristics are mostly true of Ivy College as a whole; others are based more on the seven variable aspects previously discussed. In varying amounts and combinations, these five characteristics are also true of most other liberal arts colleges. At the right of the figure are the observed

Figure 6. Integrated Model of the Effects of Liberal Education at Ivy College

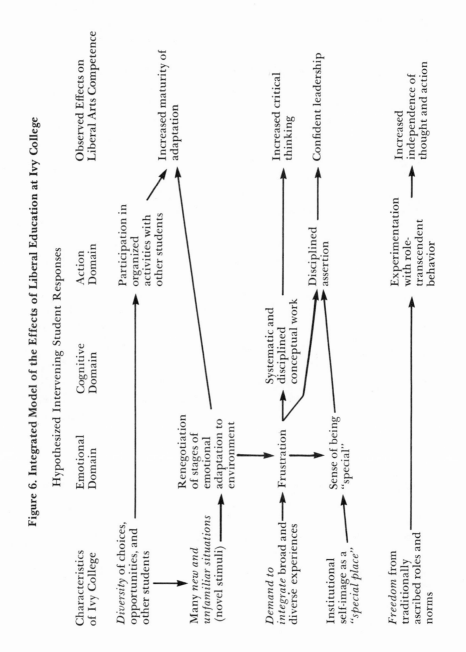

gains in liberal arts competence. In the middle, we have hypothesized some student responses in the domains of emotion, cognition, and action that intervene between the inputs of institutional characteristics and the outputs of student growth. The
arrows represent relationships—some are demonstrated in the
findings presented previously and some are estimates consistent
with these findings—among institutional characteristics, student
responses, and observed effects. Overall, the model assumes
both that institutions have powerful impact and that students
vary in how they perceive and adaptively respond to that impact.

To illustrate the model, let us begin with two of the most
important characteristics of Ivy College: It presents an enor-
mously diverse environment, and it demands integration of that
diversity of experience. As a direct result of the diversity, students are more likely to find (often after some searching) other
students with whom they can join in organized activity in an
area of interest. Diversity enlarges, in other words, the "cafe-
teria" from which students select activities. At the same time,
this diversity puts students into largely unfamiliar situations,
forcing them to renegotiate the stages of emotional adaptation.
This renegotiation, like the participation in organized activity,
has the long-run effect of increasing adaptive maturity; but in
the short run, it creates a sense of frustration that is only further heightened by the demand to integrate the diversity of intellectual, personal, and social experience. Many students respond to such frustration with disciplined conceptual effort
that in the end enhances overall critical thinking abilities. Disciplined assertion may be a further response, both directly and
as a result of the sense of being special that tries to recover self-
esteem lost in the initial frustration. At Ivy College, self-esteem
is also enhanced directly by an institutional sense of superiority
that sometimes borders on arrogance. All these cognitive, emotional, and action responses combine to enhance the leadership
motive pattern, a confident assertion of controlled power.
Finally, the Ivy College tradition of freedom and nonconform-
ity encourages students to go beyond the behavioral styles,
roles, and norms they brought to college. With this liberation

comes enhanced independence of thought. As previous research with one measure of this independence, Self-definition, has shown, thinking patterns that are not constrained by traditional roles and norms are more likely to be instrumental, adapted to the situation and problem at hand, and therefore effective.

This model is generalized and abstract. The institutional characteristics and student responses we include in Figure 6 are broad categories that would apply to a wide variety of more detailed specific situations and responses in the lives of particular students at particular institutions. Other colleges, for example, might present students with a different mix of diverse experience, express a sense of superiority in different terms, or foster role transcendence in different ways. Each characteristic would get a different emphasis at different institutions. Thus while the present model is only preliminary, doubtless lacking in some necessary elements, it can be applied to a wide range of different colleges and universities. Let us return to the results presented in Chapter Three as an example. We might speculate that State Teachers and Community colleges expose students to *some* diversity and novelty and give them *some* freedom from the roles and norms of American high school culture; hence there is some growth in maturity of adaptation and Self-definition, although in each case, significantly less than at Ivy College. The lack of significant freshman-senior differences in critical thinking and confident leadership at these other two institutions, however, suggests that they do not make the same demand to integrate diversity of experience, that they probably arouse less initial frustration, and that they do not convey as great a sense of being special.

Finally, the model can help us understand positive and negative adaptations in individual students. A freshman at Ivy College who recoils in isolation from the diversity of experience, for example, will probably not show much growth in maturity of adaptation. A student who selects a challenging program of varied interdisciplinary courses will likely develop more sophisticated critical thinking ability and perhaps even better leadership potential. If we want to help frustrated and discouraged freshmen become confident and conceptually sophisticated leaders, we might steer them toward courses and activities that involve systematic, disciplined practice in conceptualization and assertion, as well as encouraging their sense of being important. The sequence of stages in adaptation to the novel environment could even become a framework for sophisticated student academic advising and personal counseling.

Notes

1. Statistically minded readers may question our use of simple gain scores to measure change in college. While it may seem obvious that the way to measure growth is to subtract initial (freshman) score from final (senior) score, there is in fact a considerable controversy about how best to measure change. (See Lord, 1963; Cronbach and Furby, 1970; Werts and Linn, 1970, 1971; Huck and McLean, 1975; Kenny, 1975, 1979; Linn and Werts, 1977; Nunnally, 1975; Cook and Campbell, 1979, for exposition of the main positions and discussion of the main issues.) Recently, some statistical theorists (for example, Bryk and Weisberg, 1977; Weisberg, 1979) have argued that there is no single best way to measure change. Any method of calculating true change scores in nonequivalent control group studies of the present type, they argue, runs into technical assumptions that may be impossible to justify and conceptual problems that are difficult to resolve. After reviewing the discussion and the alternatives, we decided that using simple change scores was the most defensible procedure for this study because, with the assumptions it seemed appropriate to make about our subjects, data, and design, this method involved the least likelihood of serious distortions.

2. Following the advice of Cohen and Cohen (1975, pp. 97-98, 102-104), we used the simultaneous model for regression. We had no logical or theoretical basis for considering any variable to be prior to any other, as is required by the hierarchical model, and we did not want to miss any suppression effects, as can happen with the stepwise model.

3. For reasons of theory, sample size, and ease of presentation, we have used successive splits of the whole sample rather

than adding interaction terms to the regressions. We also believe that a regression coefficient significant for a single group (for example, among women) may be meaningful for understanding and important for policy regardless of whether the coefficient of the college aspect-by-group interaction term is significant.

4. Why becoming absorbed in a thesis should make men less mature is not fully clear, but the association of precocious intellectual activity with male immaturity recalls the testimony of a defense psychiatrist in the 1924 Leopold and Loeb murder case, testimony that may have fueled a generation of anti-intellectualism in America: "He appears to have the intellect of a man thirty years of age who has been a student all his life. One is next impressed with the disparity between his intellectual development and his emotional life, because there is an emotional poverty, compared with an intellectual wealth" (Higdon, 1975, p. 225).

5. This and following statements are true only in relative terms. An additional level of complexity, which is too subtle to consider in our analysis, is raised by the fact that many actions that are role transcendent or role deviant with respect to American society as a whole are probably role normative or conforming at Ivy College. With cross-pressures of this kind, it is often difficult to distinguish genuine independence of thought and action from simply marching in tight conformity to a different drummer without doing a much more intensive study of students as individuals.

6. This discussion is based on Freud ([1916] 1957). The general line of interpretation was, of course, further developed by Adler and has again emerged in more recent psychoanalytical formulations of narcissism (see, for example, Kohut, 1977). If wounded narcissism is one cause of the leadership motive pattern in college students, we do not suggest that it is the only cause or that narcissistic wounds in childhood would have the same effect (see McClelland and Pilon, 1979).

SIX

Comparing Institutional Characteristics and Student Development at Other Colleges

While the analysis presented in Chapter Five suggests some causes for the effects of Ivy College, it was only a first step toward a general theory of how and why colleges work and what special impact a liberal arts college may have. The sample of students studied was not large, and the dimensions of Ivy College experience were rather crudely measured. More fundamentally, most Ivy College students share an overlapping set of environmental influences, opportunities, stresses, values, emotions, and beliefs about themselves and their college. Even allowing for individual differences in experience and activity—often inflated by a tradition of individualism and even idiosyn-

151

cracy—Ivy College is nevertheless a single, relatively homogeneous institution. If any significant and important effects of liberal education at Ivy College involve the institution as a whole, which seems plausible and even likely, they could not be detected by studying only individual variation within Ivy College. The next step, therefore, is to expand our study to other institutions.

In this chapter, we extend our research outward to the study of several other institutions and backward in time to Ivy College as it was in the early 1960s. We use a cross sectional design in each case, taking freshman-senior differences at each institution as an estimate of how that institution affects the growth of liberal arts competence and taking into account the problems of cross sectional designs discussed in Chapter One. We look for relationships between the varying change effects (or "yields") of the different colleges and other differences in institutional characteristics. Here the college as a whole becomes the unit of analysis; we are looking for features of the college, to which all of its students are exposed, that may be associated with the magnitude of comparative freshman-senior differences.

This research is complementary to the investigation reported in the previous chapter. First, it is an attempt to cross-validate the results of the internal analysis of Ivy College. Do the same general factors, whether measured at the level of the individual's college experience or at the level of the institution, cause the same kinds of changes? If we can find such convergence when we look at a wider range of colleges, then we will have made considerable progress in refining our conceptions of the complex term *liberal education* down to some carefully circumscribed and defined institutional characteristics and educational effects. Finally, the research reported in this chapter shows how our general procedure and measures can be applied more broadly in higher education—to th evaluation of different institutions and programs within institutions.

Studying Seven Other Institutions

The Sample of Colleges. As part of a larger project on the evaluation of competence in higher education that one of us carried out at McBer and Company, cross sectional studies similar to those presented in Chapter Three were carried out at seven other four-year colleges. We discuss all details of design, procedure, and data analysis in the methodological Resource B. Although they vary widely in many characteristics, these seven institutions are neither a random nor a systematic sample of American colleges. They came to be included in the project as a result of many factors, such as personal contacts, interested institutional research directors, and so forth. Taken together, however, they include many variations on the theme of liberal arts higher education.

We begin with a brief description of each college, including some tabular data comparing them to each other and to Ivy and State Teachers colleges. In order to preserve a measure of institutional anonymity, we have used pseudonyms and disguised details of the institutional descriptions and numbers in Table 14 while preserving the essential features of each college. Any statistical analyses, however, were always done with the exact real data. We are interested in drawing accurate general conclusions but not in making invidious comparisons among particular colleges. Four of these seven institutions are liberal arts colleges in the classic sense of the term, since they embody most of the defining features suggested in Chapter One.

• *Liberal College* is a medium-sized private college located in a small city in the East. It has a tradition of both excellence and moral consciousness that dates back to its founding in the middle of the nineteenth century, as well as a more recent reputation for academic innovation. Liberal draws students mostly from the Northeast and Middle Atlantic regions. Academic standards are very high. Most students live in dormitories or other campus housing.

• *Elm College,* located in a small Midwestern town, is a medium-sized church-related college with associated arts and health sciences schools. It was founded in the middle of the nineteenth century. Most students come from the North Central region. Academic standards and competition are moderate. Elm College is traditional in many respects: The fraternity system is strongly established; interest in athletics is great; and the college exercises considerable control over student life and conduct. Al-

Table 14. Characteristics of Seven Institutions (Ivy and State Teachers Data Added for Comparison)

Institution	Students					Faculty			Facilities and Life		
	Size of Student Body	% Applications Accepted	% Accepted Who Enroll	% Entering Freshmen Who Graduate	Average Freshman SAT Scores	Faculty Size	% Faculty with Ph.D.	Books in Library (000's)	% Students Living in Dormitories	% Fraternity/Sorority Members	Tuition and Fees in 1977-78 (dollars)
Ivy	5800	20	75	93	685	550	80	2500	90	0	4600
State Teachers	4450	60	35	50	425	295	35	90	0	0	950
Liberal	2200	30	45	85	625	205	75	780	90	10	4500
Elm	2200	80	60	90	525	140	55	300	94	75	3900
New South	1300	60	75	50	530	80	40	95	80	20	2100
Jordan	500	85	70	40	490	35	25	25	75	0	2500
North State	6300	60	30	55	485	290	45	250	80	20	1100
Clare	1000	80	80	45	475	65	20	75	40	0	2250
Becket	1400	70	45	65	500	90	23	95	60	0	3100

most all students live in dormitories or fraternity/sorority houses.

• *New South College* is a small church-related college located in a large, growing Southern city. It was founded shortly before the Civil War and continues to draw almost all its students from the Deep South. New South has attempted to transform itself financially with several major fund drives and academically with an independent liberal studies program involving off-campus work and self-created majors. Academic standards and competition are moderate. Most students live in dormitories, although about one fifth commute.

• *Jordan College* is a very small church-related college in a medium-sized Midwestern town. It developed out of its theological seminary origins into a separate college forty years ago, but the devout religious influence continues to be strong. Chapel attendance is required, and there are very strict rules about student conduct and living arrangements. Most students come from the Middle West. Academic standards are relatively easy. Out of a concern for the educational and financial implications of proliferating courses and departmentalism, Jordan recently abolished departments and developed six broadly based interdisciplinary programs in which students major. It now emphasizes team-taught general education courses.

The remaining three institutions are variants on the liberal arts theme.

• *North State College* is a medium-sized branch of the state university system in a large Northern industrial state. Founded in 1890 and located in an isolated small town, over the past thirty years it has expanded from its teacher's college origins into a general purpose institution, housed on a new and strikingly modern campus. Academic standards and competition are moderately high. The administration is dynamic and the faculty, active.

• *Clare College* is a small college for women located in a large Northern city. It traces its origins back to a church college founded just before the turn of the century, and while it was formally secularized about fifteen years ago, the religious tradition and influence are still strong enough for it to be classed as church related. Most students commute from the surrounding area, although some live in dormitories. Almost half are preparing for nursing or teaching, while the rest take a general liberal arts course. In the late 1960s, Clare College redefined its curriculum in terms of student competences such as "effective social interaction," "problem solving," and "commitment to values," although the usual academic departments continue to exist along with the competency-based approach. (See Grant and others, 1979, for an extensive theoretical and historical discussion of competency-based education.) Clare College sees its special mission as fostering direction and self-management in its women students. Academic standards and competition are moderate.

• *Becket College* is a small church-related college in a medium-sized Northern industrial city. It was founded at the turn of the century with a strong classical and theological orientation and still retains the flavor of a religious community. Most of its students come from the nearby region, and about two thirds live in dormitories. A health sciences program exists within the general liberal arts context. Subjects for the present research were drawn from this program in order to see whether the effects of such a vocationally oriented program were enhanced by the surrounding liberal arts setting.

Table 14 compares these seven colleges, along with Ivy and State Teachers colleges, in terms of facts and numbers taken from the usual guidebooks to college and other statistical sources. At each institution, the dimensions of liberal arts competence were measured by the three major test instruments discussed in Chapter Two: the Test of Thematic Analysis to measure critical thinking, the Analysis of Argument test to measure intellectual flexibility, and the Thematic Apperception Test to measure Self-definition, Stages of Psychological Adaptation to the Environment, the leadership motive pattern, and achievement motivation. (Although this last measure showed no freshman-senior differences in Chapter Three, we included it because of its conceptual links to liberal arts competence, as discussed in Chapter Two.) For reasons of time, only the TAT was given at Jordan and Becket colleges. Because of the heterogeneity of sampling and testing conditions, various adjustments were made in order to ensure comparability of data across the seven institutions. These procedures, as well as other data-analysis details, are discussed in the methodological Resource B.

Results. Table 15 presents the freshman-senior differences on all measures at each institution. Because of differences in administration procedures, test forms, and TAT pictures, these scores and differences are not directly comparable to the results presented in Chapter Three. We can draw some informal conclusions from Table 15 and raise some further questions. For example, at Liberal College, which of the seven is the most like Ivy College, each of the measures shows freshman-senior differences that are in the same direction as at Ivy. At North State College, however, only the Analysis of Argument test difference holds up (and is, in fact, the largest Analysis of Argument test effect of the five colleges where the test was given). Is this because it is a state-controlled college, because it has a less-eminent faculty, or perhaps because it is located in a small town? The greatest differences in the leadership motive pattern are at Jordan and Clare colleges, both of which have a strong religious emphasis; yet the three other church-related colleges do not show large differences. The religious emphasis at Jordan and Clare does seem to be more "energetic," militant, or activist; yet the results at highly "secular" Ivy and Liberal colleges suggest that this activist religion cannot be the only cause of the leadership motive pattern.

Relation of Institutional Goals to Observed Effects

Are the freshman-senior differences shown in Table 15 related to what the seven colleges say their goals and purposes are? While most liberal arts colleges make broad, sweeping, and rather vague statements of purpose in their catalogues and bulletins, there are actually many differences among colleges in the goals that they emphasize and elaborate. Are these differences in emphasis at all related to the observed differences in effects?

To explore this question, we looked for statements of goals or purpose in the catalogues, bulletins, or other material that each college typically sends to prospective freshmen. We

Table 15. Freshman-Senior Differences in Liberal Arts Competence at Seven Colleges

Institution	Thematic Analysis		Analysis of Argument		Self-definition[a]	Achievement Motivation[a]	Leadership Motive Pattern		Modal Stage of Adaptation	
	Freshman Level	Freshman-Senior Difference	Freshman Level	Freshman-Senior Difference	Freshman-Senior Difference	Freshman-Senior Difference	Freshman Level	Freshman-Senior Difference	Freshman Level	Freshman-Senior Difference
Liberal College[b]	1.99	+.23	-2.04	+.17	+1.92	-.77	27%	+14%	3.00	+.16
Elm College	1.75	-.36	-2.46	-.06	-1.35	-2.60	14%	+ 6%	2.93	+.47
New South College	1.34	-.32	-1.91	+.28	+ .45	-3.40	19%	+ 8%	2.98	-.07
Jordan College					-2.46	+ .02	18%	+24%	2.87	+.22
North State College	1.48	-.13	-2.63	+.52	- .39	- .41	11%	+ 4%	3.09	-.05
Clare College	1.04	+.48	-2.58	+.24	-2.06	+1.99	18%	+23%	2.83	-.14
Becket College					+4.66	-1.77	22%	- 4%	2.88	-.29

[a]Because scores on this variable were standardized separately by institution, initial freshman levels are not comparable across institutions.

[b]Freshman levels and gain scores estimated, as discussed in the methodological Resource B.

were concerned with broad general purposes rather than specific skills or distribution requirements. We then coded and grouped these goal statements into the four abstract categories originally developed by Parsons and Platt (1973) that we used in Table 5 to group our measures in summarizing our results. These four categories are a further abstract reduction of the list of nine liberal arts goals that we presented in Chapter One. We prefer the fourfold table here because it is much easier than the nine-goal list to apply to the vague and exalted language of college. (For example, a catalogue may mention cognitive skills or intellectual development in general rather than more specific goals such as critical thinking or intellectual flexibility.) Although some statements were difficult to classify because they were so vaguely worded, two coders working independently on the same material achieved 90 percent category agreement.

Most catalogues give the impression that the college promotes truth, beauty, and goodness while being all things to all people. Nevertheless, the paraphrases represented in Table 16 show that there are clear institutional differences in the extent to which each of the four major categories is emphasized and elaborated. We shall discuss briefly the relationship between catalogue goals and measured freshman-senior differences (from Table 15) for each college.

Liberal College is the only one of the seven institutions with explicit goals from each of the four categories; correspondingly, it is the only college showing gains on all the measures. In terms of both its professed goals and its actual effects, therefore, of all the seven colleges in our sample, it most closely approaches the broad liberal arts idea.

Elm College emphasizes three areas but neglects the area of independence and instrumentality—that is, the domain of Self-definition. Elm shows gains on measures of two of the three areas of emphasis (leadership motive pattern and maturity of adaptation) and an actual decline in the one area not emphasized (Self-definition). The correspondence between emphasis and change is not complete, however. Elm does not show a gain on either of the cognitive skill measures, an area to which it gives some emphasis in its catalogue statements.

Table 16. Comparative Elaborations and Emphases of
Institutional Goals

Abstract Cognitive Skills (Measured by Test of Thematic Analysis and Analysis of Argument test)	*Socially-Relevant Motives (Measured by achievement motivation and the leadership motive pattern)*
Liberal: Think critically, habits of imaginative and disciplined minds	*Liberal:* Active involvement in the community
Elm: Critical thinking	*Elm:* Examine values
New South: Articulate, well-informed, discriminating	*New South:*
Jordan: Informed, competent	*Jordan:* Christian values, personal vocational calling, understand social context of work
North State: Spirit of rational inquiry, developing of intellect	*North State:* Cherish privileges and responsibilities of individual in a free society
Clare: Use knowledge in different circumstances, do well what one knows	*Clare:* Manage effects of social change, responsible contributing member of society
Becket:	*Becket:* Observe Christian standards

Defining and Maintaining the Self (Measured by Self-definition)	*Personal Integration, Maturity (Measured by Stage of Psychological Adaptation)*
Liberal: Think and act independently, make own decisions	*Liberal:* Personal enrichment, developing moral sensibilities
Elm:	*Elm:* Living with meaning, self-identity
New South: Think, feel, and act individually	*New South:* Integrity, genuine humanity, historically rooted
Jordan:	*Jordan:* Personal growth, intellectual encounter with Christian revelation and personal commitment to it
North State:	*North State:* Growth and development
Clare:	*Clare:*
Becket: Resourceful coping with personal and social problems	*Becket:* Mature, generous, creative, freed from ignorance and indecision, dedicated to enthusiastic pursuit of truth, family spirit

New South College shows the least correspondence between stated goals and measured outcomes. It emphasizes personal maturity but shows no gain in maturity of adaptation; it shows a gain in the leadership motive pattern even though it does not emphasize motives. It is tempting to suggest that New South may have a hidden agenda, that the emphasis on being historically rooted may in fact be a euphemism for concerns with prestige, power, and dominion (see Vandiver, 1964).

Jordan College expresses strongly evangelical Christian values in its catalogue and shows large gains in both achievement motivation, the leadership motive pattern, and maturity of adaptation. To an external observer, the conservative *content* of Jordan's religious orientation might seem too parochial and restrictive to bring about growth in secular motives and maturity. The underlying religious themes of the college, however, are precisely those that possess transformative potential, in the terms of Eisenstadt's analytical extension of the Weber thesis (1968, p. 20; see also McClelland, 1961, pp. 367-373): transcendentalism, individual responsibility and activism, and an open, unmediated relationship between the individual and the sacred tradition. The latter theme is nicely illustrated by Jordan's concern that students have a personal "intellectual encounter with the Christian revelation"; the former is reflected in the emphasis on a personal vocational calling and an understanding of the social basis of work. Thus Jordan clearly motivates and matures students, even if the particular goals of the motives and language of the mature adaptation are quite different from the sophisticated secularism of Ivy and Liberal colleges.

North State College has effects that are mainly oriented toward the external world (cognitive skills and motivations). Its passing catalogue reference to growth and social development is not supported by gains in maturity of adaptation scores. North State thus embodies the practical, utilitarian tradition of the American state university, in contrast to the emphasis on inner growth characteristic of the classical private liberal arts college.

Clare College is strongly pragmatic, activist, and utilitarian in its claims and effects. Its emphasis on *using* knowledge and *doing* well, as well as on making a reasonable contribution to society—which are, indeed, the core values of competency-based education—are paralleled by strong gains in the cognitive and motivational areas. Less emphasized in formal goal statements are self-definition and mature personal integration, and in fact students show no gains on measures in these two areas.

Becket College is deeply religious, like Jordan and Clare, but in the more inward-looking direction of the contemplative monastery tradition. Eisenstadt (1968, p. 20) argues that this kind of "withdrawn" community is associated with accommodation to the existing social order rather than the transformations characteristic of more activist communities such as Clare. As would be expected, therefore, Becket shows no motivational gains. Since the cognitive measures were not given, we cannot tell whether Becket's lack of catalogue emphasis in that area is also paralleled by a lack of gains. If there were no cognitive gains, it would suggest that Becket elaborates the theme of the set-apart community in an unintellectual (or even anti-intellectual) direction. (Freshmen and juniors at Becket, however, were given the Test of Thematic Analysis and the Analysis of Argument test. There were virtually no differences on either test between freshmen and juniors, suggesting that the community theme is elaborated in this way at Becket.) In any case, Becket offers interesting contrasts—on the one hand to Jordan, another actively religious college, and on the other hand to Clare, which has in fact become formally secular in recent years.

Taking all the comparisons together, we find there is surprising convergence between the kinds of claims colleges make (or, more precisely, the goals they choose to emphasize) in their catalogues and the actual observed patterns of freshman-senior differences. When all comparisons are summed, there is evidence of actual freshman-senior gains for fifteen of the twenty (or 75 percent) emphasized goals (quadrants for which there is some relevant catalogue goal statement in Table 16). For the goals not emphasized, only one of six (or 17 percent) shows such gains. This difference in proportions of emphasized goals and nonemphasized goals showing gains is quite significant by Fisher's exact test ($p < .02$). Although there are some discrepancies, then, we can say that in a rough and general sense, there is congruence between what colleges claim they do and what they actually do. If a college emphasizes a certain class of goals, there is some evidence of freshman-senior gains on at least one measure of that class of goals. In an area where a college makes no claims, it is very unlikely that the college will show any effects.

Such a conclusion holds only, of course, for the seven institutions of the present study and must surely remain tentative because of the vague, flowery, and imprecise language in which colleges clothe their statements of goals in catalogues for prospective freshmen and the consequent difficulty of classifying goals and coding them into even the simple fourfold schema of Table 16. The measures are only a crude sampling of relevant outcomes within each quadrant, and most of the colleges also have other kinds of goals that we have not even considered. Our purpose in presenting this analytical comparison is to show that even with all these difficulties, the task can be done. How much better and fuller the analysis would be if colleges made their claims in more precise and refined language. If they were complete and explicit about what they claimed to do, and if they employed a common, standardized language for articulating their goals, then prospective students as well as prospective philanthropists would be better able to compare and contrast institutional goals. Finally, goal statements could be fairly and fully tested. Thus research of this kind could help colleges to clarify their goals and then find out whether they are achieving them.

Relation of Institutional Characteristics
to Observed Effects

Apart from the general tendency for the seven colleges to do what they say they do (however vaguely), are there any systematic relationships between objective institutional characteristics and the growth of liberal arts competence? The information reported in Table 14 is of little use in answering this question because only a few of the simple correlations between college characteristics and the magnitudes of freshman-senior differences reported in Table 15 are statistically significant. These results are scarcely surprising, given the small number of institutions studied and all the sampling and analysis problems of field research of this kind. To answer the question, therefore, we turn to our own impressions of the seven colleges and some more sophisticated measures of college characteristics, using the preliminary model developed in Chapter Five as a guide and framework.

Cognitive Skills. Within Ivy College, involvement in dormitory life was negatively associated with growth in critical thinking. Consistent with this finding are negative correlations between the magnitude of freshman-senior differences in thematic analysis and the percentage of students belonging to fraternities and sororities (rank order correlation or *rho* = -1.00, N = 5, p $<$ .01) and percentage of students living in dormitories or fraternity/sorority houses (*rho* = $-.70$, N = 5, p = .10). This latter percentage has the same negative correlation with the magnitude of freshman-senior differences in the Analysis of Argument test. Apparently, then, college life (at least in its informal collegiate sense) tends to work against at least some aspects of conceptual development.

What promotes this development? In Chapter Five, we made the very tentative suggestion that cognitive growth (especially growth in critical thinking) might be facilitated by a curriculum that required students to integrate complex and divergent experience, materials, and concepts. Like most American colleges, the institutions studied in this chapter have some kind of distribution requirement. In most college catalogues, these requirements are stated merely as requirements; for example, "two courses from each of four groups" or "freshman composition, a science course, and two terms of physical education." At Liberal and Clare colleges, which had the greatest effects on thematic analysis, distribution is an essential aspect of the institution's commitment to liberal education. Liberal College avoids strict requirements in favor of persuasion: "guidelines" are to ensure "breadth of educational experience," giving the students "an opportunity to achieve an integration of their knowledge." Clare College requires two kinds of integration: At introductory levels, students must demonstrate each broad generic competence in several different disciplinary contexts; at advanced levels, a single, complex, self-designed project explicitly integrates several different competences.

Our strong impression, then, is that institutions that stress the *integration* of ideas, courses, and disciplines are the ones whose students show the greatest growth in critical thinking. Where the college merely gives a checklist of distribution requirements, without any integrative rationale—in Whitehead's (1953, p. 92) words, "the fatal disconnection of subjects which kills the vitality of our modern curriculum"—students do not seem to show as much growth.

These impressions are further supported by research on the effects of a particular integrative program at Cathedral College. (Cathedral College, located in a large Eastern city, was founded in the nineteenth century as one of the country's oldest church-related colleges. It is medium sized. Most students are drawn from the surrounding states and live on campus. While the religious tradition and an emphasis on athletics are strong, there is also a firm commitment to liberal arts undergraduate teaching.) With government financial support, Cathedral recently developed a joint humanities program, where students take a group of two or more courses from different but complementary subject areas, focused on an integrative theme relevant to the different subjects. Each group of courses has been carefully prepared by the relevant faculty members, most of whom attend the classes of all courses in the group. Clearly, this program involves the same kind of conscious integration of curriculum that we found at Liberal and Clare colleges. The program should therefore enhance students' growth in critical thinking.

In a study of the effects of this integrative program, we gave the Test of Thematic Analysis to sixty-six students from the joint humanities program at both the beginning and the end of the group of courses. As a control, we also tested sixty-seven students in regular courses in the same general area, or covering some of the same material, at the same two times. While the program students started out scoring higher than the controls (average score of 1.66 versus 1.22), they also tended to show greater gains from before to after the courses (average increase of +.50 as compared to +.08 for the controls, p of difference in gains < .10 in the predicted direction). This suggests that the actual experience of having to integrate two or more disciplines at the same time, guided by faculty committed to and encouraging such integration, brings about greater cognitive growth than does studying the same material in separate courses without the consciously designed integrative rubric.

Thus the format and instructions of the Test of Thematic Analysis seem to capture an important cognitive principle of liberal arts education. As students are encouraged to compare and contrast deliberately diverse facts, methods, principles, and points of view, they grow in the ability to think critically—to construct and articulate careful, sophisticated comparisons. Our conclusion, that critical thinking depends on the integration of complex, varied stimulation and experience, is consistent with a good deal of other psychological evidence about the importance of varied experience for optimal functioning (see Fiske and Maddi, 1961; Maddi, 1976).

Independence of Thought. The Ivy College finding that independence of thought is encouraged by transcending traditional role prescriptions—in simplest terms, by freedom of thought and action—is confirmed among the seven colleges in a rather simple and obvious way. Colleges that encourage individual freedom of action tend to promote Self-definition; more restrictive colleges retard or even lower it. A simple measure of institutional freedom (+1 each for having coeducational dormitories and allowing students to live off campus after freshman year, and —1 each for requiring chapel attendance and forbidding alcohol) is associated with the magnitude of freshman-senior difference in Self-definition (*rho* = .62, p < .10). With more detailed information, of course, we could develop a more comprehensive index of freedom-restriction, but this measure makes the point clearly enough. Liberal College, which shows a large Self-definition effect, has quite a reputation for encouraging students to "do their own thing," while Jordan College (where seniors score considerably lower than freshmen) has a whole series of restrictive and traditional customs: controlling sunbathing; forbidding tobacco, dancing, and public displays of affection; and maintaining a candlelight ceremony to honor newly engaged women.

Interestingly enough, the size of a college's campus is also correlated with its effects on Self-definition (rho = .75, p < .05). Can this be more than a coincidence? Perhaps physical space on campus has more than a metaphorical relationship to the students' sense of space to develop their definition of self. In any case, the effects of campus geography and architecture on students are neglected topics of environmental psychology that deserve more careful investigation.

Leadership. What causes increases in the leadership motive pattern? Jordan, Clare, and Liberal colleges show the greatest effects, with freshman-senior differences as large as those at Ivy College, as reported in Chapter Three. We have the impression that in different ways, students at each of these three institutions think of themselves as being special. This feeling goes beyond the usual school spirit, institutional chauvinism, or even admissions competitiveness. At Jordan, for example, the sense of being set apart from the rest of the world is explicitly expressed in the language of fundamentalist Christian doctrine, especially in terms of the doctrine of divine election.[1] At the other colleges, the sense of special mission is expressed in secular terms. Liberal College rhetoric emphasizes its institutional uniqueness, both in general, on account of its innovative tradition, and in particular, on account of its many unusual programs. An urgent sense of educational and social mission pervades the atmosphere of Clare College. Women students are told that they must learn skills and acquire self-confidence to lead because they will be responsible for managing the complex social changes of coming decades. At Ivy College, students continually remind themselves that they have been "chosen" (somehow in a more profound sense than merely having survived a rigorous admissions scrutiny); so in whatever they do after college, they are expected to become national leaders.

One of the objective measures lends some support to this conclusion based on our impressions. Freshman-senior differences in the leadership motive pattern are significantly correlated with the percentage of accepted freshmen applicants who actually enroll, or the "admissions yield" (rho = .71, p < .05). The enrollment percentage is not related to how difficult it is to get into the college, the eminence of the faculty, or even the cost of attendance. Thus it seems to measure the attractiveness of the college to prospective students, a quality that seems akin to a sense of being special, on whatever basis or for whatever reason. Apparently, being special has more to do with a college's sense of calling and its mythology than with its material resources and objectively measurable characteristics. While our conclusion about the sense of specialness gives some support to Botstein's (1977) interpretation of the effects of Ivy College, we must point out that specialness as we use the word here is different from Botstein's meaning of "elite" or "high quality." Moreover, the sense of specialness helps to explain the development of only one motivational pattern and not the growth of all aspects of liberal arts competence.

In Chapter Five, we found that those Ivy College students who had experienced a lot of early frustration were especially likely to develop the leadership motive pattern. We argued that the sense of being special may develop in reaction to the wounded pride of this early frustration, but the results of this chapter also suggest that it can be transmitted directly by the college.

One final institutional characteristic that seems to enhance growth in the leadership motive pattern is opportunity for participating in intercollegiate sports, which is also consistent with our longitudinal findings, at least among women at Ivy College. Obviously, there is a strong relationship between the size of a college's student body and the number of varsity teams it has. When we correct for this correlation statistically (by subtracting from the actual number of teams the number predicted by the correlation with student body size), we still find a nearly significant correlation between adjusted number of teams and magnitude of freshman-senior differences in the leadership motive pattern ($rho = .63$, p $< .10$).

Personal Maturity. In Chapter Five, we found that growth in maturity of adaptation at Ivy College was associated with exposure to new experiences. While it is difficult to develop a single measure of opportunities for exposure to new stimuli that can be applied to the seven colleges of our study, the proportion of a college's student body coming from out of state is one simple index of its diversity. (Because Becket College is located only fifteen miles from the state line and actually draws more students from the more populous neighboring state, we count students from both states.) This percentage is positively correlated with freshman-senior differences in modal Stage of Psychological Adaptation score (rho = .64, p ~ .06). Conversely, the percentage of students who live at home and commute—presumably an index of both the college's homogeneity (or even insularity) and also of the proportion of individual students who are not faced with the novel stimuli of living with other students instead of family—shows the expected opposite relationship to effect on maturity of adaptation (rho = −.79, p < .05).

Although there is a significant negative correlation between size of the city in which the college is located and magnitude of the stages effect (rho = −.79, p < .05), we take this to mean that colleges in large cities often have more commuting students rather than that small cities as such increase maturity of adaptation. (Recall that Ivy College is located in a very large metropolitan area but has very few commuting students.) So far as they go, then, these results are consistent with the interpretation of Chapter Five, as well as with other research evidence using the Stages of Psychological Adaptation measure, that novelty and life changes increase the subsequent maturity of adaptation.

Contributions of the Seven-College Study. Several important conclusions can be drawn from the seven-college comparisons. First and most simply, there are variations in the growth of liberal arts competence at different institutions. This means that the effects of liberal arts education are not a single, unified pattern of growth in skills and personal qualities. (And if there were such a single pattern, we would be inclined to attribute it to simple maturation effects.) Rather, liberal education brings growth in a series of overlapping but distinct components, involving cognition, emotion, and motivation. Growth in these components is not a simple function of higher education in itself, but rather can now be linked to specific characteristics of the liberal arts college. Using different measures and research techniques, the Ivy College study in Chapter Five and the seven-college comparisons have produced consistent and convergent findings about the effects of two different kinds of institutional characteristics: consciously articulated goals and objectively measured institutional aspects.

We want to emphasize that these characteristics are not alternative explanations, but rather complementary ways of describing the same features and processes. For example, the generic quality of institutional freedom may be expressed in a college's conscious commitment to developing students' individuality (a catalogue goal), in widespread student participation in activities not traditional for their sex, social class, or other role (Ivy College study in Chapter Five), or in a relative lack of college rules about student conduct (seven-college comparisons). Or in support of a consciously stressed goal of broad intellectual growth (catalogue goal), a college will be likely to structure the curriculum to encourage (or even require) students to integrate diversity (seven-college comparisons), while paying less formal attention to student social life (seven-college comparisons and Ivy College study in Chapter Five).

Continuity and Change: Ivy and Hillside Colleges in 1960

A further test of the generality of some of our findings can be made with a secondary analysis of data collected on male students at Ivy and Hillside colleges in 1960. Hillside is a large private liberal arts college located in a large city in the East. Founded in the mid 1800s, it is now part of a larger university with professional, technical, and specialty schools. Although academic standards and competition are high and attrition is low, Hillside suffered then from its image as a second-choice college. About two thirds of the students live on campus. Fraternity membership is low, and there are no sororities. In the autumn of 1960, TATs were given to one hundred randomly selected male students at Hillside, half freshmen and half seniors. (The Thematic Analysis and Analysis of Argument tests had not, of course, been developed at that time.) Forty-nine male

Ivy students were also tested, and for comparison purposes, a random sample of fifty male freshmen tests was drawn from the large sample of Ivy College freshmen discussed in Chapter Four. While adding yet another institution to the list of colleges studied, these comparisons also enable us to see whether the Ivy College effects of the 1970s had occurred at the same college fifteen years earlier, at the end of the Eisenhower era—the time of the "silent generation," McCarthyism, and traditionally pre-scribed sex roles.

We scored and analyzed the TATs in the usual way, with separate standardization at each institution. Table 17 presents

Table 17. Comparison of Male Freshmen and Seniors
at Ivy and Hillside Colleges in 1960

| College and Group | Mean Score on | | | |
	Self-Defini-tion	Achieve-ment Motiva-tion	Modal Stage of Adapta-tion	Leader-ship Motive Pattern
Ivy College				
Freshmen (N = 50)	44.05	48.09	2.38	16%
Seniors (N = 49)	56.07	51.96	2.50	39%
Freshman-Senior Difference	12.02***	3.87[+]	+.12	23%*
Hillside College				
Freshmen (N = 50)	42.71	44.26	2.57	14%
Seniors (N = 50)	57.29	55.74	1.80	22%
Freshman-Senior Difference	14.58***	11.48***	−.77***	8%

[+]p < .10

*p < .05

***p < .001

the scores on the TAT-based variables for freshmen and senior men at Ivy and Hillside colleges, as tested in 1960. Self-defini-tion scores show very significant freshman-senior differences at both institutions, as expected from the results presented in Chapter Three and the relatively unrestrictive atmosphere of Hillside. The leadership motive pattern goes up at Ivy in the late

1950s, as it does fourteen years later. There is only a small difference at Hillside, but this can be accounted for by its second-
choice image, the opposite of a sense of being specially chosen.
Thus there is a good deal of continuity in the effects of Ivy College over fifteen years. The results for achievement motivation
and maturity of adaptation, however, diverge sharply from the
findings for the 1970s. On the Stage of Psychological Adaptation measure, Ivy shows only a small, nonsignificant difference
instead of the substantial gain shown in the 1970s; but Hillside
seniors actually score significantly lower than Hillside freshmen.

Why should Ivy and Hillside both have had so little effect
on maturity of adaptation in 1960, compared to the large gain
observed at Ivy in the 1970s? Have the colleges changed during
this interval in ways that would promote maturity of adaptation?
Obviously they have, most notably in the relations between
men and women. In 1957 (the freshman year of the seniors
tested in 1960), both colleges were predominantly male. Men
and women lived in widely separated dormitories, with a few
hours of regulated "intervisitation" in the afternoons and on
weekends. Women guests in the men's dining rooms drew stares,
gestures, and sometimes cheers. Men and women got to know
each other mainly through the complex, stylized nexus of dat-
ing, so vividly recounted in the novels of and about the period
(for example, Kaufman, 1957; Updike, 1968). Fifteen years
later, much had changed at Ivy College. (Many of the same
changes have doubtless occurred at Hillside, but our impressions
are not as full or as current, and we have no 1970s test data.)
More women were being admitted; dormitories were coeducational; men and women mingled at every meal; and continual
and varied informal contact had diminished the surpassing significance of the stereotyped Saturday date. (Ivy College continues, however, to have an exceptionally low proportion of
tenured and untenured female faculty.) In psychological terms,
then, the Ivy College climate had moved from male assertion
and exhibition toward the integration of love (or at least
friendship) and work. It is not surprising, therefore, that male
students began to show greater gains in maturity of adaptation,
toward the integrated stage, during their years at Ivy College.

(Regrettably, we do not have TAT data from freshmen and senior women at Ivy College in 1960, to see whether similar changes have taken place.) Some further support for the connection between companionate (rather than traditionally stereotyped) relations between the sexes and enhanced growth in maturity comes from the seven-college study. The magnitude of freshman-senior differences in maturity of adaptation score was significantly correlated with how close the ratio of male and female students was to fifty-fifty (rho = .71, p < .05).

Beyond the changes in male-female relationships, though by no means unrelated to them, Ivy College student culture and student values seem to have "grown up" in recent years. Spooner's (1980, pp. 34-38) nostalgic recall of Harvard in the 1950s documents the old ways in terms that were just as true of Ivy College at that time:

> The attitudes of Eastern establishment prep schools remained important in the Harvard of the Silent Generation. . . . I remember being fascinated . . . and delighted to be part of their games, which emphasized, as far as I could tell, two words: pleasure and irresponsibility. These words were impossible to resist. Violence and destruction were also part of this world—violence and destruction for the sheer hell of it. . . . There was status to be achieved by tossing what was called "the biggest horror show." Social exhibitionism was an area of competition. Who could be the most outrageous? . . . The feeling of invincibility . . . is unique to youth. But we felt certain that this was only the beginning of our triumphs, that . . . we would leave our roistering behind us and move on to accomplishments that were serious, far-reaching, and special. . . . The Silent Generation is still good at retreating into the fantasies fostered by Harvard.

Why has college life at Ivy, and probably at most other colleges, grown up in recent years, so that students now show increased maturity of adaptation as they go through college? Society as a whole has changed dramatically in the two decades

since 1960. Stewart's (in press) theory of the relationships between change and the growth of maturity suggests how these
dramatic social changes could affect the maturation process in
college. The greater the prior experience with change, Stewart
argues, the quicker the adaptation to further change, in the
sense of both more rapid negotiating of the stage sequence and
also reaching a higher ultimate stage level. The seniors of 1960-
61 experienced a relatively stable and even tranquil life during
their adolescent and young adult years. While they undoubtedly
experienced *personal* changes (family moves, new schools, and
such), they grew up during the quiet, steady Eisenhower years.
In stark contrast to this were the twelve years of major and
continuous social change experienced by the seniors of 1974-
75: political assassinations; the Vietnam War; drugs; the sexual
revolution; urban riots; Watergate and a presidential resignation;
strife and turmoil in the universities; movements for the liberation of oppressed blacks, women, ethnic groups, and homosex-
uals; concerns about the environment; and the first major stir-
rings of the energy crisis. There is no doubt that by graduation,
the class of 1975 had lived through much more social and personal change than had the class of 1961. One would predict,
therefore, that they should adapt more quickly to the changes
of college, ending up at a higher final stage level—which is exactly what the results show. In terms of the Stage of Psychological
Adaptation to the Environment scoring system (see Stewart,
1977b), it is no surprise that the Ivy College seniors of 1975 are
more likely to view authority as limited, to express ambivalent
feelings, to see others as differentiated individuals, and to be involved in preparation for work—all categories of the fourth and
highest integrated stage.

The same considerations would lead us to predict that the
"veterans' classes" immediately after World War II also showed
relatively large gains in maturity during college, because of their
prior experience of great changes. Perhaps TATs from students
of that era exist in data archives; so our prediction could even
be tested. In any case, the energy and maturity of that generation of college students is a fond and vivid memory of the faculty who taught them.

Achievement motivation shows freshman-senior differences at both Ivy and Hillside colleges in 1960 but a slight decrease at Ivy in the 1970s. (We have no explanation for the greater size of the effect at Hillside.) No institutional changes at Ivy College during this period seem to be relevant to the change. The difference can readily be interpreted, however, in the light of broader social trends. Veroff and others (1980) compared motive scores from TATs administered in national sample surveys in 1957 and 1976, dates that bracket the college years of the two Ivy College samples. They found a significant drop in achievement motivation among American males.

In general, the effects of Ivy College show continuity over time. Where these effects have changed over the past two decades, the differences can be accounted for in terms of a combination of changes within the institution and wider social and psychological changes within the larger society. Over time, then, the effects of the liberal arts education at Ivy College have grown and developed out of institutional evolution and in response to broader social trends. The observed effects of Hillside College in 1960 are about what one would predict, given the basic findings of Chapter Three and the relationships between institutional characteristics and outcomes presented earlier in this chapter.

The Growth of Liberal Arts Competence in a High School Advanced Studies Program

We also extended our explorations to the secondary school level through additional scoring and analysis of data first collected in 1959-60 as part of a study of the summer Advanced Studies Program (ASP) for gifted high school students at "St. Grottlesex," a pseudonym for an elite New England boarding school. (The original research was reported in Winter, 1960, and Winter, Alpert, and McClelland, 1963.) While covering a year's work in one subject during the six-week program, students were also exposed to the upper-class mores and "classical" personal style of the school: polished manners and self-control, detached and yet benevolent authority, and sophisticated, cynical humor.

How did the program actually affect students' scores on our new measures? To answer this question, we rescored the TAT's written before and after the summer program by a small sample of ASP students and a control group of equally intelligent students from the same high schools who did not attend the program.

Like Ivy College, the St. Grottlesex program was highly selective and elite, so we would expect the ASP students to show gains in the leadership motive pattern. Also like Ivy College, it was a new and strange environment, so it should increase maturity of adaptation. In both cases, that is exactly what happened: The ASP students showed significant gains, compared to the control group. Unlike Ivy College, however, St. Grottlesex maintained a tight schedule of academics and activities, and enforced a strict behavior code. We would therefore expect the ASP students to show significant *losses* in Self-definition, and this also occurred. In terms of both its positive and negative effects, then, the ASP results further confirm our model that ties the effects of liberal education to specific institutional characteristics.

Summary

In this chapter, we have expanded our initial study of Ivy College outward to other institutions and backward in time in order to generalize from our original results and to determine what characteristics of colleges and of students' experiences promote different dimensions of liberal arts competence. We can now summarize our results by refining the model introduced at the end of Chapter Five to explain the effects of Ivy College.

Most of the relationships hypothesized in Figure 6 are confirmed in the seven-college study, and several additional relationships are suggested. For example, students' maturity of adaptation is enhanced by companionate relationships between the sexes and retarded by male-female interaction patterns that are based on traditional sex-role stereotypes—a finding fully consistent with Freud's definition of maturity as the integration of love and work—and varsity sports promote leadership ability for both sexes and not just for women, as our longitudinal data from Ivy College suggested. (This is also consistent with the strong athletic emphasis and demonstrated increase in the leadership motive pattern at the St. Grottlesex Advanced Studies Program.)

We can summarize our findings by sketching the process underlying each of the changes in liberal arts competence at Ivy College noted in Chapter Three. We will phrase our explanation in terms of "liberal arts education" not because these several dimensions of competence and these processes and characteristics are unique to the liberal arts college or even true of all liberal arts colleges—clearly they are not, as our own results have shown—but because we believe that the liberal arts college is the fullest and most characteristic expression of *all* these features and dimensions of competence, combined into a single institution.

First, *liberal arts education increases students' capacity for mature adaptation to the environment when students encounter new experiences*: that is, experiences involving novelty, variety, and meaningfulness. In terms of Fiske and Maddi's theory (Maddi, 1976), the ideal liberal arts college would have high institutional impact, transmitted in each of these three different modes. Summarizing across our various studies, we can say that students who live a long way from home, attending colleges with a diverse student body, who become involved in new and unfamiliar intellectual activities and cultural interests, show the greatest gains in maturity of adaptation. Liberal arts colleges can best help this growth by providing an environment with the greatest possible diversity of opportunity.

Second, *liberal arts education increases students' critical thinking and conceptual skills by demanding that they integrate broad ranges of this novel experience,* especially the novel academic experiences. Students must come to compare and contrast the different aspects of their diverse environment rather than merely absorbing the complexity into isolated, separate compartments of the mind. The most obvious way to promote integration of this kind is through curriculum design. So far as critical thinking goes, it apparently makes little difference whether integration is a requirement, as at Clare, or a set of suggested guidelines, as at Liberal. (For growth in Self-definition, however, it probably makes a difference.) What is important is some kind of aggressive faculty thought about the curriculum, going beyond a mere list of requirements lacking coherence or rationale. The major obstacle to conceptual growth—the enemy, as it were, of critical thinking—is informal student social life centered in dormitories or other living units. Why should this be so? Partly, it may reduce diversity of inputs; more generally, it may lead to segmentation or segregation of experience rather than integration. Given that many American colleges and universities are committed to housing their undergraduate students and have invested heavily in dormitory bricks and mortar, perhaps the best way to have both dormitories and conceptual growth is to introduce intellectual activities and values to dormitory life, in addition to sports and bull sessions. Ivy College has tried to do this to some extent. Yet such a policy raises many problems and is not always successful, as Vreeland (1964) and Jencks and Riesman (1962) discuss in their analyses of the Harvard Houses.

Third, *liberal arts education increases students' independence of thought, instrumentality, and Self-definition by setting them free from elaborate restraints on behavior and thought.* This is liberal education in the sense of "liberating" education. Dress codes and prohibition of dancing are only the most obvious kinds of restriction. We believe that more subtle forms of constraint, whether from church doctrine, the watchful eye of a state legislature, or the insistent demand to learn something that will be vocationally "useful," may well have the same effects. Students do not become instrumental in thought and action unless they are set free to discover their own abilities, tastes, and reactions—in short, to define themselves instead of accepting others' definitions.

Finally, *liberal arts education increases students' motivation for leadership by endowing them with a sense of being special.* Apparently, a college's resources and opportunities (mechanisms) do not by themselves create new motives or goals. Rather, students develop motivation for leadership out of a new vision of themselves. (McClelland and Winter, 1969, pp. 19-25, discuss the difference between the mechanisms of rational opportunities, incentives, and resources and motivations.) This has an important policy consequence: While instruction in techniques may facilitate the growth of the *skills* of leadership, it does not seem to produce the relevant motivation to *use* these skills appropriately. Perhaps this is why the British Empire was ruled so long and so successfully by men who were not trained in leadership skills (as at West Point or as in recent American management training) but rather who were convinced of their inherent right and mission to rule.

This raises a problem for liberal education in American society because success in creating motivation for leadership may work against the deeply held value of equality. (The "Oxbridge mystique" is less of a challenge to English values; hence equality of *access* rather than of outcome was the major political issue in reforming English higher education after World War II.) Students plucked out of mainstream America for four years at an elite institution like Ivy College may become overly sophisticated, cynical, and arrogant, at least in the perception of the wider society. Perhaps in America the small, church-related colleges have made the best solution of this dilemma, thus accounting for their extraordinarily powerful impact on American higher education. By remaining small, these colleges are not a very visible challenge to egalitarian values. In the pluralism of American religious life, moreover, being special in the eyes of the deity is a privilege everyone can enjoy in his or her own way. In a more secular age, sports may provide some of the same sense of legitimized specialness through the highly ritualized apparatus of institutional competition.

Is it ever possible, we wonder, for a legitimate sense of being special to arise from an institution's special characteristics (such as a unique location or an outstanding program), from its unique engagement in the problems of our society (or of our psyches, our economy, or our world polity), or even from the unique rhythm of excitement and discipline of intellectual inquiry itself?

Note

1. The connection between the Calvinist sense of election and the desire for leadership—controlled power—that constitutes the leadership motive pattern can be found in Calvin's own writings: "[Paul] states both that power is an ordinance of God, and that there are no powers except those ordained by God. . . . Accordingly, no one ought to doubt that civil authority is a calling, not only holy and useful before God, but also the most sacred and by far the most honorable of all callings in the whole life of mortal men" (Dillenberger, 1971, p. 477).

SEVEN

From Evidence to Action: Research-Based Educational Policy

The preceding six chapters have been links in a chain of argument. We began Chapter One by arguing that a good deal of the crisis of confidence in higher education generally and liberal arts education specifically resolves down to a *crisis of evidence*: In the crossfire of claims and counterclaims, no one is really sure whether liberal education has any effect; even more seriously, no one is sure how to ask and answer the right questions. In Chapter Two, we described a group of new measures of important cognitive skills and personal qualities and proposed some general standards for measures of educational effects. In Chapter Three, we established that students at Ivy College, an academically eminent traditional liberal arts college, show greater freshman- to senior-year differences on several of these new measures than do students attending two other kinds of college

181

—a teacher-training institution and a community college—even taking account of differences in intelligence and social class. Most of these effects hold up in a longitudinal study of Ivy College students from freshman to senior year. In Chapter Four, we traced the long-range impact of some of these skills and personal qualities over fourteen years on students' lives and their contributions to society. We then sought to isolate the causes or mechanisms for these changes by further analysis of Ivy College longitudinal data in Chapter Five and, in Chapter Six, by cross sectional studies at seven other, very different liberal arts colleges and by a brief glance back at Ivy College and another institution in 1960. The results are a model of how we believe liberal education changes students, as developed and elaborated in the conclusions of Chapters Five and Six.

Now that we have completed this chain of argument, what are the practical implications of our findings? What do our results mean for the liberal arts, for the evaluation of higher education, and for the improvement of educational policy making?

Implications for the Liberal Arts

We believe that our findings help to establish a base of evidence to support the ideal of liberal arts education. At one liberal arts institution, and probably at others, liberal education seems to have at least some of the important effects that it claims to have. We have not, of course, isolated and identified all the complex causes of these effects. We are not completely certain how much they have to do with the liberal arts curriculum as such or with any particular aspect of the form and content of the curriculum. For example, the evidence from Chapters Five and Six suggests that a scientific and technological institute of very high academic quality and resources, also located in a large, diverse, and confusing city and giving its students a strong sense of being in a special place, might show the same effects as Ivy College, and yet such an institution would not ordinarily be thought of as a liberal arts college. Conversely, merely adding a few liberal arts courses to the catalogue of an institution like State Teachers College probably would not bring about any substantial change in its effects on students. And still unidentified factors, such as faculty dedication and morale or the dynamism of an especially far-sighted and persuasive college president, behind our clusters of variables may be the "real" causes behind our effects. In spite of these problems and gaps, we believe that we have established the claim of the liberal arts on a plausible and scientific basis. Each aspect of the argument needs further specification and validation in future research, but the framework has been constructed and is in place for this research.

Our results can also be read as making a case for increased (if selective) support of liberal arts education. From the evidence in Chapter Four, we see that while the beneficial effects of liberal arts education are partly personal (for example, increased maturity of adaptation leading to greater life satisfaction), they are also very much social (for example, increased leadership motive pattern scores leading to involvement in voluntary organizations and more effective leadership and management). In years past, having a higher income was one of the personal benefits of attending a liberal arts college, but recent studies have cast doubt on the extent of this income advantage, especially if computations involve the ultimate net return on money spent for college (see Bird, 1975; Freeman, 1976). (Along these lines, incidentally, we found no relation between any liberal arts competence measures and income levels in the longitudinal study of Ivy College graduates. Liberal arts competence may make Ivy College graduates more satisfied with their lives, but it does not appear to make them richer.) Yet liberal arts colleges are expensive, especially considering costs for features or programs such as an integrative (and therefore usually "hand-tooled") curriculum, extensive extracurricular opportunities, such as athletics, and residential facilities. This raises some provocative issues of equity. If liberal arts education confers benefits to society through better leadership and management skills and more vigorous voluntary organization activity of liberal arts graduates, but if it does not confer financial benefits to these graduates that are commensurate with its costs, society, as a major, if not the principal financial beneficiary of liberal education, should assume a large share of increased college costs. Our results, therefore, can be read as making a case specifically for increased public support of liberal arts education, either by direct grants to private, high-quality liberal arts institutions or by changing public institutions so that they have these qualities.

Implications for Educational Evaluation

We believe that any good measure of liberal education outcomes should meet five criteria or standards better than existing measures of liberal arts competence and that our new measures of liberal arts competence meet this test.*

First, *a measure of liberal arts competence should seem to measure what it purports to measure; that is, it should have face validity.* To many professors and educators, this requirement of face validity is absurdly obvious, for they recognize no other kind of validity. Given the politics of higher education, face validity is necessary for a measure to be taken seriously, even if on psychometric grounds it is unimportant or even undesirable when the measure arouses "response set" or faking tendencies ("psyching out" the question or test) in students. Professors simply will not consent to evaluation of their teaching (especially as part of a tenure decision) or their students' learning by measures that do not, in their view, do justice to what they are trying to teach.

For example, according to Feldman and Newcomb (1969), psychology classes tend to make students more theoretical and perhaps less religious. Some researchers might try to assess this presumed change with items such as the stained-glass versus sense-of-reverence question from the widely used Allport-Vernon-Lindzey *Study of Values* that we quoted in Chapter One to see if, after taking a course, students tended to respond in terms of the aesthetics of stained glass rather than a sense of reverence. But as professors ourselves, we would protest that this choice of answers really has nothing directly to do with our

---

*This section is based on Winter (1979b).

educational goals and that such measures use a meat cleaver where a scalpel is required. As professors rather than as research psychologists, we would not consent to have our careers and reputations rest on check-mark answers to questions like that. And, along with parents, employers, and the courts, we take a dim view of that kind of evidence for students' grades, degrees, or job prospects.

If this example seems valid, it suggests that most traditional psychological tests are not good measures of liberal arts competence, over and above the operant-respondent issue raised in Chapter One. They are "objective," quick, easy, cheap, and mindless to score; but as serious measures of the effects of liberal education—measures that could be used to provide credentials to students and to evaluate programs—they simply will not work because faculty do not believe in them, regardless of whether psychometricians argue that they "ought" to believe in them. Most faculty will insist that measures of effects look like they measure what they claim to measure and that they measure outcomes at the same levels of complexity, sophistication, and subtlety as those outcomes are taught.

Second, a measure of liberal arts competence should be generic, applicable to different levels and across different fields. This standard conflicts a little with the previous one because one easy way to enhance the face validity of a measure is to tie it closely to a specific content area. Letting "a thousand measures bloom," however, makes it difficult to establish convergence. For example, is a test of critical thinking for experimental social psychology measuring the same thing as a critical thinking test for physiological psychology or other tests custom designed for use with macroeconomics, German romantic poetry, or Wittgenstein's philosophy? And how do these measures at College A compare with other, different ones tailored to the different reading lists at College B? The greater the proliferation of outcome measures, then, the greater the work necessary to demonstrate convergence and equivalence (in order to establish fairness). The more generic the measures, the more quickly we can move on to satisfy the rest of the standards.

Third, a measure of liberal arts competence should be

based on criteria that are public; so different evaluators would make approximately the same assessment of the same student performance. In psychometric language, this is called "scorer reliability" or "interobserver agreement," but we prefer the term "public criteria" for several reasons. First, two observers can sometimes agree on how to apply what are nevertheless essentially esoteric, intuitive criteria. Public criteria are necessarily criteria on which observers can agree, but they are much more. They are explicit. They are known in advance. Students therefore know the goals toward which they are studying and working; so liberal learning becomes a little more of a collaboration between student and professor instead of a hide-and-seek game in which students try to find they-know-not-quite-whats that professors hide they-know-not-quite-where. When evaluative criteria are public, evaluations can be questioned by students and defended by professors in a straightforward fashion that damps down students' suspicions of favoritism, fate or futility.

Fourth, a measure of liberal arts competence should have educational validity. That is, it should be shown to change as the result of educational programs and interventions. Students at the end of the program should score higher than other students (or than themselves) at the beginning of the program. This standard seems obvious; yet it is often neglected or treated casually in practice. It implies several things. First, it implies careful coordination between curriculum design and competence measurement. We should try to test what we have taught; and if we evaluate students' performances with respect to criterion X, then we should design our teaching to be sure we emphasize X, either explicitly or implicitly.

Second, however, it implies the use of measures that are *capable* of showing change. Measures that appear to reflect stable traits, such as intelligence, abilities, personality, or abstract stylistic traits, will therefore not be very useful for measuring the competences of liberal education. In fact, because the canons of personality and ability testing require that these measures be stable or reliable—that subjects give the same answers on a second testing that they gave on the first testing—they have a built-in bias *against* showing educational change. When mea-

sures of this kind are used to evaluate students' performances or
program effects, they tend to work against showing any change,
not necessarily because there has been no change but because
the component items of these measures have been screened so
that only the most stable (resistant to showing change) survive.

If we accept this fourth standard, then we must realize
that many, if not most, traditional measures of ability, such as
are used for screening students at entry, are not very useful as
measures of learning, liberal arts competence, or educational
effects.

*Fifth, a measure of liberal arts competence should be
demonstrably relevant to performance in later life.* Here the
issue is not whether the measure is relevant, but rather the ade-
quacy of the evidence brought forward to back the claim. All
liberal arts educators believe that their measures or evaluations
are relevant to later life. The question is whether this belief
rests on an a priori faith or on some kind of demonstrable evidence about the measures.

How well does our new battery of measures meet the five
standards we have proposed in comparison, say, to traditional
examination questions or to more recent measures used by
"competency-based" programs? Consider first the traditional
classroom measures.

Traditional Examination Questions. To illustrate the
ways that professors usually evaluate students, imagine a hypothetical example of a course in personality. The professor has
given a final examination that includes the following essay question: "Compare and contrast the theories of motivation of
Freud and Maslow, with special attention to the notion of unconscious motivation." It is late at night, the day after the final
grades were already due at the registrar's office, and many
exams are left to plow through. Overworked and underpaid, the
professor picks up the next bluebook and reads it, with
thoughts perhaps running something like this: Well, it says most
of the right things about Freud and Maslow. The facts are
pretty good. The organization is OK, but it rambles a lot. That
whole first page discourse on Freud being "linear" and "irrelevant" to twentieth-century America is off the point. All the

facts are there, but the organization just isn't up to A standards; it's not creative and crisp. But it's better than the usual B rehash of what I lectured about in class. I guess I'll give it a B+. Is it really worth an A— though? Isn't this as good as that exam I gave an A— to an hour ago? Oh my, it's so late and I have so many more exams to do. B+ it is then. How does this familiar measure of liberal arts competence fit the five standards? First, what is the competence being measured? Is it factual knowledge of Freud and Maslow? Apparently so, but there also seems to be some implicit competence involving organization, synthesis, and writing style, at least so far as the threshold between A— and B+ goes.

Is the exam question face valid? The professor obviously believes that it is; and subject to the usual parochialisms within and across departments, most professorial colleagues would agree. This measure "looks like" it measures students' ability to remember and then use factual knowledge about Freud and Maslow. Certainly it is better than an "objective" question such as "The unconscious played a more important role in Freud's theory of motivation than it did in Maslow's theory of motivation. True or False?"

Is the exam question generic? It is tied to particular subject matter (Freud and Maslow), but the professor certainly believes that the ability to marshal, organize, and use facts that it reflects is a generic one and that students' answers to this question would be of about the same quality as their answers to any other similar essay question, assuming some minimal mastery of the relevant facts.

Are the criteria public? Yes and no. Professors can usually defend their grading to a disappointed student, although they are often not very explicit about what they expect, especially in the areas of organization of facts and clarity of writing. Would colleagues agree with the evaluation? It is an interesting question: Normally, professors do not grade each other's exams, although they do discuss and compare students' performances in different classes. (One of us remembers a sense of elation when a colleague agreed that a certain student was always just on the borderline of B+/A—. Both of us always opted for B+.

Of course, we never bothered to establish explicitly just what was involved in this border between B+ and A−.)

Does this measure show change as a result of education, in this case, the personality course? The professor does not know, never having given the final exam on the first day of class. *Presumably,* a student who had learned nothing about Freud and Maslow would not write a very good answer; so the "facts" aspect of the measure does reflect the teaching of the course. But it is not certain that the "use and organization of facts" or "clarity of writing" aspect of the measure (the A−/B+ borderline area) has anything to do with the personality course or that it would show change as a result of the course (controlling somehow for factual knowledge). Within the context of a single course, many professors tend to treat writing style as a stable trait rather than as something they can hope to change.

What about relevance to later-life performance? Like most academic people, our hypothetical psychology professor believes that exam grades (and the letters of recommendation based on these grades) are very important and relevant to students' later lives. How can someone who cannot answer a question about Freud and Maslow dare to turn out a success in politics, business, or law—let alone as a professor of psychology? Yet there is not very much evidence that college grades—from any professor—have any strong relationship to competence in later life (see McClelland, 1973; Heath, 1977). More important, professors are usually not very interested in gathering such evidence systematically. Generally they are satisfied to remember a few "star" students with whom they have kept in touch, students who answered their questions well and who went on to be successful.

In summary, the traditional method of measuring liberal arts competence—typified in this hypothetical but realistic example of exam grading—is a *series of private judgments backed by undemonstrated personal confidence about later-life relevance.* Its strongest point is its face validity; almost by definition, professors believe that what they do is an appropriate way of doing what they explicitly say they are trying to do. They have generally convinced students, parents, and employ-

ers, too, although the doubts have recently spread. With respect
to the other criteria, however, especially interrater agreement
and later-life relevance, the traditional method has problems.
This is not to say that the way a professor grades exams would
or could not be replicated by colleagues, only that we do not
know if this is true and that professors rarely ask the question
systematically. This is also not to say that their grades predict
nothing worth predicting in later life: Their exam grades *might*
predict the ultimate destination of students' souls. Rather, this
is to say that the later-life relevance of the exam grades rests on
faith or casual reflections about particular striking students rather than on any systematic demonstration of such a relationship.

    Assessment in a Competency-Based Program. The com-
petency-based movement stresses the explicit definition of
learning goals and the careful breaking down of broad, abstract
objectives into specific skills that in turn are measured by students' performances. The emphasis on explicit goals is often
paralleled by an emphasis on innovative and nontraditional
ways of measuring outcomes. One example is *simulation*: Students perform in a task-oriented small group discussing a simulated real-life administrative problem; or they write letters, give
speeches, or observe videotaped situations about simulated
problems. Another example is *production*: Students create a
product or a multimedia presentation of a point of view or a
message. *Performance* is a further example: Students actually
carry out the real-life adult behavior for which they have been
trained, whether it is making medical or nursing rounds in a
hospital, playing a piano concerto, or helping a legal services
client. Students may even take over the *self-assessment* of their
own performance. (See Grant and others, 1979, for other examples.) How do these innovative methods relate to the five standards?

    Face validity is largely subjective. If faculty in a compe-
tency-based education program have devised a certain kind of
measure, then they probably agree that it looks like it measures
what it ought to. Because of the nontraditional methods often
used, it will be harder and take more time, we believe, to arrive

at such agreement (that is, mutual satisfaction with respect to face validity) for competency-based measures.

Are the nontraditional competency-based measures generic? This is a problem. Given the emphasis upon explicitness and measurability, the result is often a series of highly specific criteria for a particular performance. Did the student show critical thinking in a simulated report written on a controversial issue (for example, by stating the main points of each side of an argument in parallel form and stating the underlying issue on which each side differed)? If this report was written in a biology class, is it equivalent to the measure developed by a professor of German literature for articulating the comparison between Goethe and Schiller? And are either of these equivalent to a medical or nursing student's diagnostic comparison of two clinical cases? Obviously, some measures are generic and some not; but there is nothing *intrinsic* about competency-based measures that makes them generic, and the pressures for explicitness and detail may actually work against it. This is not to say that competency-based measures are less generic than the traditional grading outlined previously (where the generic quality of the method is almost wholly assumed but not demonstrated), only that such a quality cannot be taken for granted.

Are competency-based measures based on public criteria? Yes, if the categories and standards used to make evaluations are explicitly spelled out, broken down, and rigorously defined, especially if there are systematic procedures for training evaluators and monitoring their agreement. But there is nothing intrinsically public about competency-based measures if the evaluation of a student's performance is a simple, subjective, undifferentiated, and unexplained Yes/No (Pass/Fail, Credit/No Credit, or Meets criterion of competence/Does not meet criterion of competence) made by some internal or external evaluator.

What about validity? Neither educational validity and later-life validity nor relevance is guaranteed merely because a measure is competency based. If measures are systematically given before and after instruction or practice in the relevant competence, then educational validity is demonstrated; but such validity cannot be assumed just because the competency-based measure, being nontraditional, somehow looks more relevant than traditional measures do. Relevance to later life, as well, is not automatic. One may design the most realistic simulation of real-life on-the-job performance that one can; yet without further evidence, the conclusion that this measure has real-life relevance involves the same leap of faith that the traditional professor made about the Freud versus Maslow question. No matter how realistic, a simulation is a simulation and not a real-life performance; and college is college and not a career. Factors such as evaluation apprehension and test anxiety are intrinsic possible contaminants of performance. (Even real medical rounds made with an evaluator or with the knowledge that the evaluator is monitoring the performance are not the same thing as the real rounds of a real doctor.) Of course, it seems reasonable to believe that these simulations are pretty close to real life or that they are obviously closer than are traditional methods. (Students usually say that the new methods feel more relevant.) Such beliefs are, however, just that—beliefs. Of course, evidence can be gathered for any measure, traditional or nontraditional, explicitly competency-based or not, to demonstrate its relevance to real-life careers and roles. The point is that without such evidence, even the measure that feels or seems most relevant rests on the same faith that the traditional professor has.

We suggest, then, that there is nothing special about a measure just because it is called competency-based. The new, fashionable label does not magically solve the problems of evaluating and measuring performance, in the liberal arts or in any more applied context. In philosophical, epistemological, and scientific terms, competency-based measures are not *intrinsically* different from traditional measures with respect to the five criteria we have presented. They can be different and better on most of these standards, but this requires further work that goes well beyond the application of fashionable new labels such as competency based. Huff, Klemp, and Winter (1980) surveyed the practices of competence assessment at a variety of educational institutions, concluding that only a few programs spend much effort developing explicit manuals and checking agreement among evaluators. Very rarely is research on the relationship between competence measures and real-life performance carried out. Research and training of this kind are time-consuming; and in the context of ongoing institutional life and real-life settings, they cannot always be carried off with the psychometric precision of laboratory experiments, although they continue to be valid standards or goals.

New Measures of Liberal Arts Competence. In terms of face validity, readers can easily make their own judgments about whether our new battery of measures seems to measure what it claims to measure. Since the Test of Thematic Analysis and the Analysis of Argument test were consciously designed to duplicate the processes that actually go on in the liberal arts classroom (and examination room), we believe that many educators will readily acknowledge their face validity. These two instruments are also generic, both in the sense that they do not depend on knowledge of particular subject matter and also in the sense that they can be readily adapted to particular course material. In using the Analysis of Argument, for example, a professor could present students with one side of a scientific controversy, a dispute about historical interpretation, or an ethical dilemma—whatever is germane to the course being taught. The thematic analysis scoring system could even be applied to the essays written to any compare and contrast question, as in the following examples: Compare and contrast Moliere's *Don Juan* and Mozart's *Don Giovanni.* What are the essential differences and similarities between normal and malignant cells? Distinguish between Freud's and Rogers's conceptions of the normal adult personality. Boyatzis and Burruss (1977), for example, used two sets of counseling situations instead of stories in the Test of Thematic Analysis and found that successful alcoholism counselors scored higher on the test.

The measures adapted from previous research are also generic in the sense of being independent of particular subject matter, but their face validity may be more open to question. Educators and researchers who are experienced and familiar with psychological assessment procedures will probably accept that these instruments measure what they purport to measure. Readers who are dubious about the worth of any psychological tests will probably have doubts about these as well; but perhaps the empirical validity established in earlier chapters has resolved some doubts about face validity.

All the measures we use are objective—based on clear-cut and public scoring criteria that are spelled out in detailed manuals, where necessary. In most cases, scorers can, after training, attain agreement with experts at the level of 85 percent or higher. Because the measures use explicit and public criteria, they can also be used for curriculum design, as we discuss later in this chapter.

What about educational validity and real-life relevance? The pilot studies used to develop the Test of Thematic Analysis and the Analysis of Argument test are a step toward meeting the first of these standards, but the main evidence that these measures show change from before to after liberal arts education was presented in previous chapters. For many measures, the existing evidence about relevance to real-life performance and outcomes was also presented in previous chapters. Nevertheless, some of the measures are so new that their real-life validity credentials need to be more firmly established by further research.

A Typology of Educational Outcome Measures. We have suggested in previous paragraphs that the problems and standards of measuring liberal arts competence are the same whatever the mode of evaluation, and that these same standards also apply to measures used in research on higher education (including our own). Table 18 summarizes our discussion in terms of perhaps the two most important standards: public objective criteria and demonstrated real-life relevance. In the upper left-hand quadrant of the table, we locate the typical professor reading an essay, characterized as a private judgment the relevance of which to the student's later-life performance rests on an undemonstrated faith. In this quadrant also are those competency-based assessments and other nontraditional measures that call for global judgments by observers and assessors, without providing any detailed criteria or training, and that have only a presumed relevance (even if it is an "obvious" one) to later life.

The lower left quadrant contains measures that involve

Table 18. Classification of Several Methods of Measuring Liberal Arts
Competence and Outcomes Along Two Dimensions or Standards

Criteria Used in Making Evaluation	Relevance to Later Life	
	Assumed; Based on Personal Faith or Persuasion	Based on Demonstrated Evidence
Private or intuitive	Traditional professor's grading of papers and exams Many competency-based assessment measures	Letters of recommendation from a professor with an established track record as a good "talent scout" Clinical judgments with established validity cretials
Public and trainable	Competence measures with detailed, clear-cut criteria and intensive assessor training SAT and GRE scores Some new measures (for example, Analysis of Argument), where there is little evidence as yet about real-life relevance	Competence measures with public criteria *and* empirically demonstrated relationships to real-life outcomes Some new measures (for example, Self-definition, Stage of Psychological Adaptation to the Environment, perhaps Test of Thematic Analysis)

public criteria but that have not yet attained demonstrable life relevance. Many traditional outcome measures, such as SAT and GRE scores, also belong here.

What is in the upper right quadrant? Can any measure have demonstrated validity, or relevance to real life, without being based on public criteria? We think so. There are probably some professors who, in their intuitive (and private) wisdom, can pick students who will turn out to be the scholars, business achievers, or political leaders of tomorrow. Their letters of recommendation are eagerly sought by students and are taken seriously by graduate schools, scholarship committees, and corporate executives. If we only knew the criteria they used for making their judgments. Here would go the interview situations that have demonstrable capacity to pick those who will succeed but are not based on any clearly articulated cues or criteria. Also belonging here are intuitively made clinical judgments for which there is, nevertheless, evidence of life relevance or validity (see McClelland and Winter, 1969, p. 268, for an example).

In the lower right quadrant are those measures that have met both standards. Movement toward the lower right quadrant, then, is desirable in terms of the point of view we advance in this book because this is movement toward attaining the two most critical standards for evaluating any outcome measure. The College Outcome Measures Project (COMP), conducted by the American College Testing Program, began with measures in the upper left quadrant and has tried to move them toward the lower right quadrant both by calibrating faculty ratings and by testing effectively functioning adults (Forrest and Steele, 1977; American College Testing Program, 1979). Some of our own tests are already in this cell; others are somewhere along the way.

Evaluating Liberal Arts Competence in the 1980s. Up to this point, we have discussed our measures in the language of statistical inference and laboratory research, but the dimensions of liberal arts competence are real abilities and traits in real people. How are these dimensions likely to be expressed in the lives of students in the years to come?

First, we would expect an effect on students' ideas and conceptions of what is happening to the world, to American society, and to themselves. Instead of having incoherent and jumbled impressions of events, students with high scores on the major dimensions we have discussed would develop clear and coherent concepts of the changes that are taking place and the deeper problems that these changes represent. Before college, they might have described recent changes in a confusing array of emotionally tinged personal complaints: "My life isn't as much fun as it used to be because I don't have as much real money." "I can't get the gas to drive my car where I want to go." "I feel frustration and rage at OPEC [or at the government, the driver ahead of me in the gas line, and so on]." With the development of thematic analysis skills, however, they would be able to conceptualize problems in abstract and objective terms that subsume superficially unrelated elements. Discrete concepts such as energy, inflation, and international relations might be linked in a broader theme, for example, the imbalance between America's share of world population and its share of world consumption, with a resulting sense of injustice and deprivation in other nations. With increasing Self-definition, they would become more aware of causal relationships within and across these complex concepts. In terms of cognitive mapping theory (Axelrod, 1976; Hart, 1977), their conceptual structures would have higher causal density. Thus they would apprehend (for example) the interdependency of resources, population, consumption, and the environment in broader concepts such as the limits to growth (whether or not in the exact terms of the Club of Rome report; see Meadows and others, 1972). In even broader terms, the American experience of 1946-1974 might be seen as a temporary burst of consumption made possible by the time gap between the influx of resources and skills from an exhausted Europe in the 1940s and the full emergence of a powerful and nationalist Third World, as symbolized by the precipitate American departure from Vietnam in 1975.

Second, we would expect a higher level of maturity in the liberally educated students' reactions to these events. Instead of waiting passively for a powerful and good authority to fix everything up or feeling helpless, incompetent, and at the mercy of a conspiracy of evil authorities (as might have happened in freshman year), they would now be more aware of the limitations of authority. They would see leaders as neither beneficent parents nor evil demons, but rather as human beings of mixed will, constrained by the limits of their ability and knowledge as well as by the situation. Their own feelings would balance positive emotions against the painful readjustments that the future will require, for example, by realizing the pleasure of a simpler life or feeling the inner satisfaction of nonmaterial values.

Through the time of discontinuities and frustrations, the liberal arts students' more mature adaptive responses would also mean that they would be able to sustain the capacity for close, mutual relationships with others rather than displacing frustrated rage on family members and other people, as might have happened before college. They should be able to work instrumentally and effectively, avoiding the paralysis of doubt about

competence, the distractions of obsessive rituals, and the temp-
tation to flee from the world as it really is, in search of personal
pleasure. With the combined development of Self-definition and
the leadership motive pattern, their work would have discipline,
instrumentality, and effectiveness: At least in a small way, they
could marshal society's undoubted material, human, and intellectual resources to develop institutions that are enduring, popular, and just.

Throughout this slow and sometimes painful process, the
liberally educated students' greater intellectual flexibility and
ability to analyze arguments would help them to resist dema-
gogic appeals for simplistic diagnoses and intemperate actions—
arguments to which they might have been more vulnerable before college or as freshmen. They would be able to pick ways
through the ideological and emotional crossfire of public and
private rhetoric, gathering whatever truth is to be found from
all sides.

In the crises and stresses of our own time, therefore, all
liberally educated students who approach this ideal type would
be able to form coherent and sophisticated conceptions of the
world and its problems. They would be able to act maturely and
responsibly on behalf of the larger society while retaining the
capacity for mutuality within their own face-to-face groups.
They would keep their emotions under control and grasp the
logic behind the emotions in others' arguments. In short, they
would be educated citizens. As in times and crises past, such
citizens would be a social resource of inestimable value.

Implications for Educational Policy

Although we believe that our research results support the
ideals of the educated citizen and the liberal arts college, it
would be most fortunate if educators merely accepted these results, relegated them to their public relations departments (as
Botstein, 1979, proposes), and then lapsed back into faith or
personal testimony as the basis of their beliefs, policies, opera-
tions, and liberal arts curriculum. Our real concern is not so
much to establish a definitive case for the liberal arts as it is to

establish a climate in which educational goals, choices, and policies are formed, articulated, and adapted on the basis of research evidence about their educational effects. The studies that we have presented in this book demonstrate how that kind of research can be done. We believe that existing ways of making educational policy are long on rhetoric and short on evidence and that there is therefore a great need for a different approach.

We cannot improve on the humorous and vivid accounts of Cornford (1922), Adams (1976), or C. P. Snow's *The Masters* (1951) to illustrate traditional educational policy making: reliance on exalted but vague educational platitudes, expressions of moral indignation and outrage, statements of personal conviction, anecdotes about student success or satisfaction, frantic overreactions to unanticipated crises, and continual administrator-faculty infighting and recrimination. There is nothing wrong with lofty ideals, anecdotes, personal conviction, or even moral indignation as initial parts of the process of forming educational policy. All have their uses. Taken only by themselves, however, they are not adequate as guides. Systematic evaluative research can make a more useful contribution to the formation of educational policy, even if it cannot measure every effect and answer every question. While plans and programs will always be affected by ideals, testimony, prestige, and simple academic politics, the application of systematic knowledge about effects can sharpen and improve educational policy. To this end, we have developed the measures and carried out the research reported in this book.

Who should do educational research of this kind? The simplest answer is anyone who wants to know how well a particular educational venture is doing. More specifically, within higher education four interested groups can use such tests: (1) faculty members, both as individuals and as members of committees; (2) administrators responsible for individual institutions; (3) decision makers interested in several campuses or institutions; and (4) groups serving students, their families, and their future employers—the ultimate consumers of higher education.

Faculty Research on Educational Effects. As individuals,

professors can use measures of liberal arts competence of the sort described in this book as a supplement to more traditional measures of student performance, such as examinations, term papers, standardized objective tests, or competency-based assessments of performance. Curious or adventurous professors can go beyond these evaluative uses to conduct small-scale, informal research studies. For example, which students get the most out of a particular course, in the sense of showing the greatest gains in thematic analysis or Self-definition? Which way of teaching the course gives the greatest average gain among all students? Where are improvements most urgently needed? Thus a philosophy professor interested in knowing whether his or her course in logic improves students' critical thinking ability and skills at analyzing the logical structure of arguments could, with a little technical assistance in administering and scoring tests and analyzing data, use some of the instruments described in this book to test his or her students at the beginning and the end of the course. To isolate changes that were specific to the logic course, rather than changes due to studying philosophy or learning how to write, and to control for maturation and the effect of taking the same test twice, he or she could also test students from other courses as controls at the beginning and end of the term. This research would give the professor new knowledge about the effects of the course and some ideas about how to change it to have different effects. What he or she would then do with this knowledge would depend upon his or her goals and values. The *research would not automatically produce educational policy; instead, it would assist in the clarification and implementation of educational policy.*

Faculty members could also use the new measures in designing courses to teach liberal arts competence directly. For example, the compare and contrast framework of the Test of Thematic Analysis could be adapted to raw material from course content in fields as diverse as art history, sociology, and geology, with the categories of the scoring system covered explicitly in class. Given, for example, a painting by Leonardo and a painting by Michaelangelo (or the concepts of *Gemeinschaft* and *Gesellschaft*, or two different strata of rock), what overarching categories or characteristics apply to both? What contrasting elements are present in each one but not the other? What are examples or illustrations of each of these points? Are there exceptions or qualifications to be made? Can subjective, emotional reactions to these two paintings (concepts, strata) be reworked into more objective, parallel, and therefore communicable terms? By encouraging students to use this framework in learning and organizing their knowledge, professors would be teaching the competence of critical thinking directly instead of implicitly, while they are also teaching the traditional subject matter of the discipline. The component variables and scoring categories of the leadership motive pattern could be developed into an explicit way of teaching leadership motivation and skill. (See McClelland and Winter, 1969, for examples of how training programs of this kind can be developed.)

Faculty committees could use these tests in more systematic research addressed to the familiar questions of educational policy: How should the curriculum be structured? Do students really get more out of college if they have to meet specified distribution requirements rather than being completely free to choose any course? Is a senior honors thesis worth the faculty time and student effort in terms of any demonstrable educational effects? Does the new interdisciplinary program live up to its claim? The latter question suggests that program evaluation is an area where this kind of educational effects research could be especially important. At most colleges and universities, new programs are given faculty approval with provision for some kind of review and evaluation by a faculty committee after a certain number of years. Often these reviews are never carried out; but when they are, they are usually based on the familiar appeals to personal testimony or self-selected opinion. Accomplishments of students in the program are pointed to with pride but with little effort to determine whether the new program actually changed the students or simply selected the good students. It is obvious that research on program effects will (and should) never be the *sole* basis for program evaluation, but it is equally obvious that such research could play a useful role in evaluation when taken together with other considerations. The study of the joint humanities program at Cathedral College, discussed in Chapter Six, is an example of how research can contribute to these program evaluations. As a matter of standard policy, for example, some proportion of a new program's cost (say 5-10 percent) could be budgeted for such evaluations.

Administrative Research on Educational Effects. Administrators can use research of this kind as a guide to their most difficult problem: allocating scarce resources among departments, individuals, and activities with competing claims. Whether the decisions involve creating new programs or cutting existing ones, information about the actual educational effects of programs can contribute to the quality of the decisions and thereby maximize the overall efficiency and effectiveness of the institution.

Of course, the mention of research-based decisions about cutting programs raises both anxiety and hostility in any loyal liberal arts professor. The language of efficiency and measurable results, like the earlier notions of performance contracting, seems jarring and inappropriate when applied to something as complex and subtle as liberal education. Yet it is perfectly obvious that every institution will have to reduce or eliminate some programs over the next decade if it is going to have the resources to add any new programs. Many colleges will have to cut drastically just to survive; more than a few private colleges will not survive in any case. No doubt many of them will go down full of ideals and dedication to the end—trying, in the words of the president of one recently deceased institution, to create a curriculum that makes educational sense. The introduction of research results into the decision-making process does not cause, prevent, or exacerbate the need to make cuts. But it can cause decisions about these cuts to be made in more equitable and objective ways.

Obviously, research is never going to replace the traditional forces that shape decisions about educational policy. Colleges and universities are social systems, and as such they must respond to internal bureaucratic needs for system maintenance and member commitment as well as to external needs for efficiency and effectiveness in defining, measuring, and performing their formal mission. As Garvin (1980) points out, the quest for institutional prestige (or a reputation fo excellence among academic and professional colleagues) guides a good deal of faculty and administration behavior, whatever the catalogue claims about affecting students may be. We are only proposing that research on educational effects be *added* to the other factors affecting educational decisions. Where, for example, two out of four programs must be eliminated or where a college can do either X or Y but not both, some objective and extensive attempt to untangle change effects, selection effects, and eloquent mythology may be of use even if it may not be decisive.

Ivy College administrators, for example, might find the results in Chapter Five useful in considering how to allocate resources among diverse programs such as integrated curriculum programs, dormitory life, and sports. Administrators elsewhere might find it useful to invest in special studies of particular programs, along the lines of the studies at Cathedral College, or even of all major programs. Research of this kind is not cheap. In the present financial climate, these costs may appear to be one more avoidable administrative expense. In fact, however, investment in careful research on educational effects is an investment in the effective and efficient attainment of institutional goals.

Other Decision Makers' Use of Research. Policy makers involved in education at a level broader than individual campuses include chancellors of multicampus systems, officials of state boards, foundation officers, legislators, and philanthropic businessmen. All share a concern with allocating resources among different campuses or different institutions.

Research results will never fully displace political and social considerations in such concerns, and there is no reason why they should. Research results, however, can become one element in interinstitutional choices and the give-and-take of political bargaining, as Keppel (1980) has proposed for systematic national testing of student learning. For example, with the spread of desegregation in recent years, traditionally black colleges have been more and more called upon to justify their "separate" existence. Their leaders have argued that they provide a supportive environment for many black students, who can thus perform better than they would at a predominantly white college. From what we know about the subtle effects of white institutional racism, as well as what psychologists have found about fear of success among blacks (Fleming, 1975), this argument seems plausible. But to know whether it is really true (and how important it is if it is true), research is needed on the gains of black students at different kinds of institutions. Fortunately, a research project addressed to this issue has recently been completed. A preliminary analysis of the results from nine institutions suggests that the claim of the black colleges is, if anything, an *understatement* of their actual effects: "In general, the results indicate that black students in black schools show substantially better intellectual as well as psycho-social development than counterparts at predominantly white schools. . . . While gains in psycho-social development may have been predicted from the previous literature, gains in intellectual and cognitive domains are surely contrary to all expectations" (Fleming, 1979, p. 4). It looks as though this research will generate a strong case for the unique role—and therefore the special claims for financial support—of the traditionally black colleges.

It is easy to see that similar studies could be made of the educational effects on women of women's colleges versus coeducational colleges or, more relevant to the era of coeducation, the effects on women of varying intrainstitutional modes and practices having to do with coeducation. In Chapter Five, for example, we noted that the elaborate traditional life associated with the dormitories at Ivy College seems to be of little benefit and some harm to women. It may be unrealistic and even undesirable to split Ivy into male and female component colleges, but it is surely possible to find ways to redesign the Ivy College dormitory system in order to increase its benefits and decrease its weaknesses.

Other subinstitutional programs, ranging from ethnic studies to innovative ventures of cooperation between the college and the community, can be evaluated by research of this kind. Funding agencies both public and private could assist in this trend by requiring that perhaps 5 percent of a grant to

establish any new program be spent on an independent exter-
nally conducted research evaluation of the program's change
effects on students. Often a particular program's goals will not
fit completely and adequately within the framework of the liberal arts competence measures that we have used here; in these
cases, additional funds should be budgeted for the development
of new measures. For example, a program might emphasize the
development of empathy, careful listening, or complex scheduling and planning. Evaluating such a program fairly would
require suitable new measures of these competences. While
developing customized measures to order is difficult and time-
consuming, it often produces the most useful results, as the College of Human Services in New York City illustrated in working
with McBer and Company on the development of outcome measures that are tailored to its own educational goals and curriculum (Grant and others, 1979, pp. 308-309).

  Consumer Protection Through Research. Students, their
families, and their future employers can also use educational research of this kind. A college education is very costly, even for
the family of a student with a large scholarship. As an investment, its cost is probably surpassed only by a home; yet how
much less objective information is available about what the college "buyer" is getting. Houses can be checked for structure and
condition by licensed building inspectors; lawyers check the
validity of titles and the existence of liens. None of this is available for a college education. Consumers have to be content with
objective data about *characteristics* instead of *effects,* to which
is added varying amounts of institutional prestige, economic
necessity, family tradition, and peer group fashion.

  We believe that this state of affairs can be changed. Measures of the type introduced in this book can be developed to
provide systematic data on institutional effects. We see no reason in principle, for example, why a future *Barron's Profiles of
American Colleges,* a *Lovejoy's College Guide,* or a College
Board *College Handbook* should not begin to show comparative
profile information about college change effects on a standard
series of liberal arts competence measures that are face valid,
generic, reliably scored according to public criteria, and relevant

to both educational and later-life goals. Prospective freshmen, parents, counselors, and others would then have some more objective basis for estimating the abstract skills, competences, and personal qualities that could be expected of graduates from a given college. Perhaps federal and state governments, concerned as they are with both stewardship of tax money and social equity, should require that each recipient college and university produce, maintain, and follow an affirmative documentation plan to demonstrate their claimed effects, as a minimum standard of institutional accountability (not to say of truth in advertising). As Chait (1979, p. 36) has put it, "a catalogue could be enriched as a document to read and a device to recruit were there as many examples of results as expressions of aspirations."

For anyone interested in using our battery of tests, further details about their availability, cost, and administration may be found in Resource A.

Assessing Liberal Education

In summary, we hope that the dissemination of these measures and, more important, the creation of a climate in which research informs and contributes to educational policy, will converge with the efforts of liberal arts educators to improve knowledge about what is happening in their colleges and assess the attainment of competence in liberal education.

In the past, psychology has not had much of value to contribute to policy making in higher education, especially in the liberal arts. Traditional "objective" tests, which have been the basic tools of so much educational research, will not suffice as adequate measures of the goals of the liberal arts. And while the competency-based education movement has contributed fresh ideas and valuable perspective on the goals of liberal education, its assessment procedures do not necessarily offer an improvement on either traditional grading or "objective" tests (see Huff, Klemp, and Winter, 1980). Instead, another kind of measure, drawn from several traditions in psychology that look at what people do spontaneously and creatively, holds more promise for assessing achievement in liberal education. These new "operant" measures (see McClelland, 1966, 1972, 1980) have roots in such diverse sources as Skinner's (1938) behaviorism and the projective tests developed within the psychoanalytic tradition (Murray, 1938). Because they are closer to the actual situation of the college student, they are better able to reflect the abstract and wide-ranging goals of liberal arts education.

The measures of liberal arts competence that we have introduced here are not perfect, and they certainly do not exhaust all the goals that could be assessed. They require care to administer; in relative terms, they take a good deal of time, effort, and money to score; and some educators will protest that they capture the essential spirit of the liberal arts no better than any other psychological test or assessment procedure. We believe, however, that these measures not only identify liberal arts competence but also demonstrate growth in this competence in the liberal arts college. No longer do we have to rely on mere faith or personal testimony as the foundation for our belief in the liberal arts. A better response, with better evidence, is available to articulate goals, to allocate resources, and to adapt programs during the demographic and economic times of troubles in the decades to come. If we are to preserve and defend the liberal arts ideal, should we ever try to do it with less than our best response and our best evidence?

How To Use
the New Measures
of Educational
Outcomes

Many readers who have followed the accounts of our research and who believe that educational policy, planning, and evaluation ought to be guided by appropriately designed and rigorous research will now want some practical information. How can they acquire and use the new measures of liberal arts competence? Who should be tested? What will it cost? Where should they begin?

The first step is to decide what questions to ask and then to translate these questions into a research design. We have given in Chapter Seven several examples of educational problems and issues that can be addressed with the liberal arts competence measures. Some research experience, or else consultation, is usually required in order to develop an appropriate and efficient research design. Here there is no single best way to proceed. Social science faculty members from within an institution who are experienced in this kind of research can often give assistance, but not all professors will be interested in what they see as applied research. Other resources are in-house directors of institutional research and interested and competent faculty from other institutions. Although their services may be expensive, contract research companies with experience in evaluation research can be used for anything from consultation at the research design stage to design and execution of the entire project. Finally, educators with some research training and experience will be able to work out their own designs. We encourage all readers to be as actively involved as they can be at the research design stage and suggest that they consult one or more of the following sources for introductions to research and technical advice on specific issues (listed in approximate increasing order of complexity): *Educator's Guide to Research* (Crosby, 1977, written to be accessible to the nonspecialist and available from McBer and Company); *Experimental and Quasi-Experimental Designs for Research* (Campbell and Stanley, 1963); *Quasi-Experimentation: Design and Analysis Issues for Field Settings* (Cook and Campbell, 1979); and the *Handbook of Evaluation Research* (Struening and Guttentag, 1975).

For educators who want to use the new measures discussed in this book, we give information about sources, administration times, costs, and scoring. The prices quoted were current at the time of writing (late 1980); and although they will obviously change over time, they give the potential user a rough idea of costs. In some cases, readers may want to learn how to do their own scoring (or have a research assistant learn to score). This can be very time-consuming; for example, learning a single scoring system may take two to three hours per day for ten days. Thus many readers will find it easier and even cheaper in the long run to have materials professionally scored by trained experts, through the scoring services listed later.

The Test of Thematic Analysis and Analysis of Argument

test are available through McBer and Company (Test and Scoring Division), 137 Newbury Street, Boston, Massachusetts
02116. Each test costs $1.50 per copy for materials and $4.00
per copy for expert scoring. The former test normally takes
thirty minutes to administer (although it can easily be cut back
to fifteen minutes), and the latter test takes fifteen minutes.
The Thematic Apperception Test can be obtained in several
ways. For researchers who want to create their own tests, sample instructions and pictures are given by McClelland (1975, pp.
384-388) and McClelland and others (1972, pp. 360-367). (We
recommend using at least four pictures in the TAT.) McBer and
Company distributes a six-picture version called "Picture Story
Exercise," costing $.75 per copy for materials. McBer provides
expert scoring of the TAT at a cost of $.55 per motive per story
for achievement, affiliation, or power motivation, and $.67 per
story for Self-definition or Stage of Psychological Adaptation
to the Environment. (Activity inhibition and story length each
cost $.22 per story.) Materials for learning to score the TAT
variables are available as follows: Achievement and affiliation
motivation are given in Atkinson (1958, Appendix 1). Power
motivation materials are given in Winter (1973, Appendix 1).
Self-definition and Stage of Psychological Adaptation materials
are available, at cost, from Professor A. J. Stewart, Psychology
Department, Boston University, 64 Cummington Street, Boston, Massachusetts 02215.

The Profile of Nonverbal Sensitivity (PONS), described
by Rosenthal and others (1979), is available in various audio-
and videotape versions from Irvington Publishers, 551 Fifth
Avenue, New York, New York 10017. The Uses of Objects and
Meanings of Words tests are simple to reproduce and score from
the examples and instructions given by Hudson (1966, p. 165).

Table 19 summarizes the information on administration
times and costs for the various measures. As a rough guideline, a
researcher who wanted to give the main tests of liberal arts competence that showed differences in Chapter Three and that were
used in Chapter Six could assume that the test battery would
take about an hour and a half to administer and that materials
and expert scoring costs (for all variables, including activity in-

Table 19. Administration Times and Costs for the Liberal Arts Competence Measures

Instrument	Approximate Time to Administer	Cost of Materials	Cost of Scoring
Test of Thematic Analysis	30 minutes[a]	$1.50	$4.00
Analysis of Argument test	15 minutes	1.50	4.00
Thematic Apperception Test	35 minutes for six pictures (5 minutes per picture, plus 5 minutes)	.75	.55 per story for each story .67 per story for Self-definition and Stages of Adaptation .22 per story for activity inhibition and story length

[a]Can be cut to 15 minutes, but scores should not be compared to those obtained from 30-minute administration.

hibition and story length) would be $25.46 per student with a four-picture TAT and $32.33 per student with a six-picture TAT. These operant measures of liberal arts competence are more expensive to give and score than are traditional objective tests; but as we have pointed out throughout this book, the two kinds of measures simply do not converge. They measure different things. The costs of using the new operant measures can be reduced in two ways: first, by training in-house scorers to do some of the scoring and, second, by sharpening the research questions and carefully sampling students to be tested (or selecting only some of the completed tests for scoring). The second step should be taken only in accord with good principles of research design and data analysis.

If the Thematic Apperception Test is used as a part of any test battery, it should be given before any other procedure, as close to the beginning of the testing session as possible, and in as neutral a manner as possible. These precautions are necessary because the TAT is so sensitive to the effects of the situa-

tion in which it is administered. In this context, a neutral setting means one in which nothing is done to arouse any particular motive or other concern and in which the TAT is *not* described as any kind of "test." (The descriptions of relaxed and
neutral settings in McClelland and others, 1953, pp. 100-102,
may be consulted.)

Researchers at McBer and Company have developed several other new measures of competence, such as (1) the *Focusing Exercise,* a measure of the ability to attend to feelings that
are concrete although cognitively unclear; (2) the *Scheduling
Exercise,* a measure of the ability to coordinate and arrange several different complicated tasks in order to achieve the greatest
efficiency in the use of time and resources; and (3) the *Life History Exercise,* a measure of accurate and efficient processing of
information about other people, as a component of human relations skills. (Further details on these and other new measures
can be obtained from McBer and Company.)

RESOURCE B

Methodological Considerations

Testing and Analysis Procedures in the
Three-College Study (Chapter Three)

Testing. Students at Ivy, State Teachers, and Community Colleges were tested in small groups of between 20-50 subjects each. Each testing session was conducted by two graduate students (one male, one female), who explained that the research was intended "to try out some new instruments and procedures." Subjects were assured that their responses would be treated as confidential and not read by any college officials. Because it is the most sensitive to situational effects, the Thematic Apperception Test was given first in all sessions, using standard "neutral" arousal procedures (see Atkinson, 1958). The other tests were printed in several test booklets, with the Test of Thematic Analysis and the Analysis of Argument put first because they are operant measures. At the end of each session students were paid and thanked for their participation.

Data Reduction. In those cases where the correlation was significant, all variables derived from the written TAT stories were corrected for the effects of correlation of score with length of stories. This was done to ensure that students who wrote longer stories did not get higher scores merely because of the (presumably extraneous) factor of having produced more material that could be scored. Corrections were done with a technique (Winter, 1973, p. 146; 1979a) in which the regression of raw score on length of stories is used to calculate a predicted score (given length), which is then subtracted from the actual score to give a corrected score. Such corrected scores are uncorrelated with length of stories. Finally, all motive scores and Self-definition scores were standardized, with overall means of 50 and overall standard deviations of 10 for each variable in order to facilitate comparisons across variables and across colleges. The correction and standardization procedures were carried out on the entire pooled three-college sample.

Analysis of Variance. It can be argued that the technically correct data analysis procedure is to examine first the results of an analysis of variance, separating out the significance of variation due to college, to class (freshman versus final year), and to interaction of college by class. This latter interaction tests whether freshman-senior differences are themselves significantly different at the three colleges. We did in fact carry out such analyses for all variables, including co-variance adjustments for SAT scores and father's education (the single best measure of social class) in a further effort to remove any spurious effects of these two variables that have such different levels at Ivy College and the two other colleges. We did not, however, insist that the college-by-class interaction effect be significant before examining and interpreting freshman-senior differences at Ivy College. The reason is that the other two colleges were primarily intended as controls for expected changes. Also, the unweighted means analysis of variance that would be necessary because of the very unequal numbers of cases per cell seriously underestimates the contribution of the Ivy College samples to the significance of the interaction term. By using the harmonic mean of cell size for all cells, the unweighted means analysis of variance assumes their numbers to be much less than they are in fact.

Length of Test of Thematic Analysis Responses. Although thematic analysis scores were significantly correlated with length of response (r = .46, p < .001 for the total sample), on theoretical grounds it is not clear that thematic analysis scores should be corrected for length of response. Longer answers in a task of this sort may be an intrinsic part of improved ability, rather than a "spurious" factor that only suggests higher scores. That is, length of response may be part of a "developmental sequence" rather than "spurious." In such a case, one could argue that writing a longer response was part of writing a better response; thus, the effects of length should *not* be removed. Thematic analysis has a much lower correlation (r = .21) with TAT story length, which may be a better measure of verbal fluency. Nevertheless, when thematic analysis scores were corrected for length by regression of score on length of protocol, Ivy College seniors still score significantly higher than Ivy College freshmen.

Definitions of Selected Male Life Outcomes
(Chapter Four)

Early Success. Separate criteria used for each of the four most common occupations: professor (having tenure); doctor (having some responsibility for teaching or supervising interns); business (being owner, president, or director of a business grossing over $1 million annually, or being at a high level of a large corporation); and lawyer (having a connection with a prestigious firm).

Entrepreneur. Same criteria as used by McClelland (1965).

Publications. Each article counted as one point and each book counted as two points.

Career Satisfaction. Responses to each of the following nine items were first standardized and then summed: "How satisfying is your present job?" and "How frustrating is your present job?" (each answered on a 5-point scale); and feeling that the following things are true of current job (each on a 4-point scale): "your work is intrinsically interesting," "the social environment at work is pleasant," "you have a chance to do what you do best," "you leave work each day with good feelings," "your supervision is competent," "your job measures up well to the sort of job you wanted when you left college," and "your achievements have been fully recognized by your co-workers." This cluster of items emerged from a factor analysis of the 1974 follow-up questionnaire.

Dual-Career Family. Spouse has a full-time career (versus part-time career, unstable career pattern, or no career). Single men were coded "no" on this variable because our interest was in predicting a particular kind of family style versus all alternative family styles.

Children. Whether the person has had any children, regardless of present marital status.

Self-Image Variables. Subjects were given a list of 22 adjectives and asked to choose the four that "best characterize your current life-style."

Testing and Analysis Procedures in the Seven-College Study (Chapter Six)

Selection of Subjects and Testing Procedures. At each of the seven colleges, groups of freshmen and senior students were tested. At two of these institutions, freshmen and seniors were selected by the simple expedient of testing large and comparable courses having a heavy concentration of either group. At the other schools, freshmen and seniors were recruited directly for group testing sessions. At three sites, students were paid to participate. At Liberal College, for example, it was necessary to pay students $10 in order to ensure an adequate turnout from certain groups that were carefully selected to include certain academic programs of research interest to Liberal College administrators. At five colleges, freshmen were tested in the fall term and seniors in the spring term in order to maximize the chances of detecting college change effects. All Liberal College students, however, were tested in the fall term, and all Jordan College students were tested in the spring term.

At each college, the testing sessions were conducted by a faculty member or member of the institutional research staff in accordance with a standard set of written instructions. The Thematic Apperception Test was always given first in order to make the situation and arousal effects as similar as possible across the different testings, and as unaffected as possible by the other two instruments. The Test of Thematic Analysis was always given last. Each testing session took about an hour and a half. At North State College testing sessions were limited to fifty minutes. Since a large number of subjects was available, the test battery was divided into two forms—one with the Thematic Apperception Test and the other with the Test of Thematic Analysis and Analysis of Argument. These two forms were randomly mixed together and passed out to students so as to ensure equivalent groups and numbers for each form. In all cases, students were told that the tests were new procedures that were being developed to study the effects of higher education. They were assured that their responses would be treated confidentially, handled by code numbers only, and never seen by anyone at their college.

While test conditions varied, we know of no *systematic* differences in test administration procedures that could spuriously affect the kinds of conclusions drawn from these data. Nevertheless, these testing situations were not as controlled and standardized as those in the three-college study reported in Chapter Three, where the test administrations, rationale, timing, procedures, and payment were uniform, and freshmen and seniors were tested together.

Data Processing and Analysis. All test responses were sent to McBer and Company for scoring and analysis. First, groups of freshmen and seniors (as close to 60 of each as possible) were randomly selected for each college. Freshmen and senior tests were mixed together and scored for all variables by trained, expert scorers who were blind to the name or college class of any subject. All TAT-based variables were corrected for the effects of any correlation with the total length of the stories and then converted to standard-score form by the same technique described earlier. These corrections and standardizations were carried out separately for each site because of the inter-site variability in testing conditions (that is, length of stories and correlations of scores with length). For the TAT-related variables, the pooled freshmen and senior scores at each site thus had an average of 50 and a standard deviation of 10. Of course the *differences* between freshmen and senior averages varied from site to site, because these differences reflect the (presumably differing) effects of college. Since the TAT-based scores were standardized separately for each college, these difference scores are less likely to be affected by different initial levels among the colleges than would raw scores.

Interactions between sex and college class were checked by analyses of variance to see whether men and women showed significantly different changes. There were no sex by class interactions, so the male and female data were analyzed together. Because the Liberal College testing was part of an evaluation of two sophomore-to-senior year programs, sophomores were tested instead of the usual freshman samples used elsewhere. To estimate what the freshman scores would have been, to make the Liberal College differences comparable to the others, we simply assumed that change is equal in each year. Thus the presumed freshman-to-senior changes used in Chapter Six are taken to be 1.5 times the observed sophomore-to-senior changes. This is conservative, because the true changes are more likely to be negatively accelerated functions.

References

Adams, H. *The Academic Tribes.* New York: Liveright, 1976.

American College Testing Program. *COMP Prospectus.* Iowa City, Iowa: American College Testing Program, 1979.

Astin, A. W. "The Measured Effects of Higher Education." *Annals of the American Academy of Political and Social Science,* 1972, *404,* 1-20.

Astin, A. W. "Measurement and Determinants of the Outputs of Higher Education." In L. C. Solomon and P. J. Taubman (Eds.), *Does College Matter?* New York: Academic Press, 1973.

Astin, A. W. *Four Critical Years: Effects of College on Beliefs, Attitudes, and Knowledge.* San Francisco: Jossey-Bass, 1977.

Astin, H. S. "Factors Associated with the Participation of Women Doctorates in the Labor Force." *Personnel and Guidance Journal,* 1967, *46,* 240-246.

Astin, H. S. *The Woman Doctorate in America.* New York: Russell Sage Foundation, 1969.

Atkinson, J. W. (Ed.). *Motives in Fantasy, Action and Society.* Princeton, N.J.: Van Nostrand, 1958.

Atkinson, J. W., and Raynor, J. O. (Eds.). *Motivation and Achievement.* Washington, D.C.: Hemisphere, 1974.

Axelrod, R. M. *Structure of Decision.* Princeton, N.J.: Princeton University Press, 1976.

Aydelotte, F. *The Vision of Cecil Rhodes.* London: Oxford University Press, 1946.

Babbitt, I. *Literature and the American College.* Boston: Houghton Mifflin, 1908.

Bailyn, L. "Family Constraints on Women's Work." In R. B. Kundsin (Ed.), *Women and Success.* New York: Morrow, 1974.

Barton, A. H. *Studying the Effects of College Education: A Methodological Examination of Changing Values in College.* New Haven, Conn.: Edward W. Hazen Foundation, 1959.

Baruch, R. "The Achievement Motive in Women: Implications for Career Development." *Journal of Personality and Social Psychology,* 1967, *5,* 260-267.

Becker, H. "What Do They Really Learn at College?" *Trans-Action,* 1964, *1,* 4, 14-17.

Bernard, J. *The Future of Motherhood.* New York: Dial Press, 1974.

Bettelheim, B. "Individual and Mass Behavior in Extreme Situations." In E. L. Maccoby, T. M. Newcomb, and E. Hartley (Eds.), *Readings in Social Psychology.* (3rd ed.) New York: Holt, Rinehart & Winston, 1958.

Bieri, J. "Complexity-Simplicity as a Personality Variable in Cognitive and Preferential Behavior." In D. W. Fiske and S. R. Maddi (Eds.), *Functions of Varied Experience.* Homewood, Ill.: Dorsey Press, 1961.

Bieri, J. "Cognitive Complexity and Personality Development." In O. J. Harvey (Ed.), *Experience, Structure and Adaptability.* New York: Springer, 1966.

Bird, C. *The Case Against College.* New York: McKay, 1975.

Birnbaum, J. "Life Patterns and Self-Esteem in Gifted Family-Oriented and Career-Committed Women." In M. T. S. Mednick, S. S. Tangri, and L. W. Hoffman (Eds.), *Women and Achievement.* Washington, D.C.: Hemisphere, 1975.

Birney, R. C. "Research on the Achievement Motive." In E. F. Borgatta and W. W. Lambert (Eds.), *Handbook of Personality Theory and Research*. Chicago: Rand McNally, 1968.

Block, J. "Advancing the Science of Personality: Paradigmatic Shift or Improving the Quality of Research?" In D. Magnusson and N. S. Endler (Eds.), *Personality at the Crossroads: Current Issues in Interactional Psychology*. Hillsdale, N.J.: Erlbaum, 1977.

Bloom, B. S. (Ed.). *Taxonomy of Educational Objectives. I. Cognitive Domain*. New York: McKay, 1956.

Bok, D. C. "The President's Report." In *Official Register of Harvard University*. Vol. 75. Cambridge, Mass.: Harvard University, 1978.

Botstein, L. "Are You Better Off at Harvard?" *New York Times Magazine,* April 17, 1977, pp. 81-86.

Botstein, L. "Comment on 'Describing and Measuring the Competencies of Liberal Education.'" Paper presented at the conference of the American Association for Higher Education, Washington, D.C., April 1979.

Bowles, S., and Gintis, H. *Schooling in Capitalist America*. New York: Basic Books, 1976.

Boyatzis, R. E. "Affiliation Motivation." In D. C. McClelland and R. S. Steele (Eds.), *Human Motivation: A Book of Readings*. Morristown, N.J.: General Learning Press, 1973.

Boyatzis, R. E., and Burruss, J. A. *Validation of a Competency Model for Alcoholism Counselors in the Navy*. Boston: McBer, 1977.

Boyer, E. L., and Levine, A. *A Quest for Common Learning*. Washington, D.C.: The Carnegie Foundation for the Advancement of Teaching, 1981.

Bradburn, N. *The Structure of Psychological Well-Being*. Chicago: Aldine, 1969.

Brody, E. B., and Brody, N. *Intelligence: Nature, Determinants, and Consequences*. New York: Academic Press, 1976.

Brown, N. O. *Love's Body*. New York: Random House, 1966.

Bruner, J. S., Goodnow, J., and Austin, G. A. *A Study of Thinking*. New York: Wiley, 1956.

Bryan, A. I., and Boring, E. G. "Women in American Psychology: Factors Affecting Their Professional Careers." *American Psychologist,* 1947, *2,* 3-20.

Bryk, A. S., and Weisberg, H. I. "Use of the Nonequivalent Control Group Design When Subjects are Growing." *Psychological Bulletin,* 1977, *84,* 950-962.

Butterfield, V. "An Educator's View of Psychology." In *Fiftieth Anniversary Celebration, Psychological Laboratory 1894-1944.* Middletown, Conn.: Wesleyan University, 1946.

Campbell, D. T., and Stanley, J. C. *Experimental and Quasi-Experimental Designs for Research.* Chicago: Rand McNally, 1963.

Campbell, J. *The Hero with a Thousand Faces.* New York: Pantheon Books, 1949.

Chait, R. "Mission Madness Strikes Our Colleges." *Chronicle of Higher Education,* July 16, 1979, p. 36.

Chomsky, N. *American Power and the New Mandarins.* New York: Pantheon Books, 1969.

Cohen, J., and Cohen, P. *Applied Multiple Regression/Correlation Analysis for the Behavioral Sciences.* Hillsdale, N.J.: Erlbaum, 1975.

Coleman, J. S., and others. *Equality of Educational Opportunity.* Washington, D.C.: U.S. Government Printing Office, 1966.

Conant, J. B. *My Several Lives.* New York: Harper & Row, 1970.

Cook, T. D., and Campbell, D. T. *Quasi-Experimentation: Design and Analysis Issues for Field Settings.* Chicago: Rand McNally, 1979.

Cornford, F. M. *Microcosmographia Academica.* (2nd ed.) Cambridge, England: Bowes & Bowes, 1922.

Couch, A. S. "The Psychological Determinants of Interpersonal Behavior." In K. Gergen and D. Marlowe (Eds.), *Personality and Interpersonal Behavior.* Reading, Mass.: Addison-Wesley, 1970.

Cronbach, L. J., and Furby, L. "How We Should Measure 'Change'—or Should We?" *Psychological Bulletin,* 1970, *74,* 68-80.

Crosby, F. *Educator's Guide to Research.* Boston: McBer, 1977.

de Charms, R., and others. "Behavioral Correlates of Directly and Indirectly Measured Achievement Motivation." In D. C. McClelland (Ed.), *Studies in Motivation.* New York: Appleton-Century-Crofts, 1955.

Dillenberger, J. (Ed.). *John Calvin: Selections from His Writings.* Garden City, N.Y.: Doubleday, 1971.

Domhoff, G. W. *Who Rules America?* Englewood Cliffs, N.J.: Prentice-Hall, 1967.

Dressel, P. L., and Mayhew, L. B. *General Education: Explorations in Evaluation.* Washington, D.C.: American Council on Education, 1954.

Duncan, O. D., Featherman, D. L., and Duncan, B. *Socioeconomic Background and Achievement.* New York: Seminar Press, 1972.

Ebersole, M. C. "Why the Liberal Arts Will Survive." *Chronicle of Higher Education,* May 21, 1979, p. 48.

Eisenstadt, S. N. "The Protestant Ethic Thesis in an Analytical and Comparative Framework." In S. N. Eisenstadt (Ed.), *The Protestant Ethic and Modernization: A Comparative View.* New York: Basic Books, 1968.

Ellison, A., and Simon, B. "Does College Make a Person Healthy and Wise?" In L. C. Solomon and P. J. Taubman (Eds.), *Does College Matter?* New York: Academic Press, 1973.

Erikson, E. H. *Childhood and Society.* New York: Norton, 1950.

Erikson, E. H. *Identity and the Life Cycle.* Psychological Issues Monograph 1. New York: International Universities Press, 1959.

Faust, C. H. "The Problem of General Education." In *The Idea and Practice of General Education.* Chicago: University of Chicago Press, 1950.

Feldman, K. A., and Newcomb, T. M. *The Impact of College on Students.* San Francisco: Jossey-Bass, 1969.

Fiske, D. W., and Maddi, S. R. (Eds.). *Functions of Varied Experience.* Homewood, Ill.: Dorsey Press, 1961.

Fleming, J. "Approach and Avoidance Motivation in Interpersonal Competition: A Study of Black Male and Female College Students." Unpublished doctoral dissertation, Department of Psychology and Social Relations, Harvard University, 1975.

Fleming, J. "Comment on 'Do Women Fear Success?' by D. Tresemer." *Signs: Journal of Women in Culture and Society,* 1977, *2,* 706-717.

Fleming, J. *The Impact of Predominantly White and Predominantly Black College Environments on Black Students: Report to the Carnegie Corporation.* New York: United Negro College Fund, 1979.

Forrest, A., and Steele, J. M. *COMP: College Outcome Measures Project Annual Report.* Iowa City, Iowa: American College Testing Program, 1977.

Freedman, M. "The Passage Through College." *Journal of Social Issues,* 1956, *12,* 13-28.

Freeman, R. B. *The Overeducated American.* New York: Academic Press, 1976.

Freud, S. "Some Character Types Met with in Psycho-Analytic Work. I. The 'Exceptions.' " In J. Strachey (Ed.), *The Complete Psychological Works of Sigmund Freud.* Vol. 14. London: Hogarth Press, 1957. (Originally published 1916.)

Freud, S. "Some Psychical Consequences of the Anatomical Distinction Between the Sexes." In J. Strachey (Ed.), *The Complete Psychological Works of Sigmund Freud.* Vol. 19. London: Hogarth Press, 1961. (Originally published 1925.)

Freud, S. *Civilization and Its Discontents.* In J. Strachey (Ed.), *The Complete Psychological Works of Sigmund Freud.* Vol. 21. London: Hogarth Press, 1961. (Originally published 1930.)

Freud, S. *An Outline of Psycho-Analysis.* In J. Strachey (Ed.), *The Complete Psychological Works of Sigmund Freud.* Vol. 23. London: Hogarth Press, 1964. (Originally published 1940.)

Friedan, B. *The Feminine Mystique.* New York: Dell, 1963.

Fulbright, J. W. *The Arrogance of Power.* New York: Random House, 1967.

Gardner, J. *The Anti-Leadership Vaccine: Annual Report.* New York: Carnegie Corporation, 1965.

Garvin, D. A. *The Economics of University Behavior.* New York: Academic Press, 1980.

Getzels, J. W., and Jackson, P. W. *Creativity and Intelligence.* New York: Wiley, 1962.

Ginzberg, E., and others. *Educated American Women: Life Styles and Self-Portraits.* New York: Columbia University Press, 1966.

Goffman, E. *Asylums.* Garden City, N.Y.: Doubleday, 1961. (Anchor Books)

Grant, G., and Riesman, D. *The Perpetual Dream: Reform and Experiment in the American College.* Chicago: University of Chicago Press, 1978.

Grant, G., and others. *On Competence: A Critical Analysis of Competence-Based Reforms in Higher Education.* San Francisco: Jossey-Bass, 1979.

Halberstam, D. *The Best and the Brightest.* New York: Random House, 1973.

Hart, J. A. "Cognitive Maps of Three Latin American Policy Makers." *World Politics,* 1977, *30,* 115-140.

Harvard University Committee on the Objectives of a General Education in a Free Society. *General Education in a Free Society.* Cambridge, Mass.: Harvard University Press, 1945.

Healy, J. M., Jr. "College Environments and Psychological Adaptation." Paper presented at 50th annual meeting of the Eastern Psychological Association, Philadelphia, April 1979.

"The Heart of Harvard's Greatness." *Harvard Alumni Bulletin,* March 30, 1968, pp. 21-22.

Heath, D. H. *Growing Up in College: Liberal Education and Maturity.* San Francisco: Jossey-Bass, 1968.

Heath, D. H. "Academic Predictors of Adult Maturity and Competence." *Journal of Higher Education,* 1977, *48,* 613-632.

Heckhausen, H. *The Anatomy of Achievement Motivation.* New York: Academic Press, 1967.

Heidbreder, E. "The Attainment of Concepts: I. Terminology and Methodology." *Journal of General Psychology,* 1946, *35,* 173-189.

Higdon, H. *The Crime of the Century: The Leopold and Loeb Case.* New York: Putnam, 1975.

Hoffman, L. W. "Fear of Success in 1965 and 1974: A Follow-Up Study." *Journal of Consulting and Clinical Psychology,* 1977, *45,* 310-321.

Hoffman, L. W., and Nye, F. I. *Working Mothers: An Evaluative Review of the Consequences for Wife, Husband, and Child.* San Francisco: Jossey-Bass, 1974.

Horner, M. S. "Why Women Fail." *Psychology Today,* November 1969.

Horner, M. S. "Toward an Understanding of Achievement-Related Conflicts in Women." *Journal of Social Issues,* 1972, *28,* 157-175.

Hospers, J. *Meaning and Truth in the Arts.* Chapel Hill: University of North Carolina Press, 1946.

Hoyt, D. P. "The Relationship Between College Grades and Adult Achievement: A Review of the Literature." *ACT Research Report No. 7.* Iowa City, Iowa: American College Testing Program, 1965.

Huck, S. W., and McLean, R. A. "Using a Repeated Measures ANOVA to Analyze the Data from a Pretest-Posttest Design: A Potentially Confusing Task." *Psychological Bulletin,* 1975, *82,* 511-518.

Hudson, L. *Contrary Imaginations.* New York: Shocken, 1966.

Hudson, L. *Frames of Mind.* New York: Norton, 1968.

Hudson, L. *Human Beings: The Psychology of Human Experience.* New York: Doubleday, 1975.

Huff, S. M., Klemp, G. O., Jr., and Winter, D. G. "The Definition and Measurement of Competence in Higher Education." In G. O. Klemp, Jr. (Ed.), *The Assessment of Occupational Competence.* Boston: McBer, 1980.

Hull, C. L. "Quantitative Aspects of the Evolution of Concepts." *Psychological Monographs,* 1920, *28* (1), Whole No. 123.

Hutchins, R. M. *The Higher Learning in America.* New Haven, Conn.: Yale University Press, 1936.

Hyman, H. H., Wright, C. R., and Reed, J. S. *The Enduring Effects of Education.* Chicago: University of Chicago Press, 1975.

Illich, I. *Deschooling Society.* New York: Harper & Row, 1971.

Jacob, P. *Changing Values in College.* New York: Harper & Row, 1957.

Jencks, C., and Riesman, D. "Patterns of Residential Education: A Case Study of Harvard." In R. N. Sanford (Ed.), *The American College.* New York: Wiley, 1962.

Jencks, C., and others. *Who Gets Ahead?* New York: Basic Books, 1979.

Jowett, B. (Ed.). *Plato's Republic.* London: Oxford University Press, 1888.

Kaufman, M. S. *Remember Me to God.* Philadelphia: Lippincott, 1957.

Keniston, K. *Young Radicals.* New York: Harcourt Brace Jovanovich, 1968.

Kenny, D. A. "A Quasi-Experimental Approach to Assessing Treatment Effects in the Nonequivalent Control Group Design." *Psychological Bulletin,* 1975, *82,* 345-362.

Kenny, D. A. *Correlation and Causality.* New York: Wiley, 1979.

Keppel, F. "Strategies for Retrenchment: National, State, Institutional." *Current Issues in Higher Education,* No. 6, pp. 1-11. Washington, D.C.: American Association for Higher Education, 1980.

Kerlinger, F. N. *Foundations of Behavioral Research.* (2nd ed.) New York: Holt, Rinehart & Winston, 1973.

Kerr, C. *The Uses of the University.* Cambridge, Mass.: Harvard University Press, 1963.

King, S. H. *Five Lives at Harvard.* Cambridge, Mass.: Harvard University Press, 1973.

Kohut, H. *The Restoration of the Self.* New York: International Universities Press, 1977.

Krathwohl, D. R., Bloom, B. S., and Masia, B. B. *Taxonomy of Educational Objectives. II. Affective Domain.* New York: McKay, 1964.

Lifton, R. J. *Thought Reform and the Psychology of Totalism.* New York: Norton, 1961.

Linn, R. L., and Werts, C. E. "Analysis Implications of the Choice of a Structural Model in the Nonequivalent Control Group Design." *Psychological Bulletin,* 1977, *84,* 229-234.

Lord, F. M. "Elementary Models for Measuring Change." In C. W. Harris (Ed.), *Problems in Measuring Change*. Madison: University of Wisconsin Press, 1963.

McArthur, C. C. "Personalities of Public and Private School Boys." *Harvard Educational Review*, 1954, *24*, 256-262.

McArthur, C. C. "Personality Differences between Middle and Upper Classes." *Journal of Abnormal and Social Psychology*, 1955, *50*, 247-254.

McArthur, C. C. "Subculture and Personality During the College Years." *Journal of Educational Sociology*, 1960, *33*, 3-11.

McClelland, D. C. "Methods of Measuring Human Motivation." In J. W. Atkinson (Ed.), *Motives in Fantasy, Action and Society*. Princeton, N.J.: Van Nostrand, 1958.

McClelland, D. C. *The Achieving Society*. New York: Van Nostrand, 1961.

McClelland, D. C. *The Roots of Consciousness*. Princeton, N.J.: Van Nostrand, 1964.

McClelland, D. C. "*N* Achievement and Entrepreneurship: A Longitudinal Study." *Journal of Personality and Social Psychology*, 1965, *1*, 389-392.

McClelland, D. C. "Longitudinal Trends in the Relation of Thought to Action." *Journal of Consulting Psychology*, 1966, *30*, 479-483.

McClelland, D. C. "The Two Faces of Power." *Journal of International Affairs*, 1970, *24*, 29-47.

McClelland, D. C. "Opinions Predict Opinions: So What Else is New?" *Journal of Consulting and Clinical Psychology*, 1972, *38*, 325-326.

McClelland, D. C. "Testing for Competence Rather Than for 'Intelligence.' " *American Psychologist*, 1973, *28*, 1-14.

McClelland, D. C. *Power: The Inner Experience*. New York: Irvington, 1975.

McClelland, D. C. "Inhibited Power Motivation and High Blood Pressure in Men." *Journal of Abnormal Psychology*, 1979, *88*, 182-190.

McClelland, D. C. "Motive Dispositions: The Merits of Operant and Respondent Measures." In L. Wheeler (Ed.), *Review of Personality and Social Psychology*. Vol. 1. Beverly Hills, Calif.: Sage Publications, 1980.

McClelland, D. C. "Is Personality Consistent?" In A. I. Rabin and others (Eds.), *Further Explorations in Personality*. New York: Wiley, 1981.

McClelland, D. C., and Boyatzis, R. E. *The Leadership Motive Pattern and Long-Term Success in Management*. Boston: McBer, 1980.

McClelland, D. C., and Burnham, D. H. "Power Is the Great Motivator." *Harvard Business Review*, 1976, *54* (2), 100-110.

McClelland, D. C., and Pilon, D. "Sources of Adult Motives in Patterns of Parent Behavior in Early Childhood." Unpublished paper. Cambridge, Mass.: Harvard University, 1979.

McClelland, D. C., and Winter, D. G. *Motivating Economic Achievement*. New York: Free Press, 1969.

McClelland, D. C., and others. *The Achievement Motive*. New York: Appleton-Century-Crofts, 1953.

McClelland, D. C., and others. "Obligations to Self and Society in the United States and Germany." *Journal of Abnormal and Social Psychology*, 1958, *56*, 245-255.

McClelland, D. C., and others. *The Drinking Man*. New York: Free Press, 1972.

Maddi, S. R. *Personality Theories: A Comparative Analysis*. (3rd ed.) Homewood, Ill.: Dorsey Press, 1976.

Meadows, D. H., and others. *The Limits to Growth*. New York: Universe Books, 1972.

Merton, R. K. "Puritanism, Pietism and Science." In *Social Theory and Social Structure*. (Rev. ed.) New York: Free Press, 1957. (Originally published 1949.)

Mischel, W. *Personality and Assessment*. New York: Wiley, 1968.

Morgan, C. D., and Murray, H. A. "A Method for Examining Fantasies: The Thematic Apperception Test." *Archives of Neurology and Psychiatry*, 1935, *34*, 289-306.

Munschauer, J. L. "Are Liberal Arts Graduates Good for Anything?" *Chronicle of Higher Education*, September 10, 1979, p. 48.

Murray, H. A., and others. *Explorations in Personality*. New York: Oxford University Press, 1938.

National Public Interest Research Group. *The Reign of ETS: The Corporation That Makes Up Minds*. Washington, D.C.: National Public Interest Research Group, 1979.

Newcomb, T. M. *Personality and Social Change.* New York: Dryden Press, 1943.

Newcomb, T. M. "Attitude Development as a Function of Reference Groups: The Bennington Study." In E. E. Maccoby, T. M. Newcomb, and E. L. Hartley (Eds.), *Readings in Social Psychology.* (3rd ed.) New York: Holt, Rinehart & Winston, 1958.

Newcomb, T. M., and others. *Persistence and Change: Bennington College and Its Students after Twenty-Five Years.* New York: Wiley, 1967.

Nisbett, R. E., and Wilson, T. D. "Telling More Than We Can Know: Verbal Reports on Mental Processes." *Psychological Review,* 1977, *84,* 231-278.

Nunnally, J. C. "The Study of Change in Evaluation Research: Principles Concerning Measurement, Experimental Design and Analysis." In E. L. Struening and M. Guttentag (Eds.), *Handbook of Evaluation Research.* Vol. 1. Beverly Hills, Calif.: Sage Publications, 1975.

Ohmann, R. *English in America: A Radical View of the Profession.* New York: Oxford University Press, 1976.

Parsons, T. *The Social System.* New York: Free Press, 1952.

Parsons, T. "Age and Sex in the Social Structure of the United States." In *Revised Essays in Sociological Theory.* New York: Free Press, 1954. (Originally published 1942.)

Parsons, T., and Platt, G. M. *The American University.* Cambridge, Mass.: Harvard University Press, 1973.

Perry, W. G. *Forms of Intellectual and Ethical Development in the College Years.* New York: Holt, Rinehart & Winston, 1970.

Pheterson, G. I., Kiesler, S. B., and Goldberg, P. A. "Evaluation of the Performance of Women as a Function of Their Sex, Achievement and Personal History." *Journal of Personality and Social Psychology,* 1971, *19,* 114-118.

Rand, C. *Cambridge U.S.A.* New York: Oxford University Press, 1964.

Rank, O. *The Myth of the Birth of the Hero.* New York: Knopf, 1959. (Originally published 1910.)

Rest, J. R. "New Approaches in the Assessment of Moral Judgment." In T. Lickona (Ed.), *Moral Development and Moral Behavior.* New York: Holt, Rinehart & Winston, 1976.

Riesman, D. "The 'Jacob Report.'" *American Sociological Review,* 1958, *23,* 732-738.

Riesman, D. "Educational Reform at Harvard College: Meritocracy and Its Adversaries." In S. M. Lipset and D. Riesman (Eds.), *Education and Politics at Harvard.* New York: McGraw-Hill, 1975.

Riesman, D. Preface to A. Miller (Ed.), *A College in Dispersion: Women of Bryn Mawr 1896-1975.* Boulder, Colo.: Westview Press, 1976.

Rosenthal, R. "On Telling Tales When Combining Results of Independent Studies." *Psychological Bulletin,* 1980, *88,* 496-497.

Rosenthal, R., and others. *Sensitivity to Nonverbal Communication: The PONS Test.* Baltimore: Johns Hopkins University Press, 1979.

Roszak, T. *The Making of a Counter Culture.* New York: Doubleday, 1969.

Roth-Walsh, M., and Stewart, A. J. "The Professional Woman: Coping with Being Outnumbered." Paper presented at the Conference on Women in Mid-Life Crisis, Cornell University, October 1976.

Sanford, R. N. (Ed.). *The American College.* New York: Wiley, 1962.

Schein, E. H. *Coercive Persuasion.* New York: Norton, 1961.

Schroder, H. M., Driver, M. J., and Streufert, S. *Human Information Processing.* New York: Holt, Rinehart & Winston, 1967.

Seidenberg, R. *Corporate Wives—Corporate Casualties.* New York: Doubleday, 1975.

Skinner, B. F. *The Behavior of Organisms.* New York: Appleton-Century-Crofts, 1938.

Skinner, B. F. *Science and Human Behavior.* New York: Macmillan, 1953.

Smith, J. E. *Value Convictions and Higher Education.* New Haven, Conn.: Edward W. Hazen Foundation, 1958.

Snow, C. P. *The Masters.* New York: Scribners, 1951.

232   References

Snow, C. P. *The Two Cultures and the Scientific Revolution.*
New York: Cambridge University Press, 1962.

Solomon, L. C., and Ochsner, N. "New Findings of the Effects
of College." *Current Issues in Higher Education.* 1978 Conference Series. Washington, D.C.: American Association for
Higher Education, 1978.

Solomon, L. C., and Taubman, P. J. (Eds.). *Does College Matter?* New York: Academic Press, 1973.

Speer, A. *Inside the Third Reich.* New York: Macmillan, 1970.

Speer, A. *Spandau: The Secret Diaries.* New York: Macmillan,
1976.

Spooner, J. D. "That Side of Paradise." *Boston Globe Magazine,* September 21, 1980.

Stewart, A. J. "Longitudinal Prediction from Personality to Life
Outcomes Among College-Educated Women." Unpublished
doctoral dissertation, Department of Psychology and Social
Relations, Harvard University, 1975.

Stewart, A. J. *Analysis of Argument: An Empirically-Derived
Measure of Intellectual Flexibility.* Boston: McBer, 1977a.

Stewart, A. J. "Scoring Manual for Stages of Psychological
Adaptation to the Environment." Unpublished manuscript,
Boston University, 1977b.

Stewart, A. J. "A Longitudinal Study of Coping Styles in Self-
Defining and Socially Defined Women." *Journal of Consulting and Clinical Psychology,* 1978, *46,* 1079-1084.

Stewart, A. J. "Personality and Situation in the Prediction of
Women's Life Patterns." *Psychology of Women Quarterly,*
1980, *5,* 195-206.

Stewart, A. J. "The Course of Individual Adaptation to Life
Changes." *Journal of Personality and Social Psychology,* in
press.

Stewart, A. J., and Winter, D. G. "Self-definition and Social
Definition in Women." *Journal of Personality,* 1974, *42,*
238-259.

Stewart, A. J., and Winter, D. G. "The Nature and Causes of
Female Suppression." *Signs: Journal of Women in Culture
and Society,* 1977, *2,* 531-553.

Stewart, A. J., and others. "Adaptation to Life Changes in Children and Adults: Cross-Sectional Studies." Unpublished paper, Boston University, 1980.

Stokes, E. *The English Utilitarians and India.* London: Oxford University Press, 1959.

Strodtbeck, F. L., and Mann, R. D. "Sex-Role Differentiation in Jury Deliberations." *Sociometry,* 1956, *19,* 3-11.

Struening, E., and Guttentag, M. (Eds.). *Handbook of Evaluation Research.* Beverly Hills, Calif.: Sage, 1975.

Trent, J. W., and Medsker, L. L. *Beyond High School: A Psychosociological Study of 10,000 High School Graduates.* San Francisco: Jossey-Bass, 1968.

Tresemer, D. W. *Fear of Success.* New York: Plenum Press, 1977.

Updike, J. *Couples.* New York: Knopf, 1968.

Vandiver, F. E. "The Southerner as Extremist." In F. E. Vandiver (Ed.), *The Idea of the South.* Chicago: University of Chicago Press, 1964.

Veroff, J., and Feld, S. C. *Marriage and Work in America.* New York: Van Nostrand Reinhold, 1970.

Veroff, J., and others. "Comparison of American Motives: 1957 Versus 1976." *Journal of Personality and Social Psychology,* 1980, *39,* 1249-1262.

Vreeland, R. S. "Organizational Structure and Moral Orientation: A Study of Harvard Houses." Unpublished doctoral dissertation, Department of Social Relations, Harvard University, 1964.

Weil, M. W. "An Analysis of the Factors Influencing Married Women's Actual or Planned Work Participation." *American Sociological Review,* 1961, *26,* 91-96.

Weiner, B. *Human Motivation.* New York: Holt, Rinehart & Winston, 1980.

Weisberg, H. I. "Statistical Adjustments and Uncontrolled Studies." *Psychological Bulletin,* 1979, *86,* 1149-1164.

Werts, C. E., and Linn, R. L. "A General Linear Model for Studying Growth." *Psychological Bulletin,* 1970, *73,* 17-22.

Werts, C. E., and Linn, R. L. "Analyzing School Effects ANOVA with a Fallible Covariate." *Educational and Psychological Measurement,* 1971, *31,* 95-104.

Whitehead, A. N. "The Aims of Education." In F. S. C. North-rup and M. W. Gross (Eds.), *Albert North Whitehead: An Anthology*. New York: Macmillan, 1953. (Originally published 1917.)

Wilkinson, R. *Gentlemanly Power: British Leadership and the Public School Tradition*. London: Oxford University Press, 1964.

Wilson, C. A. "Familiar 'Small College' Quotations: Mark Hopkins and the Log." *The Colophon*, 1938, *3*, 194-209.

Winter, D. G. "Personality Effects of a Summer Advanced Studies Program." Unpublished honors thesis, Harvard University, 1960.

Winter, D. G. *The Power Motive*. New York: Free Press, 1973.

Winter, D. G. *Correcting Projective Test Scores for the Effects of Significant Correlation with Length of Protocol*. Boston: McBer, 1979a.

Winter, D. G. "Defining and Measuring the Competencies of a Liberal Education." *Current Issues in Higher Education*, No. 5. Washington, D.C.: American Association for Higher Education, 1979b.

Winter, D. G., Alpert, R. A., and McClelland, D. C. "The Classic Personal Style." *Journal of Abnormal and Social Psychology*, 1963, *67*, 254-265.

Winter, D. G., and McClelland, D. C. "Thematic Analysis: An Empirically Derived Measure of the Effects of Liberal Arts Education." *Journal of Educational Psychology*, 1978, *70*, 8-16.

Winter, D. G., and Stewart, A. J. "Content Analysis as a Technique for Studying Political Leaders." In M. G. Hermann (Ed.), *A Psychological Examination of Political Leaders*. New York: Free Press, 1977a.

Winter, D. G., and Stewart, A. J. "Power Motive Reliability as a Function of Retest Instructions." *Journal of Consulting and Clinical Psychology*, 1977b, *45*, 436-440.

Winter, D. G., and Stewart, A. J. "Power Motivation." In H. London and J. Exner (Eds.), *Dimensions of Personality*. New York: Wiley, 1978.

Winter, D. G., Stewart, A. J., and McClelland, D. C. "Husband's

Motives and Wife's Career Level." *Journal of Personality and Social Psychology,* 1977, *35,* 159-166.

Woodruff, P. *The Men Who Ruled India.* London: Jonathan Cape, 1953.

Zung, W. W. K. "A Self-Rating Depression Scale." *Archives of General Psychiatry,* 1965, *12,* 63-70.

Index

237